mountain rescue

BOB SHARP
and
JUDY WHITESIDE

foreword by
HAMISH MACINNES

HAYLOFT

First published 2005
This reprint 2008

Hayloft Publishing, Kirkby Stephen, Cumbria CA17 4DJ

telephone: +44 (0) 17683 42300
fax: +44 (0) 17683 41568
email: books@hayloft.eu
web: www.hayloft.eu

A catalogue record for this book is available from the British Library.

Front cover photograph Bob Sharp
Back cover and fly leaf photography Chris Boyles, Rohan Holt, Bob Sharp,
Barry Robinson, Pete Hill MIC and Ian Dawson.
Maps drawn by Bob Sharp and Judy Whiteside.
Illustrations by Judy Whiteside.

Printed and bound in the EU.

Papers used by Hayloft are natural, recyclable products made from wood grown in sustainable forests. The manufacturing processes conform to the environmental regulations of the country of origin.

contents

preface

Most people have heard about mountain rescue. Recent years have seen a variety of television programmes devoted to the subject – from 999 reconstructions, through fly-on-the-wall documentaries following rescue teams about their work, to Rockface – about the lives, loves (and, incidentally, rescues) of a fictional Scottish mountain rescue team.

Mountain rescue conjures up images of daring adventure, high drama and people putting their lives on the line in dreadful weather when the rest of us are tucked up in bed asleep. But is this the reality? When the Press report on yet another climber plummeting to his death or a family group wearing just trainers and summer clothes trekking along a narrow mountain ridge in winter, oblivious to the risks, how do we know the stories are accurate? Well, we know there is an element of misinformation.

Half truths, sketchy details and spin designed to paint a colourful picture aimed at boosting newspaper sales all help to give mountaineering a bad name and feed the impression that it's a high risk sport.

But consider this. The actual statistics show that if a walker wishes to be carried off a mountain on a stretcher, then he (for most are men!) would have to walk every hour of every day non-stop for 300 years before he had an accident! An implausible example, maybe, but one which demonstrates just how (un)risky the mountains really are. And here's another example. Slips are relatively common in the mountains, but not as common as in the home. If you want to slip and hit your head on something sharp – then stay at home!

This book is all about mountain rescue – from the inside out. We aim to give you a complete and

accurate picture about what we do, who we are, how we train, the risks we encounter and how we are organised. And yes, we will inject some of the gory details because life for a mountain rescuer is not always a bed of roses. There are hardships and there are risks. Life is often uncomfortable and sometimes the raw edge which divides life and death surfaces when least expected.

We'll tell the story from a variety of perspectives. All the groups involved – rescuers, casualties, family members – have a say. We've gathered comment and stories from people who have witnessed accidents, rescued people and also been casualties. They tell it as it is. One thing we have learned is that those who have had the misfortune to become lost or injured are more than happy to tell their tale. And they do it rather well.

We've divided the book into a number of key areas – the use of dogs in search and rescue, the role of helicopters, medical matters, training and so on. It's not been easy, since the great majority of rescues involve so many dimensions. For example, one of the authors was recently involved in the search for a young mother. The ensuing incident took place over two days and required three rescue teams and a police diving unit, as well as local forestry workers and a police helicopter. A number of search dogs and their handlers were also mobilised along with medical experts whose task was to predict the woman's likely state of mind and possible whereabouts. Because the protracted search took place in difficult terrain and in poor weather, communication links and resource management were critical. And when the woman was found, a complicated technical rescue involving a high degree of risk and sensitivity had to be executed to recover her body. Altogether, it was a very complex rescue involving over sixty people from many different agencies using a wide variety of skills.

With luck, we'll answer all the questions you ever wanted to ask about mountain rescue and then some. No stone unturned. It's an absorbing story about how people react when the chips are down. And one we hope will leave you confident in the knowledge that if you're ever caught out in the mountains and need assistance, help will be on hand from a group of willing volunteers who show resolve, professionalism, kindness and compassion.

An early Alpine Mariner stretcher held by Glenmore Lodge MRT

PHOTO: BOB SHARP

The very first SARDA training course, held in Glencoe. From left to right, Kenny Mckenzie and Fran, Sandy Seabrook and Rorie, Willie Elliot and Corrie, Catherine MacInnes and Rangie and Tiki.

foreword

When I read the proofs of this book I must admit that I had misgivings. Though mountain rescue is a fascinating subject, its structure, factions and debates can be tedious to say the least. I was well aware of this, having been belayed for years to soulless committee room tables when I should have been on the crags.

After reading *Mountain Rescue*, I admit that I was wrong, for it is a well-structured blend of facts and action, interspersed with actual rescue accounts. The result is a work which covers the country and all aspects of search and rescue and  how it evolved – not just the work of rope technocrats. Those injured in flat country are just as grateful to their rescuers! Another thing I like about the book is the way the historical aspects of this voluntary service have been covered – a subject much neglected. Some lighthearted comments I found nostalgic, such as the shaggy dog one; that of the SAR hound –

'....will happily snaffle all your butties, pee on your boots and give you a generous face wash in the time between indicating your whereabouts to its handler, toiling up the hill in its wake...'

Some things we now take for granted such as the early rescue pioneers who had to fight to get morphine for those injured on the hill, how the first dedicated mountain rescue stretcher came into being and the formation of the early teams. RAF Mountain Rescue is justly portrayed and is given space on the world's highest mountain and a rescue thereon. This book, in its wide appraisal together with the quantum leaps in technology, will be a godsend to the rescue student, the rescuer and the statistic aspirant who may in the future be rescued, or even those who abide by the axiom –

'...look well to each step and from the beginning think what may be the end.'

I think that my favourite passage in the book is that of a farmer, two boys, penicillin and our most illustrious Prime Minister – read on.

When you finish this book you may wonder why a rescuer leaves his warm bed to sample a blizzard in the call of duty or perhaps it may be a false alarm – or both! A well-known mountaineer's reply as to the sanity of scaling a mountain was, 'because it's there.' Perhaps the rescuer's answer to the why do it question should be, 'Because we're here.'

Hamish MacInnes, Glencoe

chapter one

MUCH MORE THAN MOUNTAIN RESCUE...

Who has the hills for friend
Has God speed to the end.
His path of lonely life
And wings of golden memory.
Geoffrey Winthrop Young

Saturday afternoon, 31 January 1987, the weather was unseasonably mild. But with Scotland set to hammer England in the annual Calcutta Cup, members of the Killin mountain rescue team could have been forgiven for drawing the curtains against the sun, and settling down in front of their television sets. The mountains could wait. Not one of them could possibly have foreseen the dark cloud looming.

Over on the slopes of Beinn Tulaichean, it was a different story, as walkers took advantage of the spring day and a chain of events unfolded which would have dreadful consequences.

It began when reports came through that a walker had collapsed and died. A helicopter from RAF Leuchars was tasked to pick up two team members, including team co-ordinator Sergeant Harry Lawrie, to assist in the recovery. Shortly afterwards, a second incident occurred on Ben More, near Crianlarich, where a climber had fallen. Five miles as the crow flies from the team's current position, by road, this was a thirty mile journey that

would take at least an hour. The Wessex helicopter, already returning to Leuchars, was asked to divert to Ben More.

Meanwhile, from their rendezvous point at a farm near Crianlarich, eight members of the Killin team set out up the north face of the hill where the climber, a female, was reported to have slipped on a hard snow slope onto rocks just below the summit. She was thought to have sustained very serious injury. On arrival at the farm for briefing, the Wessex crew agreed to take Harry Lawrie and Ian Ramsey, the local police officer, to help pinpoint the location. By now, the light was failing, although weather conditions were good.

Once the position of the casualty and her companion was identified, it was agreed that team members would move them to a suitable place for the helicopter to land on the hill and achieve evacuation. Harry and Ian would be dropped off on the hill to assist the rest of the team, by now making good progress up the mountain.

In an ideal world, the Wessex might have landed

PHOTO: CHRIS BOYLES

on a conveniently open, flattish slope. But this was Ben More in winter – one of the fifteen highest mountains in the UK and among the best known and most popular in the Southern Highlands – the only option a single wheel touchdown on the steep, snow covered hillside - a routine manouevre. Except that, on this occasion (as the subsequent accident enquiry board ascertained) the main rotor struck a rock as the crew attempted touchdown. In an instant, the helicopter spun away from the hillside, crashing into the snow slope, debris flying as it slithered towards the still ascending rescue team members. The eight rescuers instinctively dived for cover as the helicopter slid on past them to rest on a ledge just below.

Back at base, team members, including Harry's wife, Jean, heard the crash and saw the flash of fire on the hillside. If there was any evidence at all of the accustomed easy camaraderie, the quiet confidence in the process of mountain rescue, of a life being saved – perhaps, even a lighthearted exchange on the state of that crucial game – it must have hung, chilled and idle in the afternoon air. But, very quickly, the urgent need to deal with an obvious, and unexpected, emergency kicked in, each member mentally assessing the implications, a plan of action drawn up. Questions were asked of the aircrew remaining at the base. Would it be safe to enter the cabin? Was the Wessex likely to explode? In the event, the team decided to enter the cabin and pull clear the flight crew and team member, Ian Ramsay, before fire took hold and destroyed the wreckage.

A search of the immediate area found a slide mark – Harry Lawrie's body at the bottom of the slide. Ian Ramsay later recalled that both he and Harry had released their safety belts on touchdown

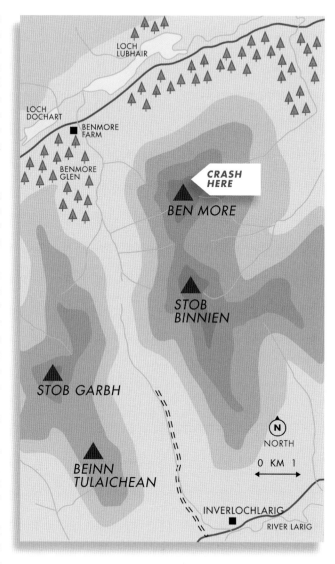

and that Harry was thrown out when the helicopter spun out from the hillside. Ironically, Ian survived because the pick of the ice axe he was holding caught the leg of a seat as the helicopter spun out of control, preventing his escape.

RAF Wessex hovering ready to winch casualty from cliff

As luck would have it, members of the RAF Leuchars MRT, returning to base from Glencoe, saw the burning helicopter on the mountain and provided immediate assistance. A Sea King from RAF Lossiemouth also attended. Between the two RAF teams, the injured crew and Ian Ramsay, who had very serious injuries, were evacuated from the mountain, leaving shocked Killin team members to recover Harry Lawrie by stretcher.

The climber who triggered the initial rescue, meanwhile, had sustained fatal injuries – a new, unused set of crampons in her rucksack. The team returned at first light the next day to recover her body.

Members of the crew, team leader Billy Stitt, and deputy team leader Stewart Ingles of Killin MRT and other team members, were later recognised at a ceremony in Stirling Castle when they were awarded the Queen's commendation for brave conduct. Tragic though it was, the accident had positive repercussions for the RAF and mountain rescue far beyond those bravery awards. It brought about change. As a result of the enquiry into the crash, all RAF rescue helicopters had one main rotor blade painted yellow to allow the rotor 'disc' to be more easily seen when the aircraft was hovering close to the mountainside.

When it comes to helicopters, Ridley Scott has a lot to answer for. Remember Thelma and Louise? The scene that spawned a hundred imitators? Sand blown desert bowl, blasted war zone, ice capped peaks – sure, the view might vary a little but that heart snapping tug on the emotions remains the same. Hope is in short supply. The girls have played all their cards and their enemy knows it. Or so it would seem. The viewer, sensibilities shredded by two hours' fevered concentration, grips the edge of his seat, petrified with anticipation, diaphragm suspended, jaw slack, eyes unblinking. And then it happens. Cut to blue-skied, desolate horizon, dust shimmering in the heat. First it's the noise. Wop,

wop, wopp, wopp, woppp. Louder and louder. And then we see it. In a split second. The helicopter rising from the Grand Canyon in front of the car. And the shock reminds us to breathe.

Every film director knows it – whip up the senses with a well turned helicopter shot and your audience will love you for it. Because helicopters always generate excitement. Combine them with a mountain accident and you have dramatic tension, heart-racing action and human emotion in abundance, for everyone involved. But here's a curious thing – most of us drive round in our cars every day, or move in a world dominated by cars. They're familiar, part of the fabric of daily life. And every day sees road traffic accidents reported in the press – sometimes from half way around the world. The same could hardly be said of accidents on the hills and mountains of the UK. Okay, most incidents involve nothing more than broken limbs and wounded pride (no less painful to the casualty!) requiring an evacuation to the nearest hospital. But there are many in which time is of the essence. It might be a critically injured or hypothermic casualty, to whom the skills of the mountain rescue service quite literally mean the difference between life and death. Teams will always assess the potential risks involved but, sometimes, the situation is so unstable, the environment so hostile, team members may face extremely challenging conditions to save the life of one other human being. And yet, as far as the press is concerned, these incidents have tended to attract only a passing local interest. Unless the helicopter was called, and, increasingly, these days, it is.

A common public perception is of a mountain rescue service which deals only with the few who venture onto the steep rock, snow and ice conditions of our mountains, a world away from the comparative safety of day to day life. If the term 'mountain rescue' means anything at all, it's considered to be an activity confined solely to the rugged highlands of Scotland, with the odd, highly publicised incident occurring on Snowdon in Wales or Scafell in England.

There's a view that those who venture into such hostile environments deserve to face the consequences because they are ill clad or totally inexperienced. Granted, many people do venture into the high mountains and wilderness areas without proper planning and skills and, sometimes, they are not equipped to deal with the circumstances in which they find themselves. But the vast majority of those who come to grief in the mountains of the UK are experienced people, who possess adequate clothing and equipment. Most, too, have the skills to cope with the hazards involved. Almost all accidents are just that – no-one is to blame.

That phrase 'mountain rescue' only gives you half the picture. Teams across the UK are often called to incidents, which are not strictly mountain related. Take nursing homes, for example. Many of these are housed in grand old buildings, surrounded by extensive gardens, woodlands and fields. When an elderly or sick resident goes walkabout – in the States they call it 'wandering' – police will frequently call in the local rescue team to search for the missing person.

Of course, it isn't just the elderly who go missing. Over the years, rescue teams have been involved with some pretty high profile searches for missing children. When five year old Rosie McCann was taken from the room in which she slept, police initially asked Oldham MRT to assist in the search of woodland near her home. But, ultimately, as many as 500 rescue team members from teams across the north of England, including search and rescue dogs and the RAF, were involved. In fact, it's worth dwelling on this story for a moment as it's a wonderful illustration of the versatility and capability of the mountain rescue service as a whole and the ability of teams to collaborate and work together when required.

It began on Monday 15 January, 1996. Rosie appeared to have been abducted by thirty one year old Andrew Pountney, her mother's boyfriend but, when arrested at his home, the little girl was not with him and he denied all knowledge of the abduction. As a swathe of dense fog cloaked the north west of England, the initial woodland search was extended to include police divers, scouring the lake at Alexandra Park, Oldham. The police, meanwhile, had secured a 36 hour detention order allowing them to keep the boyfriend in custody until 6.00am on the Wednesday. When he appeared in court, later that morning, he was further remanded in custody until Friday, for his own safety, as feelings in the community ran very high. By then, 'Holmes' the aptly named computer system used by the police to correlate data would have been investigating possible links with other reports of missing children. Every action would be inputted – street names, times, witness reports, vehicle details – a veritable cocktail of information through which the computer sifts and searches, making the vital links which drive an investigation. Search parties from three rescue teams were searching the four square miles adjacent to Rosie's home, and a further area close to the town centre. Even the dustbin men were asked to postpone their rounds so that dustbins could be searched for evidence – an exercise, incidentally, which has led, on occasions, to the more urban oriented search teams being dubbed 'dustbin lid lifters' by one or two of their cheekier colleagues!

As search parties combed the town centre for the third successive day, police were reluctant to extend the search beyond Oldham, believing the person responsible for Rosie's disappearance had barely enough time to take her any further before the alarm was raised and the search underway. They appealed for people to search their industrial premises. As time ticked on to a week, and the chances of finding the little girl alive were receding fast, imagine the rush of thoughts and emotions battling it out inside each searcher. Mountain rescue team members are volunteers. They may be highly trained and professional in their approach, but not all are as accustomed to the horrors of human misfortune in the way a paramedic or police officer might be.

The start of a search can be exciting, adrenaline fuelled. There's an expectation of success, every single searcher aware that he or she may be the one who finds the missing child. Many have children of their own, able to imagine, all too readily, how they would feel. But as time goes on, there's a switch. A week of searching, early morning briefings, late night debriefings, standing around in the cold and the fog for hours waiting to be deployed, making excuses to understanding employers (not to mention their own families at home!), fuelled in the main by Thermos coffee and snatched junk food, leads to fatigue and frustration. Filter through this the gradual realisation that this search is no longer about a living person, but a body and you can see the dilemma – the almost bloody-minded determination to find a child alive, against the dreadful prospect that you may be the one to find her dead.

Actually, it was some weeks before Rosie's body was found, inside a flight bag, stuffed between two walls on derelict land, a stone's throw from where the search had been. In fact, the spot was still marked on the map as being a factory – so hadn't even entered search parameters, throwing into sharp perspective the way maps are viewed in search management. As for her abductor, mountain rescue personnel were yet to play a part in his eventual conviction for murder. Caught on a garage forecourt camera, in an area he claimed not to be at the time, Pountney was seen purchasing a Twix bar and a packet of ten Benson & Hedges. Witnesses reported a young girl in his van. So, the focus moved and team members were tasked to search for the evidence of his purchases. There may well have been hundreds picked up and bagged but the empty fag packet and discarded sweet wrapper which carried Pountney's DNA were amongst them, his conviction secured.

So, besides scooping casualties from the hills, searching for missing persons, looking for evidence in murder enquiries, what else do team members do with their spare time? Well, besides the occasional road traffic accident in remote locations, body

PHOTO: BOB SHARP

Corrie of Balglass in the Campsie Fells

recovery in cases of suicide, injured forestry workers and mountain bikers, missing children on family picnics and runners on charity events, civilian and military rescue teams have played a central role in locating and recovering the bodies from very harrowing aircraft crashes. In 1988, the Lockerbie disaster involved several mountain rescue teams working for several days and nights, as well as search dog teams from around the UK – but we'll come back to that later.

And then there are the animals. A menagerie of them. Take sheep - or, to be precise, a couple of sheep in particular. Absentmindedly nibbling their way through the Corrie of Balglass in the Campsie Fells north of Glasgow, without apparent regard for their own safety, they found themselves stuck on a ledge about 300 feet up the steep side wall of the corrie. Unable to move up or down, they had remained in the same location for a couple of days, dining quite happily off the grassy ledge. A couple of people walking along the rim of the corrie had spotted the sheep and mentioned this to the farmer at the end of their walk on the hill. His initial reaction was to take his vehicle to the base of the steep wall to see if he could entice his sheep down with his border collie. But, even the dog had more sense on such steep ground, so back the farmer drove to ask if the police could find some way to help.

Their immediate response was to call the Lomond team. About a dozen team members walked into the base of the corrie and noted the sheep were in a position too steep and complicated to effect a rescue mission from below. They decided that the best chance of recovering the animals would be to lower a couple of team members from above on ropes secured using rock anchors. This proved to be more difficult than expected since the smooth ground just beyond the lip of the corrie did not provide any trees or boulders suitable for rope attachment. So, instead, the team set up a system of stakes sunk into the soft ground to provide an

OKAY DOLL... THIS IS WHAT WE DO... WHEN YOU SEE THE WHITES OF THEIR EYES... **JUMP**!!!

When this Cessna 320 developed engine trouble en route to Ireland, crashing onto a Lancashire hillside and killing the pilot, members of the Rossendale & Pendle team were tasked by police to recover the body and help manage the incident.

effective anchor suitable for two members to abseil down to the ledge, 400 feet below. Once there, they would attach rope harnesses to each sheep and gently manoeuvre them down the steep face in relative safety.

However, all did not go according to plan. As the rescue team members moved towards them, the sheep became very agitated. There was a risk that, if they moved in too quickly, the sheep would attempt to move from the safety of the ledge and possibly fall to their deaths. So – very gently – they slowed down their actions and reached across to take hold of the sheep. But there must have been a sudden movement because both sheep suddenly 'spooked'. One flung itself from the ledge to its death. The other, ever so nonchalantly and with great gymnastic ability, scrambled from one ledge to another and made its way down to the base of the corrie quite safely and none the worse for wear! The waiting farmer was delighted that one of the two had survived.

A similar rescue carried out by the Tayside team during the lambing season in 1999 had the opposite effect – double the survivor rates! When a heavily pregnant sheep became cragfast on a steep hill in Glen Clova near Dundee, the team member who was lowered about 500 feet to the waiting ewe was surprised to find he had recovered not one sheep but two, when the ewe gave birth to a lamb during the descent!

Just one month after the nibbling sheep episode, another farmer had cause to thank Lomond team members for their services, this time with a distressed cow. The animal had gone into labour unexpectedly and tumbled into a burn running through the farmyard. Whilst the farmer called for help, his son was gamely holding the cow's head above the water to prevent it drowning. The police, recalling the rescue team's recent efforts with the sheep, knew exactly who to call! Now, every rescue is different, and no two rescues require the same set of skills or procedures – though there are a number of general skills that can be applied effectively to different scenarios. Here was a two ton animal, lying on its side, about to give birth and, no doubt, in a good deal of discomfort, to be pulled out of the water and up a steep bank of about 30 feet. Clearly, what was required was a pulley system which would enable team members to lift a very heavy weight with minimum effort.

Pulley systems create a mechanical advantage, which reduces the pulling effort at the expense of pulling distance. So, the team would need to attach the cow to a harness of some kind, rig this to a pulley system and then pull over a long distance to move the cow the necessary 30 feet. The farmer supplied lengths of wide leather from which a harness was fashioned and these were then attached to the pulling ropes. Once the system was in place and the bank suitably hosed with water to enable the cow to slide uphill more easily, the team pulled on the ropes. Everything went as planned, and without any apparent distress to the expectant mother. At the top of the bank, she rallied round and struggled to her

PHOTO: BARRY ROBINSON

Desolate Boulsworth Moor where Colin Patchett's body was found, three years after his disappearance

drum the springer spaniel

One day in early spring, Drum and his owner were out for a stroll. They were walking next to Black Rock Gorge near Evanton on the Cromarty Firth, just north of Inverness. As Drum peered over the edge, he slipped and took a tumble down a steep embankment and into the gorge proper. It was quite impossible for his owner to climb down without the aid of a rope and climbing equipment. So he called the police who, in turn, tasked the Dundonnell team to see if they could recover Drum.

PHOTO: JAN MILLAR

Picture posed by model!! In the absence of the original star Buidhe the Border Collie volunteers a reconstruction...

'There I was, sniffin' about quite happily. Mmm. Hmm. The mellow whiff of rotted leaf, soft and pungent on the nose. And fungus. Mmm... definitely fungus. Crisp snaps of ever so slightly salty air. A subtle lingering dash of coconut...

'I do have a vague recollection of them calling, "Come here, Drum", but that's one of the delights of reaching a certain... er, maturity. You can just pretend to be deaf and ignore people when you feel like it. Besides, I'd been there lots of times before. Although, once I was back under the safety of my own roof (and

taking full advantage of the TLC on offer) I did have to admit that, on reflection, the grass may have been just a little slippery that day.

'Where was I? Oh yes... (They keep saying my memory's going. Can't remember when that started to happen...) Anyway, apparently I was near the path that runs alongside the Black Rock Gorge, near Evanton when I started to slip... "Dig your heels in, lad", I yelped, 'dig your heels in!' Well it usually works. But not this time. I just kept moving. Trees and bushes started flashing past. "Grab 'em with your teeth!" I thought. No good. No teeth!

'Fifty feet of this and then a fifty foot jump (well I am a Springer) then... wallop! "Houston. We have splashdown!" But there's life in the old dog yet. A quick paddle then a waterslide (humans pay money for this sort of thing!) and, eventually, some construction of logs and twigs to climb out on to. Well, it was at this point I realised that not one single person had followed me (bloomin' wimps, humans!) so I decided I'd better sit down and wait, which seems to be what a dog's life is all about these days, anyway.

'It was quite some time later when this guy I have never clapped eyes on before pats me on the head and says, in a very familiar way, "Hello, Drum." I haven't a clue where he came from but the first thing he did was tie his lead round an upright log. Then – and you are absolutely NOT going to believe this – he started to feel and prod me all over. Right from the tip of my nose to the pads of my feet. In broad daylight!

'Then another one of his breed appeared (same

kind of hard red head) and the two of them started to muck about with all kinds of leads. Thick ones. Thin ones. And shiny clanky things. Then, final indignity, they stuck me in this bag thing and I started to levitate.

'Well, really. Even I could have told them it wasn't going to work. Started to brush against the side, so they lowered me back down again. They had obviously never heard of Benji's story. Of course, he wasn't a Springer like me, but when he got into trouble, he was zoomed up in a bag on a high wire. But not me. Oh no. I was hoisted onto the second guy's back like a bag of coal and up we went over rock, moss, bushes, branches and trees. It was okay for him. He was in control and obviously finding the whole thing highly amusing because he kept laughing. But nobody thought to tell me why I was swinging about on a human's back being jolted all over the place!

'Then, when we reached the top, this female specimen started to examine me all over again! What is it with these creatures?

'Anyway, I can't complain too much because they did let me go eventually and, a few days later, when I was more settled, some humans came round and took photos of me. Fame at last! It made a real splash in the papers – they must have thought canyoning without a rope was a really good game to invent. Who said we oldies can't teach the young 'uns a thing or two?'

It took ten Dundonnell mountain rescue team members three hours to catapult Drum the Springer Spaniel to his fifteen minutes of fame.

feet. The nifty little harness was detached and the farmer led her to a byre where she gave birth thirty minutes later!

In the Rosie McCann case, the role of mountain rescue subtly evolved over a period of a few very intense weeks. It showed all too quickly how a missing person search can turn into the search for a body or, on very rare occasions the hunt for evidence. Sometimes, incidents remain on police files for months and years before resolution. Such was the case in Lancashire when a former milkman left his home in Burnley one bitterly cold afternoon in November 1997. Newspaper reports claimed (although this was never confirmed as fact) that, wearing only a lightweight zipped jacket, grey trousers and light coloured shoes, and with just two pounds in his pocket – money to make telephone calls home from the ward – he set off to return to the hospital where he was a patient. But he never arrived. An immediate search of the moors near a local reservoir by police, the force helicopter and members of the Rossendale & Pendle MRT found no sign of the missing man. He would feature in team annual incident reports for almost three years. It became a regular call out – even, on occasion, the subject of a joint exercise.

The very lack of information convinced the police and the team that he, or – more accurately at this stage – his body, would be in the locality of the initial search area, an area of open moorland on the fringes of Nelson and close to the Lancashire/ Yorkshire border. Around October 1999, and as the result of apparently unconnected discussions between the police and the team leadership, an idea was floated that a new search be mounted under the guise of a larger scale police/mountain rescue exercise. Henry Stott, police radio engineer and a former team leader, saw an opportunity to try out his radio systems. Barry Robinson, a team member and police officer involved in the original missing person case, identified an opportunity for even closer co-operation with the police.

Barry recalls, 'As a rescue team member and police officer involved in the original search, I was perfectly placed to bring the two agencies closer together. A few conversations with Barry Wilson, Lancashire police search co-ordinator, and we got the go-ahead to run a large exercise with the added bonus of a real target. A win-win situation. About this time, it occurred to me that one of Lancashire's Assistant Chief Constables, John Vine, was currently the ACPO representative to the Mountain Rescue Council. Could this be a perfect opportunity for ACC Vine to learn even more about MR?

'Another couple of phone calls and then the reply, 'Yes, certainly, the ACC will visit the exercise.'

'Two weeks later, on a chilly November morning, the exercise participants were assembling at a local outdoor activities centre – Rossendale & Pendle mountain rescue team members, the search support unit, three full police support units... and then up rolls the ACC wearing boots and waterproofs asking to be briefed as part of a fell party. From that point on he became a 'grunt' like the rest of us, allocated to a party and a role within that party, and off onto the fells for six hours' searching and lunch on the hoof.

'Nothing was found on the search but at the debriefing the ACC made it known he had gained a valuable insight into the work and commitment of the teams. For their part, team members applauded his efforts and offered him the opportunity to join as an operational trainee!'

It was one day in early July 2000, when a badly decomposed body was found, half submerged in boggy ground at the top of the moors, just two miles from Coldwell reservoir and outside the area previously searched by police and rescue team members. A post mortem later confirmed the body to be that of the missing man. The subsequent inquest heard he had long suffered from severe depression after giving up his milk round – attempting to take his own life with an overdose just days before his disappearance. His wife reported him leaving the house on several occasions saying he wanted to die but, each time, he was found by police. Poignantly, on his last afternoon at home, he rose from the settee, said 'I am going', and walked out of the house. Whatever his state of mind, we will never know. There were no marks or injury on the skeleton and, because of the length of time the body had been exposed, pathologist Dr William Lawler was unable to give a cause of death. Most likely he had died from exposure after walking away from the road and tracks.

You might think three years of fruitless searches and the discovery of a body would signal the end of the story for the rescue team? Well, yes – almost. But not quite. Because the problem now, was not in locating a missing person, but retrieving his remains from a spot so isolated that detectives had been taken to the scene in a police helicopter. When the call came through, the pager message was short and to the point. 'Body recovery. Meet base 18.00,' swiftly followed by another indicating the job could take two to three hours – clearly not a straightforward suicide recovery.

'As it turned out,' recalls team member Andy Simpson, 'the information suggested the body was that of a misper we'd looked for, on and off, for the past three years, although we'd have to wait for the autopsy to confirm this.

'Apparently, a farm worker rounding up his sheep had found the body, about a mile or so from the nearest vehicle track and a fair distance from any footpaths. It really was in the middle of nowhere.

'We left base in a convoy of three vehicles, one or two team members joining us on the way, one or two meeting at the RV point. At the farm, we were met by various police officers, the coroner and the farmer, who led us along the track. After about a mile, the farmer took an abrupt left turn straight over the moors – this would be fun with eight people crammed into our Land Rover! Sure enough, everyone crested the hill and disappeared over the horizon – except us. The first bump we hit stopped the vehicle – we were in the wrong gear. Any further attempts resulted in the same, even though we were now employing the very best in gear box engineering and four wheel drive. At this point, everyone got out of the vehicle, including the driver, and I took the wheel while everyone pushed.

'Two minutes later, smoke coming off the clutch, we reached the top of the hill and followed everyone's tracks for about half a mile. At this point, Lancashire Police Scenes of Crime Officer handed round a great big tray of butties which we all dug into whilst surveying the scene for signs of a body.

'Not seeing any evidence of a corpse, we were told the gathering of people about half a mile away – looking distinctly like a scene from Zulu – were, in fact, farm workers and police officers, waiting for us to remove the body. As if by some unseen signal, we all began to take kit off the vehicle – presumably the defib and trauma sack wouldn't be needed – but we would need the spades and stretcher.

'By now, I knew this wasn't going to be a body in the normal sense – more likely, after three years, a skeleton. What I hadn't anticipated was the preservative effect on the human body of lying down in a peat bog. Apart from the obvious effects of exposure to the elements here was a recognisable figure of a man, spectacles still gently resting on his chest.'

In the event, the mechanics of recovering this body were no different to a living casualty – a normal casualty lift – with shovels. Then into the body bag, onto the stretcher, carry off to team vehicle, transfer back down to the road head and over to the waiting undertakers.

But if the nature of that particular rescue surprises you, what about this one? There aren't many big mountains in the Scottish Borders but, back in 1990, the new motorway from Carlisle to Glasgow had just been completed. (Now, if you've just read the previous sentence and thought, 'Hang on a minute... that sentence doesn't make sense...' bear with us). The first Monday in February was not untypical for the time of year apart from the heavy snowfall. Neil Sutherland, leader of the Moffat team had just settled down for the evening, but things were about to take a sharp turn as he relates.

'It was just a regular evening, but then a phone call from Dumfries & Galloway Constabulary. 'Are you sitting in front of a nice fire Neil?' says he. 'I am, and just about to enjoy a Guinness,' I replied.

'Well you can forget that because I've got a wee job for you!'

'He went on to explain that right across the region cars and coaches were stranded with their occupants and could the team help? Of course we could help. All team members were alerted and asked to report to the nearest accessible police station from where they would be deployed.

'As we arrived at the police stations, it would be fair to say there was more than a little confusion. This was a most unusual and unexpected event. Team members quickly moved to help. Our main task was to concentrate on the new M74 (Glasgow to Carlisle) motorway. This was a sight to be seen. A seven mile queue of trucks, cars and buses, three lanes wide. Hundreds and hundreds of stranded vehicles and their occupants. We were to walk along the lines of vehicles, checking drivers were safe, delivering food and helping to evacuate the very young, old and ill – a wee bit different from searching for a missing person on the fells.

'Why is it that those needing evacuation are always the heaviest? Two of us had to carry a seventeen stone diabetic from a coach across the motorway in two feet of snow! I would have gladly swopped this for a hard evacuation off the hill any day. As we stopped by each vehicle we met people of all nationalities and temperaments. Picture the

PHOTO: ROSSENDALE & PENDLE MRT

Call this 'rush hour'? The picture shows Rossendale & Pendle team members assisting drivers stranded in heavy snow conditions in East Lancashire. Rescue teams and their vehicles, throughout the UK, are frequently called in when conditions are extreme.

scene at 2.00am in the morning. A young woman is thirsty and I give her a can of coke. 'Excuse me,' comes the response, 'I don't like coke – do you have a hot cup of tea?' When sandwiches are offered, someone replied, "I don't like white bread, do you have brown?" At one point in the early morning, a team member tried to force-feed two men from Morocco. It wasn't until they explained in very broken English the meaning of 'Ramadan' that he realised why he was getting nowhere! When we stopped at one car, a rather terse discussion broke out with a lady of eastern origin. She insisted she was going to Bradford when it was clear she was heading for Glasgow. Eventually, we persuaded her to leave her car by agreeing that we were going to Bradford

(albeit via Lockerbie in two days time). Then there was a Japanese girl who smiled and answered yes to everything – what do you do? A very elegantly dressed lady was stranded in her Rolls Royce and desperate to visit the loo. We whisked her away from her wonderful limousine and took her into town on the way to uplift more soup for the hungry mouths. We introduced her to the toilets and then returned her to her car. And I thought a Rolls Royce came equipped with everything!

'The nearby secondary school was turned into an emergency evacuation centre. Literally 1,500 people found food and shelter there. The kitchen staff treated team members like lords insisting that we had first call for available food. We carried out all the food and drinks to the motorway in rucksacks – approximately 20 gallons of soup, 800 filled rolls and sandwiches, 300 tins of cola plus huge volumes of chocolate bars and crisps.

'In the main, people were very grateful. One coach party even had a whip-round and gave us £50. Ironically, this was the first winter the new three lane motorway had experienced since opening in the summer. Will this become an annual event? I for one will be taking just a little more in the sack for future trips during winter months.'

Leaving the motorway, but keeping with the snow for a moment, probably the most frightening hazard for winter mountaineers must be avalanche.

Every single year, without fail, people find themselves avalanched. Many survive but others don't. Believe it or not, by the way, the very first recorded avalanche took place in the village of Lewes, Sussex, back in 1836 – not a place generally associated with mountain scenery! Two days after Christmas a huge avalanche descended a short slope behind the village overwhelming many houses and killing eight inhabitants. A communal grave reminds people of the event. That and the appropriately titled local hostelry – the Snowdrop Inn!

But whilst avalanches are recorded occasionally in the mountains of the Lake District, they are essentially the preserve of the Scottish Highlands. And rescue teams need to know what to do when people are trapped – another one of their many skills.

Sgurr nan Clach Geala in Wester Ross is very popular with winter climbers. A party of five men had set out together to the foot of the crags then split into two climbing groups – a pair and a group of three. The latter were about to tackle a route called 'Alpha'. The man positioned highest had set up a belay (the means by which climbers fix running ropes to the rocks to secure themselves and their climbing partners) in preparation for the climb when a vast avalanche descended the gully striking all three. The top man bore the brunt of the avalanche as he was smashed back and forth between the rock and the tumbling snow. But his belay held fast. The others were knocked down the gully – one about 80 feet and the other about 150 feet. One of them managed to avoid any kind of injury whilst the other suffered ankle injuries. Even though he was not carried down the gully, the climber at the top suffered serious head, face and chest injuries. The alarm was raised by the other two members of the group who alerted the police using a mobile phone.

In atrocious weather – strong winds, heavy snow and the distinct risk of further avalanche danger – six members of the Dundonnell MRT were transported to the base of the cliff by an RAF Sea King helicopter. Already low on fuel and buffeted about by high winds, the crew coped well, lifting the injured climber into the aircraft and ferrying him to hospital, before gearbox failure forced an emergency landing. This left those still on the mountain at serious risk as they descended the 1000 feet to the base of the mountain. As the remaining rescuers and climbers made their way down – often wading armpit high in snow – the climbers admitted they should never have attempted the climb in the first place! Whatever thoughts might have passed through the minds of their rescuers we do not have on record!

On this occasion, the rescuers found it relatively easy to locate the avalanched climbers but often, if the climbers are buried, then specialised skills and equipment are needed. The best chance for anyone who is avalanched is not to wait for a rescue team but hope that people in the immediate vicinity see their plight and begin searching immediately. Such is the short period of time you can be buried before you suffocate.

It's likely that a good many incidents are solved with a bit of teamwork from friends and other walkers. Indeed, many incidents take place in the mountains without ever being officially recorded. People become lost and eventually find their way back to the roadside without assistance from a mountain rescue team. Occasionally, a walker will fall and break an arm or leg, yet manage to hobble off the mountainside with the help of friends or passing strangers. And, every so often, that passing stranger might just happen to be a rescue team member, snatching a bit of hill time for themselves.

Andrew Dale is a retained firefighter and full time postman. He is also a member of the Galloway team. He was out walking with his family at a local beauty spot in Perthshire called the Falls of Bruar. As the family approached the Falls, a young mother ran up to them and said her son Jamie had lost his

I somersaulted and rolled several times before intermittently regaining a degree of control. Occasional flashes of daylight led me to judge that the avalanche was not very deep and it was better to attempt ice axe self-arrest than to paddle to the surface – especially as I knew there was a long way to go! Nonetheless, I repeatedly choked on snow before gasping for air again. I quickly lost both axes, even though they were attached to my arms by their wrist loops and then tried to spread myself into an 'X' on my stomach. I even remembered that I was only wearing one crampon and wondered whether I should leave my crampon-less leg down while holding the other up!

footing and fallen into the gorge. Andrew sent his wife and daughter to fetch help and first aid equipment and then proceeded to climb down the steep cliff to the bottom of the gorge – placing himself at some risk, as he had no head protection or safety rope. Unfortunately, when he arrived at the water's edge he found Jamie dead from his injuries. Andrew responded by staying with the boy and guiding the emergency services to the scene. He also played an active role in helping to recover the body. To mark his act of bravery, he was awarded the Royal Humane Society Testimonial on Vellum.

Speaking to the press about the award, Andrew commented, 'If someone approaches you out of the blue and says a child has fallen you want to help. It's fortunate that my wife and daughter were with me as they were able to call the emergency services and fetch my bag of equipment, while I got ready to climb down. I was surprised to get the letter in the post from Jamie's father, nominating me for the award. It was unexpected and I don't think I did anything out of the ordinary that day. I am proud that I have got the award but it would have been nicer to have received it in different circumstances.'

Jamie's father paid great tribute to Andrew. He commented that it was a huge coincidence the first person his wife ran into should be a member of the mountain rescue team. It was also fortunate that his wife was able to call for help, leaving him to set about things on his own.

In March 1999 Andrew Fellows, a member of the Lomond team found himself in a very traumatic and tragic situation. He and his partner had gone to Ben Nevis with the intention of climbing Hadrian's Wall – a very long and difficult climb almost 1000 feet in length. Andrew had checked on weather conditions for climbing and also assessed the avalanche risk from the sportscotland Avalanche Information

From left to right Ben Nevis North Face, Orion Direct, Zero Gully from Orion Face

Service. The risk level was Category 2 (moderate).

On arrival, they noted two other climbers on their intended route. The temperature was hovering around freezing point and the sky was overcast with

PHOTO: GALLOWAY MRT

Galloway team member Andrew Dale receives the Royal Humane Society Testimonial on Vellum for bravery

the cloud base just on the tops. Winds at the foot of the route were generally light, but strong flurries of spindrift suggested that the forecast of 30-40mph winds at 3000 feet was accurate. The start to the climb proved problematic. Andrew's partner took three hours to lead the first section and then Andrew lost a crampon at the first ice bulge. With time marching on, they decided to abandon the route, so they down climbed and prepared to walk out from the foot of the route. The time was now shortly after 4.00pm.

'We each trailed a rope to remove twists and were therefore not roped to each other (there was no need for this now). By this time the temperature had risen perceptibly above freezing point and snow conditions underfoot were very different from those during our approach. In part this was due to the accumulation of large amounts of fresh spindrift below the flanks of Observatory Ridge but, further out into the open snowfield in the lower reaches of Observatory Gully, the snow was presumably softer due to the temperature rise. I traversed out into the centre of the snowfield, about 100m below the foot of Point Five Gully with the intention of retracing our steps down to the CIC hut. At about 4.30pm, I had reached the central fall line of the snowfield and began to descend when my partner, who was still at the foot of Hadrian's Wall, shouted "Look out!" Before I had time to look round, my feet were knocked from beneath me by an avalanche from behind.

'According to my partner I was engulfed by the snow for about three seconds and swept about 100 metres down the fall line. It is difficult to recall exactly what happened at this point, but I somersaulted and rolled several times before intermittently regaining a degree of control. Although it was clearly a wet slab rather than a spindrift avalanche, occasional flashes of daylight led me to judge that the avalanche was not very deep and that it was therefore better to attempt ice axe self-arrest than to paddle to the surface – especially as I knew there was a long way to go! Nonetheless, I repeatedly choked on snow before gasping for air again. I quickly lost both axes, even though they were attached to my arms by their wrist loops and then tried to spread myself into an 'X' on my stomach. I even remembered that I was only wearing one crampon and wondered whether I should leave my crampon-less leg down while holding the other up!

'The snow mass came to rest and I managed to surface and sit up. I was immediately aware of a body on the surface about five metres below me, which I assumed was my partner as there had been nobody else on the snowfield and visibility was still good. I called his name but there was no response. After regaining my composure (as much as possible under the circumstances!) I moved down to the body and realised that it was someone else – a woman.

Her face was covered in snow with traces of blood; her helmet was half off and full of snow and she was wrapped in climbing ropes. I removed my mitts, cleared the snow from her face and saw that she was breathing. I shouted again but got no response. Her eyelids and lips were swollen and purple and her gums and nose were bleeding slightly, but there were no other immediately apparent signs of injury. I cut off her helmet and examined her skull, in particular her exposed ear for blood or cerebro-spinal fluid, but could only see droplets of water. I decided not to turn her head to expose the other ear for fear of exacerbating any possible, indeed probable, spinal injury. I had by now guessed that she had fallen down Point Five Gully – up to 1000 feet – before hitting the snowfield.

'I then became aware of a second person half buried in the snow about ten feet away from the woman. This was a male climber – obviously her climbing partner – lying in a contorted position with his back arched. His face was exposed, ashen and blotchy, his eyes wide open and glassy. I could not detect breathing. There was no visible bleeding, nor any immediately apparent injury. I exposed his neck and checked his carotid pulse but could detect nothing. I did not trust this assessment as my fingers were by this time completely numb. I pinched his eyebrow as hard as I could and checked other parts of his face for capillary refill. My partner was still far away and, judging the situation to be too serious for me to cope with alone, I blew six blasts on my whistle to summon more help. I had noticed that the muscles either side of the climber's neck were unusually swollen, and guessed that he had broken his neck. I felt sure that he was dead, but could not allow myself to come to that conclusion.

'I decided to concentrate my efforts on the casualty who I knew was alive until help arrived, a decision reinforced as she began to regain consciousness. She began to say faintly, "Help me, hold my hand," so I held her hand, told her not to move, and reassured her that I was a mountain rescue team member and that she was in safe hands. I asked her if she felt pain anywhere in particular and she said that she wanted to go to the toilet. This led me to suspect a fractured pelvis, although (fortunately) this diagnosis subsequently proved incorrect. She did not complain of any other pain. I asked her what had happened and she told me that they had been avalanched above the final pitch of Point Five Gully. She then began to ask about her partner, and became increasingly distraught when I was unable to give her any reassurance. This was by far the most difficult aspect of the situation for me to deal with. She asked me to move her as she was uncomfortable, specifically to be aligned along the fall line with her head uppermost. I explained that I was reluctant to move her any more than was absolutely necessary (for the reason given before). I asked her if she felt cold anywhere, and she said no.

'Help arrived around this time, perhaps 15-20 minutes after the avalanche, in the form of two climbers who had descended off Tower Ridge. They had seen what had happened, so presumably had set off before I blew my whistle. It was difficult talking to them in her presence, but they behaved with commendable sensitivity. I began by asking the first to arrive if his hands were warm (they were) and asked him to check the climber's carotid pulse. He too could detect nothing. I then briefed one of them with my assessment of the situation and sent him down to the CIC hut to radio for help. My partner and two other climbers from Tower Ridge arrived – I now had four helpers at the scene. I left the three climbers from Tower Ridge to monitor the girl and went to the man with my partner. I showed him how to do chest compressions (I didn't think to ask the others and nobody volunteered) while I gave mouth to mouth, and attempted CPR. In all honesty, this was more to satisfy his girlfriend's concerns that something was being done for him than in any expectation of a recovery. I noticed that his tongue was unusually small and drained of colour. The girl continued to insist that we do more for him and continue CPR indefinitely, so I told her firmly, but tenderly, that there was nothing more that we could do for him.

'Although she had not complained of cold, I became increasingly concerned that she was at risk from hypothermia. One of the other climbers produced a bivvy bag, and we decided to manoeuvre her into it. We replaced her gloves with a dry pair, put more layers on her head and cushioned her neck with my spare jacket etc. We removed her crampons but not her boots, and I checked each limb before moving it. Before doing all this we cut the ropes from her but, at my insistence, left her harness on in case it was useful for securing her to the stretcher which we hoped would arrive. I explained everything to her before we did it, and she did not object to what we were doing. Her composure throughout was remarkable, perhaps because she was generally drowsy and subdued, though always conscious. I think that I subconsciously interpreted this as evidence of a serious injury, though at the time the history was enough to prompt such suspicions anyway! The whole process of getting her insulated inevitably involved moving her about quite a bit which, by working together, we hopefully kept to a minimum. I briefed the others of the risks beforehand, but they all seemed pretty competent anyway and were a tremendous help – a credit to the climbing community.

'By now we had all given up hope that the man was alive, and made no attempt to safeguard him from hypothermia. Instead, we concentrated on continuing to monitor and reassure the girl, in particular checking that her consciousness level did not deteriorate and that she was warm enough.

Almost two hours had elapsed, the light was fading fast, and I was conscious that we were sitting ducks in the event of another, perhaps larger, avalanche. I had asked one of my helpers to keep watching Point

The Devil's Pulpit

Five Gully for warning signs, but none were seen. Nonetheless, I began to contemplate the option of trying to get her down the snowfield ourselves, even though this would be extremely risky for her. Fortunately, around 6.30pm when I finally voiced my concerns, the first member of RAF Kinloss MRT came into view ascending the snowfield below us. I went down to meet him and to brief him out of earshot of the girl.

'Soon there were several members of RAF Kinloss on the scene, with Lochaber MRT not far behind. I was physically and emotionally exhausted and only too glad to let the arriving teams take charge of the situation. They radioed for oxygen and set up a bivvy bag over and around the girl. The other climbers left the scene and made their way down to the CIC hut, as did my partner and I, after assisting for a few more minutes.

'On reaching Fort William, I had a hot meal and then reported to Fort William police station to give a statement. The duty officer suggested that I return in the morning as the appropriate person would be there then, and I subsequently did so after a few welcome drams with my Lomond MRT colleagues in the bothy that evening.'

The man had died of a broken neck and there was nothing anyone on the mountain could have done to save his life. When Andrew visited the girl in hospital, a few days later, he found her on her feet and wearing a neck brace. They hugged and she thanked him for his help. It turned out that, in falling 1000 feet, she had fractured the base of her skull and damaged nearby cervical vertebrae, but suffered no other major injuries. From her account it appears that an avalanche triggered their fall – a pure accident!

We should have convinced you by now just how versatile the average mountain rescuer is required to be during any of the twenty four hours, three hundred and sixty five days (add one for luck in a leap year) that he or she is on call in a year. But why is it that they're even called upon – for such a diversity of situations, many completely unconnected with mountains, walking and climbing – in the first instance? What prompts the police to request the help of a mountain rescue team when an incident occurs only yards off the urban track and far away from high mountains? We could sum it up in three words – skill, motivation and experience.

Putting aside for a moment the specific search and rescue skills in which every team will train its membership, in order to do the job to the highest possible standard, there's the wide diversity of skills and interests possessed by the individual members. Team members come from all walks of life, backgrounds and occupations - employed, self employed and retired, aged eighteen through to seventy plus, male and female. (True – men do tend to be in the majority but, contrary to popular myth, women have been involved with mountain rescue for very many years.)

The wide and varied skill base makes rescue teams inherently versatile. Add to this the fact they often operate in extremely difficult situations in regard to weather and terrain, is it any wonder the police authorities see the mountain rescue service as an extremely flexible resource, able to assist in a wide variety of emergency situations?

Take this example. Just north of Glasgow, there's a geological feature known locally as The Devil's Pulpit. Over the years, the small river which cuts through a rib of sandstone has created a steep sided gorge about 100 feet deep. Normally, the water level is low enough to walk the length of the gorge (about one quarter of a mile) without getting wet above the waist. In fact, it's considered quite an adventure by some, as the dark, vertical walls allow little light to penetrate to the bottom, generating a highly claustrophobic and threatening atmosphere. However, a few hours of rain quickly turn the river into a torrent of life-threatening roller coasters that makes passage impossible. Not that this was enough to deter three local youths, keen to try their hand at a spot of 'canyoning'.

This relatively new sport involves throwing oneself into a swollen river – dressed appropriately in wetsuit and buoyancy aid – and negotiating the boulders, trees and other such obstacles, as skilfully as possible. Not an activity for the faint hearted! One of the boys positioned himself on the bridge to monitor his friends who proceeded to throw themselves into the deluge. Both forgot – or chose

Take the operational call out list of any one team, and the chances are you'll find a wide diversity of occupation.
To name a few...
Computer consultant
University professor
Electronics technician
Doctor
Paramedic
Teacher
Professional
photographer
Watercolour artist
Mechanic
Fire fighter
Police officer
Nurse
Pest control officer
Vet
Joiner
Marine engineer
Local government
officer
Housewife
Retired Royal Navy
officer
Accountant
National Trust warden
Musician
Fitness instructor
Chef
Pet undertaker
Builder
Vicar
Mountain guide
Shop assistant
Landscape architect
...the list is endless.

PHOTO: BOB SHARP

Just to demonstrate the variety of demands on the average rescuer's time...

- Search for a man reported missing whilst delivering turkeys. Date recorded – 22 December!

- Recovery of a man with a broken femur, tibia and fibula who fell whilst having a pee.

- Retrieval of two boys stuck at the bottom of a gorge whilst trying to catch bats.

- Carry to a waiting ambulance of a female rider thrown from her horse.

- Transport (with some urgency!) from a remote farm of a pregnant woman whose waters had just broken...

- Evacuation of a young courting couple who had fallen simultaneously into the quarry they had been romantically dangling their legs over.

- Rescue of a small family of ducklings from a flooded drain.

- Recovery of suicide victim hanging from a tree.

- Search for a light aircraft lost on the hills.

- First aid treatment for a paraglider whose canopy had collapsed.

not – to wear any kind of protective clothing or buoyancy aid. Within moments, they realised the folly of their ways, each dragged under several times by the force of the current and risked being pinned under the water by fallen trees. At the deepest part of the gorge they managed to catch hold of roots hanging from the side walls and steady themselves against the moving water. Seeing their predicament, their friend ran for help and called for the police.

The local mountain rescue team was called about thirty minutes later but, upon arrival at the scene, team members found themselves at the back of a queue of rescue services! The Royal Navy had arrived with a Sea King helicopter, which was parked in an adjacent field. Members of the police diving unit, ambulance service, fire service and police were waiting on the bridge. Even representatives from local and national TV were on scene waiting to film the spectacle. Without any hesitation, the mountain rescue team moved into action. A small group went to each side of the gorge and set up anchors to lower two of the technical experts down to the boys. Once at the bottom of the gorge they secured each boy to a rope, attached harnesses and gave the call for them to be hoisted upwards. Both boys were extremely cold and could do very little to help themselves. Another ten minutes and they would certainly have let go of the tree roots and probably been carried away to their deaths. Instead, within five minutes of being secured, they were at the top of the gorge, wrapped in warm clothing and ready to be whisked away by a waiting ambulance.

The team in question had never actually carried out this type of operation before, but they had the wisdom to recognise how to solve the problem and the general skills to put the plan into effect. Interestingly, none of the statutory emergency services present had the exact combination of skills or local knowledge to complete the rescue, though they played an important stand-by role in case they were required.

So that's the skill, what about motivation? A better word might be attitude. Mountain rescuers have it in bucket loads. Independent, individual and idiosyncratic they may be, but they tend to share a common attitude – an innate desire to help others. The more complicated, uncomfortable, physically demanding and challenging the circumstances – the better. Whilst very many walkers and mountaineers may be technically capable, there are few who possess the motivation to become involved, or be sufficiently community spirited and prepared to put the safety of others before their own. It is this kind of willpower, combined with the relevant skills, that makes a rescue team so versatile and successful.

And as for experience – well, there's sixty hard fought years of that - driven by desire, need and the sheer buzz of a job well done. From humble beginnings, gathered by the light of a single 100 watt bulb in a makeshift HQ, Nordic knitted bobble hats, improvised equipment and one man and his bike pedalling like stink round the village mustering bodies – to operational call out lists, matching team jackets, medical protocols, pagers, mobile phones and GPS plotting. The modern mountain rescue service is continually reviewing best practice, researching and developing purpose-built equipment and learning new skills. Teams have liveried vehicles and brand identities – and work alongside the statutory emergency services as a valued resource in the community. Team members are trained in advanced first aid, technical rigging for rescue procedures, search management and helicopter protocol. If those Arran-clad men in their hob-nailed boots and jaunty bobble hats could only see us now...

rescue on crib goch

Just after three o'clock, one wintry afternoon in March 2004, Nikki Wallis, Snowdonia National Park warden, SARDA dog handler and Llanberis team member, was making her way down the familiar zig zags of the Pyg track beneath Yr Wyddfa, when she heard distant faint cries for help. What had begun as a routine patrol with her dog Jacob, was to become a long and challenging ordeal – not just for Nikki, but for all concerned – fraught with communication problems and severely hampered by treacherous conditions.

PHOTO: ROHAN HOLT

Nikki with her dogs Jacob and Caleb

Before making her way to investigate, Nikki glanced round. Had anyone else heard the cries? Some way off with his group, an instructor – and fellow team member – had also heard something but continued in his work, too far away for Nikki to call out to. Unable to raise a radio response from the Warden Centre at Pen y Pass, she eventually managed to make contact with fellow warden Bob Ellis Jones (Snowflake 620) and Meirion Thomas, who were also out on the hill, underneath Lliwedd. She told them what she was doing and asked Bob to remain where he was. Meirion, meanwhile, returned to Pen Y Pass to liaise with the rescue team, and use Bob as a radio link to the Warden Centre, a position, incidentally, which he subsequently held for many hours.

Climbing up the steep, ice-rimed grass, impossible to negotiate without crampons and ice axe, she discovered two young men. Despite one of them wearing only trainers, they had somehow managed to negotiate their way across Crib Goch and Crib y Ddysgl when they lost their rucksack, which contained only a few biscuits – no torch, no map, no first aid equipment. Then, when one of them slipped and disappeared over the edge, his friend believed he must surely have died, somehow managing to climb down to where he lay, his leg broken, before crying out for help. The injured boy lay precariously across the scree gully line, gradually sliding towards it and, from the position of his leg, he appeared to have suffered a fractured femur.

From the start of the incident there were difficulties – and confusion – with communications. At 3.21pm, a call had been registered with the police from a mobile phone. The report was of a French couple, one with a broken leg, on a ridge. At 3.30pm, there was another report of a male, stuck and possibly hurt. The description was vague, but appeared to indicate Crib Goch. It later transpired that one of the boys, unsure what to do in case of emergency, had dialled up a friend in Nottingham who had, in turn, called 999. The 'French couple' was a bit of a red herring – accident reporting by Chinese whisper – but it would be several hours before that became clear. So, for the rescuers involved, there initially appeared to be two separate incidents. Through the boys' mobile, Nikki was eventually able to establish a direct contact with both the police and Pen y Pass, but there was further confusion with the radios. At the time, the North Wales teams were undergoing a changeover period from low band frequency to high band radio sets. Nikki had made her call to Pen y Pass, and her colleague, using her National Park high band radio. John Grisdale, leader of the first party to be deployed low down by the RAF Sea King helicopter, was one of the few with the National Park high band frequency on his set. The Llanberis team members who responded to the call were working in low band. Not only did they not have comms with Bob Ellis Jones, Nikki's link under Lliwedd, they were unaware he was even in position for some hours. Phil Benbow described the situation as a 'nightmare in terms of knowing who was where and doing what.'

Daylight was beginning to fade as a handful of Llanberis team members were airlifted up the hill to the Miners Track. The first party deployed had communications with Nikki via John Grisdale, but communications began to really deteriorate when Nikki's battery started to go flat due to the length of time she had been scanning and transmitting messages. Whilst still able to transmit, she took a bearing from their location straight up to her position so that when communications were finally lost, they could accurately locate them. With only a vague idea where she might be, it was agreed that Phil and another team member would go on ahead to establish where she was before darkness fell. Leaving the stretcher behind, but equipped with sufficient kit to

PHOTO: NIKKI WALLIS

deal with a fractured femur, they set off to Glaslyn and climbed up to the Pyg Track, on to Bwlch Coch, then on to the Rock Step before beginning their traverse underneath Crib y Ddysgl on the notorious sheep track. With hindsight, they started their traverse too low. Less than 200 metres from Nikki and the boys, their whistles clearly audible now, they reached a series of buttresses. It was not easy mountaineering terrain, and with the wind gusting and the difficulties of finding a solid placement for an axe, there was a real possibility of a slip becoming a fatality. Reluctantly, they were forced to turn back.

Back on the Pyg Track they met up with another group who had attempted a different route, climbing up from below, with a similar lack of success. The lead climber, finding himself strung out, with no secure placements, stuff falling off around him, had no alternative but to reverse down. 'He thought he was going to die,' said one team member. In fact, there were several occasions throughout this rescue when the possibility of losing one of the rescuers seemed all too real. Back at Pen y Pass, there were difficult discussions - and decisions to be made. Should they leave Nikki up there until conditions improved and risk losing the casualty? As time went on, it became clear that this was not a fractured femur, but a knee injury. Thus far he had supported himself with his broken leg, but he was very cold and still in danger of slipping. 'It was literally a case of cutting bucket seats in the snow, using the wet snow to form a splint as far as possible for his leg injury, and supporting him on the lower side so he didn't slide down the mountain,' said Nikki. However, there were also concerns for Nikki's well being. As a keen mountaineer, actively involved in encouraging fellow diabetics to enjoy the mountains despite their medical condition, she is well rehearsed in looking after her own sugar levels. Her team mates knew she would have spare clothing and a ready supply of food in her sack. Yet, despite her reassurances via the mobile that she was fine, there were still misgivings on the ground that she may be hypoglycaemic. Tough call.

Meanwhile, the Ogwen Valley team had been called to assist, with Aberglaslyn as back up. Under the impression that Llanberis team members were at the incident site and had with them all the kit they needed, they set off to provide back up support, expecting a 'nice simple carry off'. But things proved anything but simple. They were a strong group made up of members from Llanberis and Ogwen MRTs – every single one a competent mountaineer. They included Mal Creasey, experienced mountain guide and instructor and Tim Bird, also a mountaineering instructor - all well versed in the mountains and the conditions they found themselves in. Yet, at a point on the traverse where it became difficult to distinguish the path of the goat track, as they negotiated frozen turf and ice and a series of bluffs and buttresses, the thought occurred to Tim, 'One slip here and we're gone.'

Communications confusion continued. A message came through at Pen y Pass that all the kit was in one place and all the troops in another. The weather was deteriorating rapidly, visibility down to zero. All in all, not quite so simple as expected. As members of the two Ogwen parties met up, a message came over the radio of another job – a walker at Llyn y Cwn between Nant Peris and the Devil's Kitchen had twisted his ankle – stretching manpower capabilities even further. (And not forgetting that, at this point, they still believed this to be a third job, the mystery of the French couple and the stuck male yet to be resolved). Aberglaslyn team members were diverted to the task.

Tim (OVMRO) and Mal (LIMRT) worked together to take bearings and navigate a route up. Just past the avalanche fences on the way up to Bwlch Coch they spotted footprints in the snow and névé. At Bwlch Coch, they began their traverse line, pushed on at some pace by their group, unhampered by heavy kit and keen to keep moving. It was at this point they got the message that Phil and the other Llanberis team members had been forced to retreat.

So, while the Ogwen group were going across the top, Phil and company were back down on the Pyg Track. By this time, Nikki's radio had gone down completely. Phil had intermittent comms via mobile with Pen y Pass. Two of his party of four had decided to either go home or return to base – too cold, wet and exhausted to safely continue. The two remaining were aware of the bigger group coming in from above but didn't think they'd have an easy time of it, so decided to approach again from below then walk to the zig zags, coming back along the goat track in the other direction.

Back with the casualties, her radio batteries spent and, by now resolved to being on the hill for the night, or at least until weather conditions improved, Nikki worked hard to keep the pair awake – and hypothermia at bay – with 'I Spy', word games and Welsh lessons, oblivious to the traumas of her fellow rescuers unfolding around her. This, whilst continuing to blow SOS on her whistle. Each time the boys asked, 'How long will the rescue team be?' all she could answer was, 'Very soon.' Battered by wind and snowstorms, the situation could have been very different without the group shelter she also carries – alongside everything else – in her rucksack. Jacob, who was keen to stay outside the shelter listening for the sounds of the approaching people, was frequently completely covered in snow.

Finally, just before midnight, a very relieved Nikki heard shouts as Tim and his group approached from above. The separate groups – above and below the incident site – made contact, radio comms were established and the relevant kit taken to the appropriate locations – no mean task. The Ogwen group now realised that there was insufficient equipment at the incident location as members of the Llanberis team had not actually made it to the site earlier on. So now the teams were faced with bringing ropes and stretchers and more equipment from all the members who were below the incident site just above the Pyg Track. The uninjured lad was taken out first, and Nikki moved to a safe position up the hill, anxious not to be involved in any further decision making apart from her own safety, as by now she was also cold.

Benefiting from extra group shelters and extra basic mountain kit, two of the Ogwen troops (Clive and Adam) were able to improve the casualty's insulation from the freezing ground. The casualty examination indicated lack of long-bone injury but possible incomplete left patella (kneecap) fracture, which was appropriately strapped. Oral analgesia, to ease the pain, and glucose were provided to the casualty, followed by a further wait whilst the stretcher was assembled and secured in challenging ground and weather conditions. Then rescuers set about stretchering the casualty directly down the hill to the Pyg Track – first down a thirty metre bluff, then a series of ten to fifteen metre bluffs across steep scree – and on to the Miners Track. Thanks to the terrain, it was a hazardous descent with the continuous danger of stretcher inversion and prolonged difficult stretcher jockeying. Once on the track, there was a further stretcher carry of about thirty minutes before the party met with the rescue Land Rover. Here, the Ogwen team doctor was able to further examine the casualty, in slightly more favourable surroundings, before arriving at the Pen y Pass Warden Centre in the early hours of the morning. Once the lines were in place, what had been an epic became a routine rescue.

It was 6.00am the following morning before everyone involved was down off the hill and the incident closed - fifteen and a half hours, involving forty two team members working 611 man hours. Had Nikki not heard the boys' cries and found the pair, there is no doubt in her mind they would eventually have lost their footing on the frozen ground and slipped, with tragic consequences. Press reports later that day said they were lucky to be alive. Lucky indeed. For her part, Nikki remains adamant her actions were only one small factor in the rescue operation – that all she had to do was sit there and wait. It was her friends and colleagues – working together under extreme pressure, in extreme circumstances – who did the hard bit. In the end, despite its many problems, the rescue was successful because of the quality of people on the hill, their individual skills and their ability to work together as a team. Mountain rescue at its best.

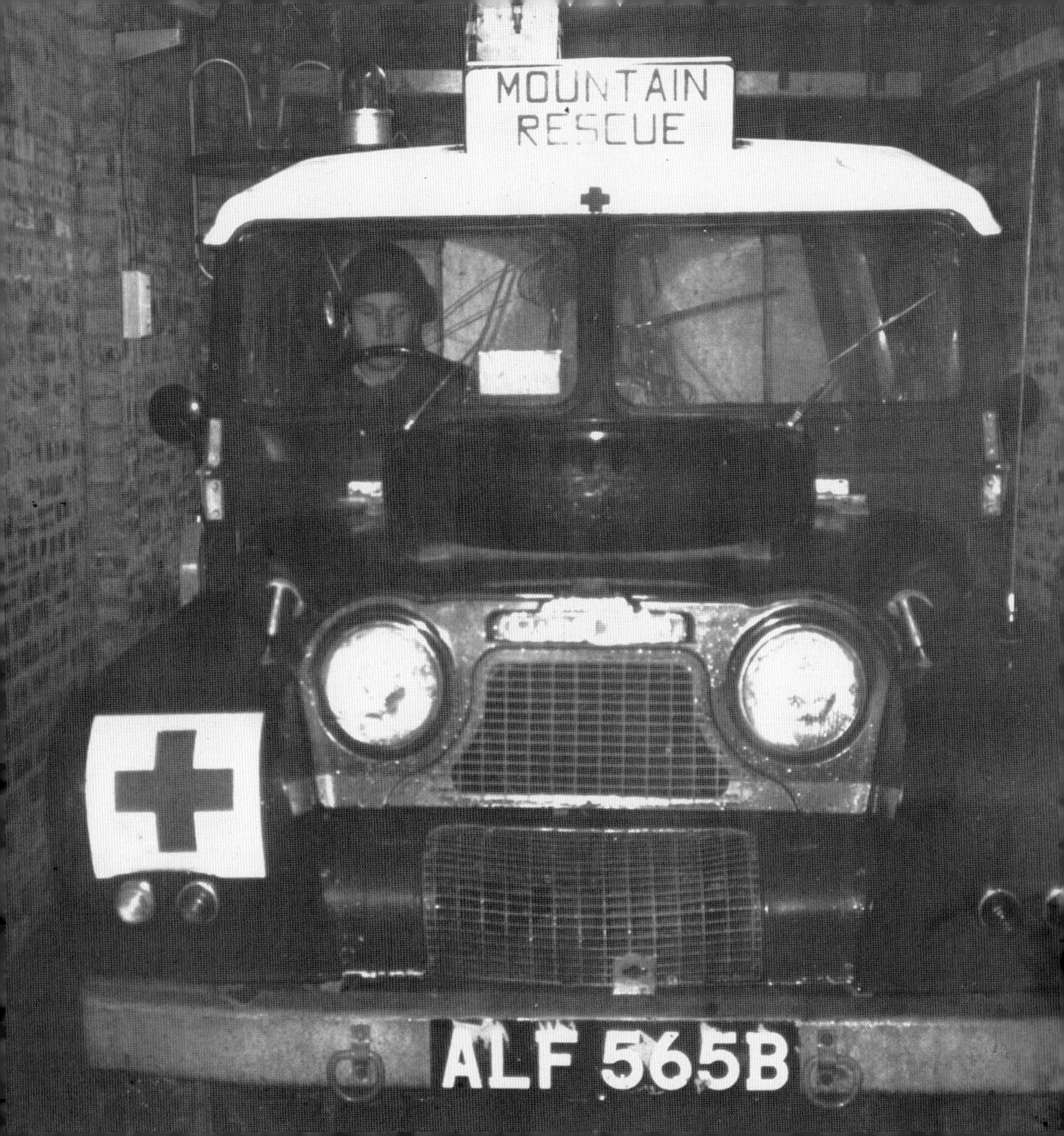
MOUNTAIN
RESCUE
ALF 565B

chapter two

THE ROAD TO DIVERSITY

Great things are done when men and mountains meet;
This is not done by jostling in the street.
William Blake

But, here's a thing: we've jumped straight in with just how diverse – and adaptable to public need – the modern mountain rescue service has become but, of course, it wasn't always that way. Whereas nowadays, the average annual incident report weaves a rich and colourful tapestry of human (and animal) misfortune – indulging in the widest possible variety of interests on or near the hills – when the seeds of mountain rescue were sown, mountaineering as a sport was centred very much on climbing. It was man against the elements, 'conquering' the mountain, pushing the boundaries of endurance. And when it all went wrong, the only people around to rescue you (if you were very, very lucky) were your mates, armed with nothing more than a five-barred gate, a bit of rope and young men's belief that they were invincible, even if you apparently weren't. The five barred gate, incidentally, doubled as a handy stretcher!

If we venture back even further, before the eighteenth century, hill walking and climbing for pleasure were virtually unknown. Life was hard enough without expending further energy pursuing the dubious pleasures of a cold, steep unforgiving landscape. But man is an adventurous animal. Inspired by the likes of Whymper and Mallory, risking their lives and livelihood in far off places, the majority could only dream about, lesser mortals began seeking adventure somewhat nearer home.

The story of Henry Wellington Starr, a thirty one year old curate from Northampton is well documented. Starr had already achieved the summit of Snowdon in late 1845, but decided to return the following year, on the advice of his doctor, to 'relax and get plenty of fresh air into his lungs.' The region was fast developing into an important tourist attraction to rival the spa towns of England, as visitors escaped the dirt and grime of a growing industrial landscape to breathe in the clear mountain air. According to Bob Maslen-Jones in his definitive book *A Perilous Playground*, Starr's disappearance, in September 1846, led to a search of 'the mountain

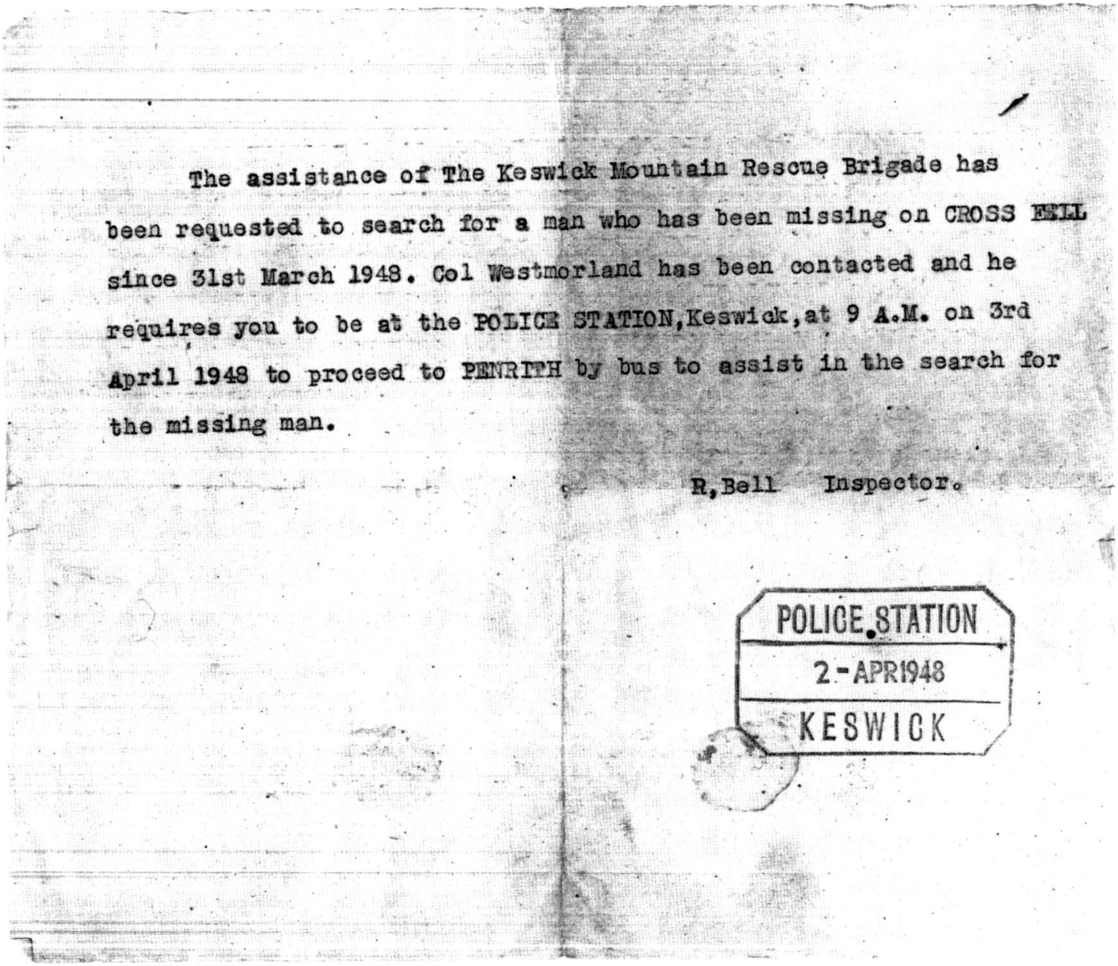

The assistance of The Keswick Mountain Rescue Brigade has been requested to search for a man who has been missing on CROSS FELL since 31st March 1948. Col Westmorland has been contacted and he requires you to be at the POLICE STATION,Keswick,at 9 A.M. on 3rd April 1948 to proceed to PENRITH by bus to assist in the search for the missing man.

R,Bell   Inspector.

POLICE,STATION
2-APR1948
KESWICK

In the 1940s, when the Keswick team was called to assist in a search for a man who had been missing for three days, team members were alerted by a letter from the local police inspector. He requested they meet the following day at 9.00am at the police station in Keswick.
Photocopy courtesy of Keswick MRT

tops, slopes and gorges, cliffs and rivers of the Snowdon massif and the Glyders' which lasted several days. A reported 900 people, probably only a few of them mountaineers 'went along for the reward rather than from a sense of duty'. In passing, Maslen-Jones draws the reader's attention to one fascinating fact – the use of foxhounds – querying whether these early 'search dogs' would have been able to resist their natural instinct to eat their 'quarry'! Eventually, as the early season snow swept across the landscape, the search was called off and it was not until June the following year that Starr's remains turned up at the end of Cwm Brwynog, at the foot of the precipice of Moel Cynghorion.

Across the UK, similar tales were unfolding. Mountain rescue had yet to be formalised. It continued in its ad hoc way with gamekeepers, sheep farmers, local doctors and police officers joining family and friends in the search for a missing climber or walker, usually against the clock and the weather, and (sometimes) with tragic consequences. Indeed, it was the mid-twentieth century before anything more formal began to emerge. Even then, rescues often took a very long time to initiate and organise – sometimes several days – with rescuers invariably travelling great distances before they arrived on scene.

Whilst the means of assistance have improved to a huge degree over the decades, the nature of those who rescue seems not to have altered at all. As Davy Gunn of the Glencoe team reflects, 'It's a testament to the early rescuers that despite probably seeing the early climbers as a somewhat eccentric bunch, it never deterred nor, I suspect, would it ever have crossed their minds, not to help someone in trouble. Often ill equipped and with only paraffin lamps to guide the way, they accomplished amazing feats. [They] would cycle round to gather a search party, perhaps including the local bobby if available. If it was an overly technical rescue,

perhaps additional manpower would be sought from any climbers in the area, or a telegram sent to the SMC clubrooms for assistance.'

Here in the twenty-first century, where the spectacular growth in instant communication has led to expectations of more instant help when in trouble on the hill, it hardly seems credible that 'team members' were assembled in such an arbitrary fashion – or that rescues were so laid back and protracted. But there were no means of calling out team members other than word-of-mouth or letter. In the 1940s, when the Keswick team was called to assist in a search for a man who had been missing for three days, team members were alerted by a letter from the local police inspector. He requested they meet the following day at 9.00am at the police station in Keswick. From here, they were to be transported by bus to Penrith to assist in the search. In the event, it proved to be unsuccessful and the man's body was found later by a group of 'boy ramblers'.

Things had first started to move on for mountain rescue in the thirties. Following a series of accidents, the climbing world began to consider the idea of developing a stretcher specially adapted for mountainous terrain, and, more importantly, a considered mountain rescue service to make use of it. One of these incidents involved a Rucksack Club member, Edgar Pryor, being knocked off his stance on the Long Climb at Laddow by a climber above him. Despite the use of an impromptu splint, fashioned from a rucksack frame, and an improvised stretcher, the rescue was described as an 'agonising business.' This despite the 'relay of runners to collect hot water bottles from Crowden to aid the victim!'

Something had to be done and, in 1933, the Rucksack Club and the Fell & Rock Climbing Club, two important mountaineering clubs of the time, formed the Joint Stretcher Committee with the specific purpose of considering the most efficient means of transporting a casualty down a

Donald Duff on Sheep Fank Wall, Glen Nevis with Duff stretcher c1956

PHOTO: COURTESY OF GEORGINA DUFF

story of Wilson Hey, a keen and experienced climber, being involved in a mountain rescue with two of his medical friends climbing on the Glyders in North Wales.

'Near the summit of Glyder Fach they came across a man who had broken his leg and needed urgent medical attention. Leaving one of their number with him the other two went down to get help and a stretcher from the rescue post at Pen y Gwryd. On the way down they came across a gate which they 'borrowed'; mindful of the fact that saving time was all important, they took the gate up to the ridge and after making the injured man as comfortable as they could, they put him on it and set off down the mountain. The journey was traumatic for the casualty; the gate was most uncomfortable, they had been able to apply a makeshift splint to the broken leg which caused him intense pain, and there were no pain killing drugs available. When they reached the road there was a long delay until an ambulance arrived and, while he waited, Wilson Hey made up his mind that his committee would ensure that the equipment held in posts must be improved.'

The new 'Thomas stretcher', designed by Eustace Thomas and produced by his company, was made of duralumin tubing with extendable handles – allowing the end carriers to see their feet and avoid stumbling and had wooden runners which gave sufficient ground clearance to allow easy movement across rock, scree, grass or snow, although it was not strong enough to be dragged over very rough ground. An adaptation, the 'Split Thomas stretcher', was split horizontally across the centre to divide into two halves, each fitted with carrying straps. Each half could thus be readily strapped onto one man's back for transport up the mountain, where they would be assembled and locked together by wing nuts. Many features of the early designs can still be seen in the modern stretchers made by current manufacturers such as Peter Bell and Hamish MacInnes.

mountainside. Two of the leading protagonists were Manchester surgeon Wilson Hey and Eustace Thomas whose engineering company, Bertram Thomas Ltd, based in Manchester, played a major part in the development and eventual production of the first purpose built mountain rescue stretcher.

Several others such as Donald Duff and Percy Unna would also be instrumental in stretcher development over the years. Unna suggested that '...the stretcher should be made rigid and non-collapsable and have full length runners with upturned ends'. And, corny though it may seem, that five barred gate we mentioned earlier proved pretty significant. Bob Maslen-Jones recounts a

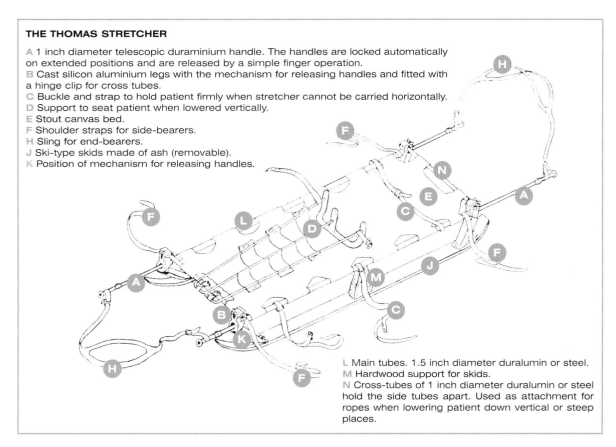

THE THOMAS STRETCHER

A 1 inch diameter telescopic duraminium handle. The handles are locked automatically on extended positions and are released by a simple finger operation.
B Cast silicon aluminium legs with the mechanism for releasing handles and fitted with a hinge clip for cross tubes.
C Buckle and strap to hold patient firmly when stretcher cannot be carried horizontally.
D Support to seat patient when lowered vertically.
E Stout canvas bed.
F Shoulder straps for side-bearers.
H Sling for end-bearers.
J Ski-type skids made of ash (removable).
K Position of mechanism for releasing handles.

L Main tubes. 1.5 inch diameter duralumin or steel.
M Hardwood support for skids.
N Cross-tubes of 1 inch diameter duralumin or steel hold the side tubes apart. Used as attachment for ropes when lowering patient down vertical or steep places.

Designated rescue posts, containing specific essential items of equipment, were set up for use by climbers, post supervisors and local volunteers. These were established in some of the more popular climbing areas - for example, in Scotland at Glen Brittle in Skye and on Ben Nevis and, in England and Wales, at Sty Head Tarn, in the Lake District and Pen y Gwryd, in the Ogwen Valley – and were managed by the various mountaineering clubs with the help of donated funds. Each post fell under the supervision of a designated individual. These 'Good Samaritans of the mountain valleys', as the 1966 Mountain & Cave Rescue Handbook later described them, were the 'foundation of the whole service.' The book exhorted those who called on the facility to 'respond to this generous spirit by doing all they can to minimise the upset and disturbance to the home and livelihood whenever a supervisor's services are called on, and to exert their influence to see that there can be no reproach of lack of good manners or considerate behaviour.' Such an expectation of respect and trust – integral to the spirit of mountain rescue – seems hardly credible now. As more and more folk took to the hills, the incidence of vandalism increased, leaving many posts without vital equipment when it was needed. Today, very few

Members of Keswick MRT on their first practice, Kern Knotts, Great Gable, 11 April 1948. Photo courtesy of Keswick MRT. From L. clockwise: Col Rusty Westmorland, Unknown, Jim Barber, Frank Barnes, Mrs C Saver, Conrad Saver, George Fisher, George Spenceley, Norman Lusby, Stan Thompson, Treeby Bolton, Vince Veevers, Unknown, Dick Fisher.

remain on the mountains. And, of course, as teams developed their own operations, the need for the old rescue post system gradually disappeared.

But back in those, perhaps, more innocent days, the posts were a huge step forward and, although pockets of growth had begun, there were still no recognised teams as such. In September 1936, the committee decided that a more permanent structure was called for to maintain and manage the posts and administer donations. Mountain rescue not yet having mastered the art of the snappy title, the grandly named First Aid Committee of Mountaineering Clubs was born.

Perhaps the most intriguing development to emerge was the introduction to the first aid equipment list of morphia. Once again, it was the dogged determination of Wilson Hey which finally saw this powerful painkiller officially authorised for use after a fifteen year, hard-fought battle. In the form of tubonic ampoules of Omnopon, the drug had been in unofficial use by one or two maverick members of the rescue community for some time. The Home Office had refused official permission for its supply – not surprising, given that rescue posts were virtually open access to anyone in need. In fact, it was 1949 before they relented, when Hey – perhaps one of the most maverick of mavericks – reapplied, freely admitting that he had been supplying the drug to the posts for twenty four years and that, to date, it had been used in fifty seven accidents. Even this final breakthrough was not without hitches, however. In the August court case in which Hey was found guilty of supplying morphia without prescription, he was fined just £10, which infuriated him. The figure was too small to generate the drama he'd hoped would strengthen his campaign. He refused to pay the fine, determined to go to prison. To make matters worse, when the

Members of the Braemar MRT practising at the Pass of Ballater 1969

Rucksack Club paid his fine for him 'his fury knew no bounds'!

By December, the Home Office had reversed their decision. It was agreed to supply ¾ grain of

Portable Pye Test on Great Gable. Photo courtesy Keswick MRT. From L. clockwise: Peter Muschin, Fred Mills, Dave Harper, Joe Graham, Joanne Weeks, Alan Ferguson, Beaut, Brian Martland, Dave Weeks, George Fisher, Derek Sandham, Alan Fisher

morphia in the form of ¼ grain tubonic ampoules to each post, but Ogwen and Glencoe might have six ampoules each due to the frequency of accidents there. The requirement for rescue teams to complete records of use, including quantity, batch number, and 'use by' date, continues to this day. That same year, the government (through the Ministry of Health in England and the Department of Health in Scotland) agreed to fund all post equipment.

The end of the Second World War brought a massive increase in outdoor activity, another step forward for mountain rescue and another – slightly snappier this time – name change. The Mountain Rescue Committee (MRC) as it was now styled, arranged for ownership of the first aid equipment to be vested in itself. By 1950, it had become a Charitable Trust with membership from a far wider, more representative, spectrum of outdoor pursuits groups. By this time, the seeds of several of the better known mountain rescue teams had been sown, notably Langdale/Ambleside and Coniston in the Lakes, Ogwen Cottage in Wales and Glencoe in Scotland. But, it was probably the example of the Keswick team – formed in 1947 by Colonel 'Rusty' Westmorland and its leader, George Fisher – and an accident on Tophet Bastion, Great Gable, that really set the scene for a more permanent, well-trained structure.

On a breezy day, in late April 1946, two experienced climbers had been tackling a climb called Shark's Fin when a gust of wind blew one of the men off his holds. He fell onto a ledge, one of his legs broken. Back at the Scafell Hotel, his companion enlisted the help of two more climbers and, armed with medical supplies, a stretcher and food, they set off to the scene of the accident. En route, they met Horace Westmorland, a local climber recently returned to Cumbria from thirty six years living, working and climbing in Canada.

In *Call Out – The First 50 Years. Keswick MRT,*

George Bott recalls that 'the three men, and three others who had heard of the incident, began the difficult task of evacuating [the fallen climber] Noyce from his precarious ledge. The loaded stretcher was gradually eased up the rock face for some 200 feet, a complicated and exhausting manœuvre which took three and a half hours. It was then lowered down a gully and eventually down 1500 feet of scree to the Sty Head track and so to Wasdale Head. The rescuers had been at work for twenty one hours, much of the time without food and in darkness.'

Concerned at the lack of any 'joined up' rescue service Colonel Westmorland decided to do something positive. While the police, acting as crown agents, would take possession of a deceased body, they were not obliged to help injured walkers or climbers, let alone being trained or equipped to do so. However, gathering volunteers was not quite as straightforward as he had anticipated. As quickly as the number of volunteers grew, so the odd few would drop out. Undeterred, he pressed on.

'The departure from the town of several of the volunteers prompted Rusty to write an appeal in the *Keswick Reminder* of 21 November 1947 asking for more names of 'willing climbers, fell walkers, young shepherds, young quarrymen and others.' For anyone worried about loss of earnings during a rescue, Rusty pointed out that reimbursement up to £1 was available from national sources which later would be claimed from the rescued individual or their family and friends. It is to the credit of Keswick employers that no such claims were made.

'It was essential, wrote Rusty, that volunteers should meet at least once indoors for discussion of methods and equipment and also carry out a practical evacuation of a patient on the crags for training and demonstration.'

Rusty, by all accounts, was a pretty formidable character, at times authoritarian and autocratic. Thirty years under his belt in the Canadian army,

serving in both world wars, he had returned to Keswick the epitome of military style – rarely seen without his polished boots and neatly trimmed moustache, his Austrian hat set at a jaunty angle. His dreams of running the team on more military principles, however, were not too keenly welcomed. At the Annual General Meeting in 1950, he proposed the team leader should be designated 'Captain', a suggestion which was subsequently quietly abandoned. The use of 'Captain' may not have sat too well with his fellow team members, but they certainly didn't have a problem with 'Rusty', the nickname he owed to an incident whilst serving with the army. A visiting general spotted some rust on the harness of one of Westmorland's horses. That night, the Commanding Officer ordered drinks all round, declaring 'Rusty will pay.' History doesn't record whether he actually did foot the bill (though one imagines he would) but the nickname stuck.

By 1948, some thirty names were on Rusty's list, mainly from Keswick and its immediate neighbourhood. With the colonel as leader, the Borrowdale Mountain Rescue Team, as it was initially titled, had their first official call out when a dozen members helped police, shepherds, farmers and other volunteers in a search for a twenty seven year old walker on Cross Fell, who had been missing for three days. Bott goes on, 'Deep snow and strong winds hampered the searchers and it was some time later that the body was discovered by a group of boy scouts on the Alston side of the fell.'

It was a story which echoed across the UK as a variety of accidents, searches and light aircraft crashes in mountainous and moorland areas galvanised the indigenous mountaineers into action. What is fascinating is that in those early days there was little communication between teams in different regions. And yet, independently, teams sprang up with similar values, similar aspirations, each subtly adapted to their own environment. The inspiration to

when is a mountain not a mountain?

When it's a hill, of course. Or you happen to be in the company of a bunch of mountain rescue folk talking about their day 'on the hill'. By which expression they could variously mean any one of an entire pick'n'mix of outdoor activities - from striding vigorously over a purple-heathered moor to scrambling gleefully up cheeky little rocks and waterfalls, every ounce of their being alive to the next move. From feigning nonchalance in the face of fear across pin-sharp ridges, hardly daring to take in the view, to idling along an early summer's lane, breathing in the blossom and sweet coconut gorse, ankles bruising the wild garlic. From pitting their wits against the most inhospitable of mountains to carving a perfect, curling ribbon through virgin powder snow. They might even have in mind the necessary two or three hour walk across fells and moorland in pursuit of a couple of hours in the dark. Underground.

It's generally accepted amongst the mountaineering fraternity (in England!) that a mountain is anything above 2000 feet (610 metres). But since metrication in the seventies, things appear to have become somewhat blurred, with a rounding down to 600 metres – and consequent drop to 1968 feet! Just to muddy the waters a little further, according to the 'Concise Oxford Dictionary', a mountain is a 'large natural elevation of the earth's surface, a large or high and steep hill, especially one over 1000 feet high.' That is half the height of our previous rule of thumb. Apply a bit of post-metric downsizing and it hardly seems worth dragging the walking boots out of the cupboard for! Incidentally, the same dictionary describes a hill as 'a natural elevation of the earth's surface, a small mountain'.

And then we have Scotland, where things are never quite the same and the 'hills' are much bigger. Bear in mind that whilst England boasts only six peaks over 3000 feet, Wales fifteen and Ireland thirteen, in Scotland there are five hundred and eleven. That's five hundred and eleven!! So, everything gets scaled up a notch. To be a mountain there, our 'large natural elevation of the earth's surface' must attain a grand 3000 feet. If we're being precise, a peak over 3000 feet becomes a 'Munro', over 2500 feet a 'Corbett' and a mere 2000 feet is a 'Graham'. And huge numbers of walkers spend their lifetime notching each and every one!

Confused yet?

Walt Unsworth stated, 'Although everyone likes to climb the highest fells 'because they are there' height is not the only means of judging a mountain. Form comes into it too. Blencathra in the northern fells is 207 feet lower than its neighbour Skiddaw but Blencathra looks a better mountain and is a finer climb. Obviously shape matters, and since the shape is largely determined by the geology, the geology matters too.'

So a mountain is a mountain if it looks like a mountain, but what about how they feel? Introduce a novice to their first 1000 foot peak, a mere training jaunt to the expert – let them savour the views, appreciate the weather, the physical exertion and the camaraderie and they will know, at the end of the day, that they have climbed a mountain.

Oh – and just one last point – every hill in the UK with a height drop of at least 150 metres all around, is a 'Marilyn'!

So now you know.

set up a team might come from anywhere – the local police officer, GP, hotelier or mountaineering enthusiast. Anyone, in fact, who saw a need for specialised assistance in first aid and search capability.

And as the popularity of climbing – and the incidence of accidents – continued to grow apace, so too did the demand for more formal training in 'outdoor skills' – a significant factor for mountain rescue. By the late 1950s, education authorities and others were seeking to establish their own outdoor activity centres. Plas y Brenin, ideally placed at the heart of Snowdonia and Glenmore Lodge in the Cairngorms were two such examples.

When Eugene Brunning, owner of the Royal Hotel in Capel Curig decided to sell the hotel in 1954, it was with the proviso that he must be the last landlord in its 150 year history, and that whoever bought the building must use it for some purpose other than as an inn. The hotel had been a popular venue for mountaineers for many tens of years and a ready source of volunteers to take part in search and rescues.

By lucky coincidence, the Central Council for Physical Recreation was looking for a suitable location for a mountain training centre in North Wales. By April 1955, the Royal Hotel had changed hands and was renamed Plas y Brenin (literally King's House), it was to be known as the Snowdonia National Recreation Centre and, with accommodation limited to forty students, the first courses were held during that summer.

Continuing the Royal tradition, students and others who came to the centre for recreation and training would regularly help out with stretcher carries and searches. By 1960, basic mountain rescue courses had been included in the programme and, in that same year, Plas y Brenin was designated MR Post No 60. Involvement with rescues, of course was purely voluntary – a huge commitment in terms of time and effort for those who already spent their professional lives out on the hill as instructors or guides and would often turn up for work straight from a rescue or turn out on a rescue after a hard day's work.

It was a similar story in the Ogwen Valley. Climbers Ron James and Tony Mason-Hornby bought Ogwen Cottage in 1959 and proceeded to open one of the first permanent private mountaineering schools. Very quickly recognised as an active mountain rescue post, the instructors automatically became members of Ogwen Cottage MRT, available for call out at any time. As the centre was open throughout the year, there was always a core of competent mountaineers available and, for the next five years, aided and advised by Flight Sergeant Johnnie Lees, leader of the RAF Valley MRT, the fledgling team carried out many rescues in their own area, and assisted their neighbours on Snowdon.

Then, as is often the way with mountain rescue, a series of coincidences prompted another step forward. Once again, education was the trigger. When Birmingham Education Authority bought Ogwen Cottage as a going concern in 1964, staff found themselves in the unusual position of enjoying regular school holidays. It was that summer, when most of the instructors were off indulging this new found freedom in the Alps, and RAF Valley team members were training elsewhere, that John Glews, a member of staff who had stayed behind, was badly injured in a fall while attempting a new route above Idwal Slabs.

Maslen-Jones recounts, 'Someone went for help and whilst John lay there waiting, he realised the need for continuous MR cover involving rescuers other than Ogwen Cottage staff and the RAF Valley MRT, either of whom might be away from the area or otherwise engaged. When a hastily assembled rescue party arrived, he was not over-impressed by their untrained skills and tried to tell them what to do as he lay injured on the stretcher. When his colleagues visited John in the orthopaedic hospital at Gobowen in Shropshire where he was still in

involved in rescue operations simply due to their presence on the hill that agreement to participate in mountain rescue was actually written into the job description. Since its establishment, the Lodge has

Members of the Millom Fell Rescue Team push the First Aid Post box up Brown Tongue

intensive care, having heard about his rescue by an inexperienced party, they decided that the need for a more permanent rescue team had become a pressing priority.'

By the autumn, the Ogwen Valley Mountain Rescue Organisation had been formed, consisting of 'a number of team leaders, mainly the instructors at Ogwen Cottage, with a large pool of skilled rescuers who would be on call round the clock. It would be a charitable and entirely voluntary commitment for... no public funds were available to cover the running costs of mountain rescue teams.'

The synergy between mountain rescue and education was also apparent in Scotland. Glenmore Lodge opened its doors as Scotland's National Outdoor Training Centre in 1947, with the Reverend Cannon Bob Clarke as its warden. Previously the Episcopalian Minister in Fort William from 1943, and a founder member of the Lochaber team, he boasted considerable mountaineering experience. Staff and students would so routinely become

continued to deliver mountain training to countless students, and mountain rescue training to thousands of team members. And, to this day, its instructors make up one of Scotland's twenty three civilian mountain rescue teams.

During the 50s, RAF Valley MRT – and Johnnie Lees in particular – conveniently based on the island of Anglesey, was clearly instrumental in the development of mountain rescue in North Wales. But, in fact, the RAF teams played a big part in the early growth and evolution of several civilian teams, essentially through the provision of equipment and training expertise, although even they'd had their moments in their early wartime days. Initially formed to rescue and recover crew from crashed or downed aircraft in the UK mountains, it bore little resemblance to the efficient RAF MRS we know today. Rescues were organised in a very ad hoc manner, a station tannoy rallying volunteers to form a rescue party. Many of the men had little or no experience of hill walking, let alone mountaineering, their equipment standard battledress, greatcoats – and rubber boots.

Two names in particular deserve a mention – Flt Lt George (Des) Graham at Llandwrog and Flt Lt David Crichton at Harpur Hill – according to Frank Card probably 'the first, certainly in the UK and possibly in the world, to establish a mountain rescue team as we would recognise it today – that is with a permanently established membership and, crucially, a regular training programme.' The template, he believes, that gave us the post-war civilian teams. Crichton, the medical officer in charge, once recalled in an interview 'going to an old retired sailor in Buxton to learn how to splice ropes.' Not a mountaineer at the start, he had to learn the skills from scratch, as did most of his team members. Both he and George Graham, over at Llandwrog were putting together scratch teams to rescue crashed airmen in the mountains from early in the war. Noel Bailey, a member of the RAF Llandwrog team during Graham's time recalled, 'It may be difficult for anybody to imagine what it was like in 1943 when you look at a present day mountain rescue team and its vast array of equipment. We had no helicopters, no fully equipped Land Rovers, no specialist clothing, no climbing boots, no walkie-talkie radios and, worst of all, no experience. What we did have was our working battledress (in fact, it has been rumoured that mountain rescue personnel could only take their berets off once they were above 3000 feet!!), rubber boots and RAF greatcoats. The Station Medical Officer, Flying Officer Graham, had his little black bag and a boy scout type compass. Transport was borrowed from our MT section.'

Incidentally, lack of suitable clothing or equipment does tend to be characteristic of newly fledged teams, with local retailers frequently cajoled into providing assistance. Gear was often freely given, or very cheap to purchase, and sometimes next to useless. Although these days equipment in general is far more fit for the purpose as new technologies continue to develop. And, in keeping with the spirit of mountain rescue, and thanks to the growth of inter-team communication, teams who are better off can now help out their less fortunate colleagues, not least with the benefit of their own experience. The most recent addition to the mountain rescue community, Cornwall Rescue Group, was helped enormously in their setting up by other teams passing on equipment, clothing and vehicles as their own was replaced. The Oban team, which was only established in 2000, quickly came up to speed through joint training with the adjacent Glencoe team.

But, back with the military, despite such basic beginnings, those early ad hoc teams – at RAF Llandwrog in North Wales, RAF Madley in South Wales, RAF West Freugh in Scotland and RAF Harpur Hill on the edge of the Peak District – successfully rescued thirty three aircrew from twenty two air crashes. Yet again, it was unhappy coincidence and a series of tragic events which led to the growth of a more formal service. On 6 July 1943, thanks largely to George Graham and his continued protestations to the Air Ministry, the Royal Air Force officially formed the Mountain Rescue Service. The very same day, an Avro Lancaster bomber aircraft crashed at Llangerniew, north of Snowdonia, three hours after take off on a training sortie – the first officially recorded training exercise for the RAF MRS. Just eighteen days later another training aircraft, this time an Airspeed Oxford, on a sortie in the Conway Valley, crashed into the hillside at Tal y Cafn. Amazingly, the pilot survived without serious injury. It was Graham's team which responded, allegedly completing the thirty mile journey in a mere thirty two minutes!

Throughout 1943 – and despite the best efforts of the rescue teams – as many as 571 aircrew lost their lives in 220 crashes across the UK. Clearly, in the face of such loss, there was a need for a more structured, co-ordinated service, properly trained and equipped for the purpose. Enthusiasm, determination and bravery, rubber boots, berets and boy scout compasses were no longer sufficient! Change was in the air – if you'll pardon the pun. At Llandwrog an instructional army team, led by Sergeant Hans Pick – an Austrian Jew and refugee from the Nazis who had joined the British army during the war – delivered two weeks of intensive training in navigation, rock climbing and hill walking. The seeds were sown for a service capable of responding beyond its original focus and, the following summer, the Llandwrog team were called to assist their first civilian climber. The RAF team was requested when police and civilians had failed to reach a young girl who had become stranded on a ledge on Cadair Idris. In the event, she was found safe and well in a farmhouse, having made her way down without help.

There was method in the Air Ministry allowing the RAF teams to assist in civilian climbing accidents. As the *Anniversary Journal* reasons, 'The most effective training for the teams was practical – that is, exercises in mountainous terrain and actual rescues. Also, the RAF had personnel who were specialists in search and rescue operations. They could provide manpower, specialist equipment and good radio communications. They were always available, no matter what day of the week or hour of the day – whensoever. And finally, it was extremely good public relations.' And you thought PR didn't exist before the twenty first century soundbite. That spirit of teamwork and collaboration continues to this day. It's a fact that the RAF helicopter squadrons spend around 95% of their time working on civilian operations.

It would be some years after the war, however, before RAF teams began to fulfil their early promise. Without the urgent demand to rescue airmen and recover aircraft, the service hit the doldrums. As late as 1951 they remained poorly equipped, the men poorly trained. Meanwhile, the civilian mountain rescue service was only barely beginning to take shape. From the RAF point of view, things may never have recovered, but for the events of 'Black Easter', as it would become known, and a major incident in the Torridon area of northern Scotland.

Easter came early that year. Maundy Thursday, 22 March. It had been a long, wet winter, with a great deal of snow on high ground, and little sign of respite for what would traditionally be the first 'walking weekend' on the calendar. The British Mountaineering Council reported 'the continued snowfall meant unusual cornices and dangerous ice slopes, which ordinary fellwalkers were unable to cope with; even with ice axes, some of the slopes, quite safe under normal conditions, had become very dangerous.' Not enough to deter some.

In North Wales, a party of seven experienced climbers were descending South Gully on Tryfan unroped (although they were carrying ropes!) even though conditions were tough – hard packed frozen snow and ice – when one of their party slipped and slid 500 feet to her death at the bottom of the gully. On the Saturday, two walkers slipped and tumbled several hundred feet whilst attempting to descend the Llanberis path, one of the most dangerous routes on Snowdon under winter conditions. Both were said to be wearing proper boots, but neither carried an ice axe, despite the prevailing conditions. When rescuers reached the couple, one was already dead from severe head injuries, the other in a serious condition. The casualties transferred to a waiting ambulance, the rescue party was en route back up the Llanberis Pass, when they were met with news of another accident – this time three experienced climbers in Trinity Gully. The three had made good progress as they climbed 600 feet, cutting steps in the hard snow, when the snow turned to hard ice and winds began to gust at gale force, sucking the energy from their bodies. Sensibly, they had decided to retrace their steps but found the steps they had cut on the way up were too steep for descent. They were forced to cut new ones, swinging the ice axe from above to strike the snow beneath their feet. Mid stroke, a gust of wind caught the lead climber blowing him off the mountain and dragging his two companions with him. Miraculously, two of them survived - sadly, one was killed instantly.

On and on it went. Back at Pen y Grwyd, team leader Chris Briggs heard of another accident at the same spot he and his team had carried out the first rescue of the day. In the evening, a solitary walker slipped on ice ascending the last 800 feet of the Watkin Path, falling about 50 feet. He was discovered some way down the slope by a party of boy scouts from Dublin who, without further ado, set about making a rope stretcher on which to carry him. They started to walk down the railway track towards Llanberis but found the going too tough and were forced to return to the shelter of the summit building. They were not alone. Twenty one people sought refuge there overnight rather than do hopeless battle with the elements and treacherous conditions. Not that Sunday dawned any better. Another group of boy scouts witnessed a couple slip and fall whilst crossing the slope, coming to rest on the railway line. When they managed to reach them, the man was dead, his girlfriend badly injured.

By the end of the Easter weekend, nine people had lost their lives on Snowdon. A further five would die before the year was out. There was a public outcry, no doubt fuelled by the press. In his summing up of the situation, the coroner was uncompromising and perhaps a trifle unfair. 'These mountains were invaded during the Easter weekend by an army of what I call novices, who were more equipped for a day on Hampstead Heath than the rigours of these mountains.' There were calls for restricted access to Snowdon, without much thought as to how that might be effected, and suggestions that 'scouts' should be appointed who could report on conditions on the mountains and issue warnings through the media. Less than a year later the National Park wardens were doing that very thing, and thoughts were crystalising about how an efficient mountain rescue service could operate in the area.

The RAF Valley team had played a key part in the events of the weekend, recovering a total of three bodies and four casualties, even lending out their ice axes to one group struggling over an icy stretch on the Snowdon Horseshoe. And, just a week prior to that, an incident in Torridon proved a turning point for the team at RAF Kinloss. When an Avro Lancaster bomber failed to return from a training exercise, several witnesses reported a red flash from the direction of Beinn Eighe, one of Torridon's highest mountains. It was five days, however, before the wreckage was sighted and the Kinloss team called to the incident. As they approached Beinn Eighe, and discovered the wreck at the base of Triple Buttress in the coire, it soon became clear that the majority of the plane was higher up the buttress. Including the crew, dead or alive.

Over several days, the attempts to locate the wreckage and the bodies of the aircrew threw the inadequacies of the RAF mountain rescue service into sharp focus. A first attempt to reach the wreckage via a gully failed miserably. Only a few had ice axes, few were properly trained for the harsh conditions or the mountains, and few had proper boots. One or two were actually wearing Wellingtons. Time after time, attempts were made to reach the wreckage, each one defeated by the atrocious weather or fatigue. The Moray Mountaineering Club had called RAF Kinloss to offer their assistance in the form of six men with a great deal of Scottish winter mountaineering experience, an offer which was declined. Yet the following day, team members who

scottish mountain rescue
the early days

PHOTO: RAY 'SUNSHINE' SEFTON

Lochaber MRT. Ben Nevis Bogie. c1958

Like most areas of Scotland, Lochaber had mountain rescues long before an official team was formulated and, in those early days, fellow mountaineers, shepherds and local men would combine to resolve the situation.

In 1934, a bunch of Glasgow men were up for the Fair Holidays when one of them slipped down No 3 Gully on Ben Nevis, breaking a leg in the process. It took two days for his friends to evacuate him – first to the CIC hut and later Fort William – Dr Isaac McIver and a Mr Murphy from the Fort were called upon for assistance.

The Rev Bob Clark was rector at St Andrew's Church in Fort William during the Second World War and, in 1944, along with local policeman Sergeant McLean, they formed the nucleus of what was eventually to become the Lochaber Mountain Rescue Team. At the end of the war, retired army officer Donald Duff was appointed surgeon at the Belford Hospital in Fort William. Not only did he bring added impetus to the mountain rescue scene through innovative training exercises on both the technical and medical side, he patented one of the first ever mountain rescue stretchers in 1946 and played a leading part in legal battles with the Home Office concerning the administration of morphia to casualties –– the government stance in 1949 being that 'morphia is bad for the man on the mountain.' An officer and a gentleman, he was leader of the Lochaber team during the late 40s and 50s.

The Lochaber section of the Junior Mountaineering Club of Scotland (JMCS) was the backbone of Lochaber MRT through the 50s and 60s, and much of their mountaineering club agenda seems to have been taken up with mountain rescue business. A meeting at the club in August 1957 expressed 'dissatisfaction' with the mountain rescue situation and a club member was asked to write and 'endeavour to arrange a meeting between the county council, police and JMCS to thrash out this sore point'. Money for equipment was the main source for concerns, of course, though there was a little light relief the following year when 'the WRVS offered clothing and refreshment facilities for mountain rescue parties'! More money was found in 1962 when, amongst other things, sixteen pairs of R Lawrie Mk IV boots were bought at £5/2/6d per pair, the 'nailing to be clinker heels, ring clinkers at toes, muggers in the centre and No 1 tricounis (about ten per boot) set in slightly from the edge.'

It was not until 1969 that Lochaber Mountain Rescue Association was set up to promote a more professional approach to rescue, raise funds for much needed equipment and training and also to manage the team in a democratic manner. That Association is still there today. The team strength has risen from twelve to forty with the first full time female member arriving in 1998! There were approximately a dozen incidents to deal with in 1969, seventy in 1999. Running costs in 1969 were £500, but this has now risen to nearer £40,000.

Mick Tighe, Lochaber MRT.

set off to Beinn Eighe on their own initiative were forced to retreat in the face of driving gales and snow. When the team finally reached the wreckage on 30 March, it was too dangerous to recover the bodies of the crew. The last body was not recovered until the end of August. Rumour had it the crew would have survived had rescuers reached them in time but the medical authorities confirmed that death would have been instantaneous.

Besides the huge press interest these incidents generated, they served another purpose. Suddenly, Whitehall was listening. The Air Ministry implemented radical changes for the RAF teams – a structured training schedule, the introduction of an annual mountaineering course in North Wales, an instruction book for mountain rescue and the secondment of experienced mountaineers to the RAF MRS.

Over the next decade, as new teams sprang up, mountain rescue in general embarked on a steep learning curve as team members gave life to their ideas and learnt from their mistakes, gaining experience and local knowledge along the way, but never losing sight of what drove them in the first place – intense camaraderie, resourcefulness and initiative, and a passionate desire to help those in need.

The 60s brought huge growth in mountain rescue. Teams were now springing up all over the UK – 'household names' such as Cairngorm and Glencoe in Scotland, Buxton and Patterdale in England. Even in the comparative lowland areas of the UK, the need for an established rescue service gradually became apparent. In the Mid Pennine region, it was two fatal moorland incidents which triggered the creation of more formal teams. The morning of Sunday 25 March 1962 dawned bright and breezy, just the sort of day for a brisk spring walk across the fells. Three teenagers, a girl aged fifteen, and her brothers aged eleven and eighteen, set off from the village of Chipping, over Parlick Hill and the Bleasdale Fells to the Langden Valley. It's an isolated valley, even by today's standards, their route a single faint footpath winding its way through the boulders and heather alongside the three mile length of Langden Beck.

PHOTO: BARRY ROBINSON

Pendle Hill, Lancashire

Absorbed by each other's company, and warmed by the exertion of the walk, maybe they failed to notice the subtly changing weather. But, by the time they came to start back home, the sky was overcast, clouds closing in on the surrounding hills and moorland. The fluttering spring breeze had gathered to gale force, driving gentle rain to sleet and snow as temperatures dropped. As an early darkness descended, the three youngsters would doubtless have felt disorientated and frightened. Certainly, they would have begun to suffer from the cold and exhaustion.

Sensibly, they found some rocks to shelter in for the night but, though the morning brought a slight improvement in the weather, the youngest boy was already unconscious with exposure. The other two decided to move on in an effort to get out of the mist and off the fells, to find help for their brother.

Meanwhile, their failure to return home had been reported to police around midnight. Local farms and roads were checked, but the deteriorating weather and darkness prevented the police and other helpers from venturing onto the hills until morning. Even then, their search had little success. Until at 10.30am, the girl struggled, exhausted and distressed, off the hills into Saddleside Farm, to report having left one brother in the shelter of rocks and the other collapsed en route with her to find help.

Following her directions, police found the eighteen year old semi-conscious at the bottom of a steep sided gully, but it was too late. Rushed to Preston Royal Infirmary, some twelve miles away, he was dead on arrival. Two hours later, his eleven year old brother was found – he had been dead for some time. The search had involved over eighty policemen, dogs and horses, farmers and a helicopter from British Aircraft Corporation at Warton.

The death of two local teenagers hit the press hard. Demands were made for some sort of fell search and rescue service for the Lancashire area, similar to that in the neighbouring Lake District. By May, the South Ribble Fell Search and Rescue team was formed, swiftly followed by the Northern Rescue Organisation, both based in the Preston area and within easy traveling distance of the Bleasdale fells, scene of the tragedy. The stage was set for a network of teams in an area which many would question the need for 'mountain' rescue – even Pendle Hill, rising conspiratorially at the heart of Lancashire's 'witch country' only manages 1831 feet on a good day – 169 feet short of official recognition as a mountain! Local team members might exchange lighthearted banter about their surreptitious efforts to tip the tape measure – but that's an awful lot of soil to carry up your trouser leg. And, truth be told, they love her just the way she is.

Whilst mountain rescue teams were emerging across Scotland at the same rate as those further south, unlike those in England and Wales it was some time before any sort of national concensus was forged. The organisation was fragmented, activity focused in the immediate area of operation with little cross-reference. Perhaps this has as much to do with the fiercely independent Scottish temperament as the nature of the land itself. Scotland has more than five hundred mountains over three thousand feet. The terrain is harsh and unforgiving, with few roads and tracks in the highland areas. It can still take hours to walk in to a favourite climb. How much more difficult then to reach an injured casualty when the gods would seem to be agin you and the weather nothing short of foul? And how much more difficult even forty years ago? Scotland needed an organisation which understood the nature of Scottish mountains, the nature of Scottish mountain rescue and, perhaps more to the point, the nature of the Scottish mountain rescuer!

By 1960, there were rumblings of dissatisfaction. Yet, even then, attempts at co-ordination resulted in the formation of not one but two organisations – one a sub committee of the Mountain Rescue Committee which would be responsible for Scottish affairs and the other the Scottish Council for Mountain Rescue, headed by Dr Donald Duff. All in all, an unwieldy twenty seven representatives from organisations as diverse as youth hostels and tourist boards – massive bureaucracy - zero effect.

But these things take time. Five years later, the Mountain Rescue Committee of Scotland was formed – an independent body which reduced the number of representative organisations to nine, alongside regional representatives from five areas in Scotland where mountain rescue teams operated, a make up which has remained more or less constant to the present day. And, perhaps not surprisingly, many of the important issues then are still high on the agenda. Mountain rescue may have moved forward in many ways, but various minutes of the time prove that paradoxically, *plus ça change, toujours c'est la même chose*! In other words, 'what goes round comes round'! There was debate as to how climbers might be better advised about avalanche dangers (the committee suggested submitting an article to a climbing magazine might help); the shelf life of nylon rope was discussed, a maximum of two years recommended; there was talk of changes to radio frequencies, the use of helicopters and the employment of strobe lights to guide them in... all as pertinent today as then.

And so it continued... through the seventies and eighties and nineties and now the noughties. Teams continued to emerge and grow, and even merge and grow. At the time of writing, the Mountain Rescue Council for England and Wales is undergoing another metamorphosis – and yet another change of name. Finally having mastered the art of the snappy title, the organisation is now simply Mountain Rescue (England & Wales). In contrast, the Mountain Rescue Committee of Scotland has not changed its label in forty years. So, will it follow suit? Will there ever be a time when north and south of Hadrian's Wall mountain rescue operates as one? Could it even be feasible given the very difference in their natures? Only time will tell.

Meanwhile from such humble and diverse beginnings, mountain rescue as a whole now boasts 85 teams comprising a membership of nigh on three thousand dedicated volunteer team members. Fifty seven teams in England and Wales and twenty eight in Scotland, including cave rescue, police and RAF teams.

But why? In a world where – should you believe the relentless waves of drivel which wash over us on a daily basis – people no longer care. Why should any human being wish to make themselves available in such a way to provide the service they do? What makes the average mountain rescuer tick?

Hard to believe, but there was a time when people did as they were told and listened without question to the words of wisdom from their elders and leaders! When procedures for behaviour were well defined and often pedantic in the extreme.

Dr Donald Duff belonged to that time. He has often been described as 'the father figure' of mountain rescue in Scotland – in particular through his involvement with both the Glencoe and Lochaber teams. It was his motivation which formalised the formation of both teams, bringing together 'local shepherds, mountaineers and forestry workers' on a more organised basis. Best known for the 'Duff stretcher', which he developed specifically for mountain use – one even found its way onto the 1953 ascent of Everest – he was renowned for his fortitude and independent spirit and commanded considerable respect from his patients and mountain rescue colleagues alike. He was typical of many of the characters to touch and influence mountain rescue over its sometimes tortuous history.

An interesting extract from the Scottish Mountaineering Club Journal in 1969 perfectly describes his character when it describes Duff battling his way to the Belford Hospital in filthy weather on an old bicycle. It would seem this typified the man. He was independent, always kept himself fit and scorned hardship – even in the coldest weather refusing to wear an overcoat or sweater to work. He loved the mountains with a passion and the Belford Hospital became known as an emergency bothy for stray mountaineers. This piece first appeared in the 'La Montagne' in May 1939, later in the 'Rucksack Club Journal' and the 'Wayfarers' Journal', in 1947.

'During the past two years we have had a most undesirable increase in the number of casualties among hill walkers and climbers. Glencoe hills have seen nine deaths in eighteen months, Ben Nevis has had one killed and one missing, presumed killed. As we have come to expect, these figures concern hill walkers rather than rock climbers. Certainly, the risk for the experienced rock climber, while properly concentrated on a rock climb, is comparatively small. It may be argued that the total number of accidents is not very large, and we may be shown figures, for example, from Oslo, indicating that in skiing weather there are, in the hills adjacent to that town, on every Sunday thirty accidents. These, however, mostly involve broken arms and legs, and so are of less significance since they should be soon mended with modern treatment. In the Swiss Alps the records kept only concern fatalities, and these average about eighty yearly among alpinists and tourists, the proportion being roughly one in winter to every two in summer months.

'In this country there is understandably much public concern over the subject, and sensational newspaper reports do nothing to mitigate the anxiety of relatives and others. There is, of course, no doubt that most of these accidents are preventable by knowledge and due care, and we may well ask, as King Edward VII did when told about infectious illness, 'If preventable, why not prevented?' Prevention in the case of climbing accidents is peculiarly difficult. We do not wish to see any diminution in the spirit of adventure in our younger generation. The survival of the nation may depend on it. But this same spirit of adventure, uncurbed by instruction and discipline, is largely responsible for accidents. Danger is delicious, but death is not. We court danger, but the real delight is in escaping. Instruction in the mistakes of others, the development of good technique until it becomes second nature, and constant awareness and calculation of the risks involved will give safe mountaineering. Such training can only be got in clubs or organisations of some sort. The development of schools such as that opened at Glenmore, or the Outward Bound School at Aberdovey will be of the greatest value. Meanwhile, despite warning notices in hotels, boarding houses and hostels, people persistently go light-heartedly on to the hills, lacking in due respect for weather and the effects of altitude, without adequate equipment or forethought and without the necessary knowledge of map reading.

'Perhaps I should try to detail actual faults which, to the best of my belief, have been responsible in the last eighteen incidents in the Glencoe and Ben Nevis area. The most frequent cause is the lack of carefulness in placing the feet. This fault, perhaps associated with lack of training, may follow a long day of ridge walking. Too much may have been attempted and insufficient regard may be paid to icy Arctic conditions. Boots may be without edge nails and the completely necessary ice axe may be wanting. There was the very serious fault of trying to climb a steep snow gully on Ben Nevis without ice axes and unroped by climbers who should have known better. There have been uncontrolled falls on snow slopes because the ice axe had been let go at the start of the slide. There have been injuries to the head and face when, during such a fall, the ice axe head has been held too close by a short wrist sling. My personal practice is to have a nylon cord of length equal to the ice axe attached with a loop to the wrist. There was one completely reckless attempt at a long climb on Stob Coire nam Beith involving step cutting far beyond the available strength. Climbing in a particularly difficult gully in wet weather with vulcanised rubber soles preceded a fall of about 40 feet, fortunately without a serious result. Apparently, careless rope technique and choice of stance, without taking advantage of a possible belay, pulled a climber to a disastrous fall. Greater attention by most rock climbers to the mechanics of stance and belay is very much wanted, and to this end I would commend the stimulating work of K Tarbuck. Taking a wrong route down a steep face from the top of a high peak, possibly in one case in mist, accounted for deaths on two occasions.

'A certain route down seems feasible, though possibly insufficient consideration has been given to its choice. Later on, there is obstinate refusal, even in the face of increasing and dangerous steepness, to change one's mind, admit error and climb up again to try a better way. Another fatal fall may have occurred from such a cause in the case of an experienced climber descending a steep gully alone after a day's good rock climbing. Mistaken map reading was, I think, the cause of the disaster in the case of one hill walker who tried to descend from Ben Nevis to the arête for Coire Leis. He is about 600 feet from the NE Buttress. Insufficient respect for the inexorable force of a Highland burn in spate caused the death of a southern member of a rescue party; another fatal result might have been prevented if the rope had been used by a novice on a moderately difficult rock climb. Lone climbing when staying alone at a remote hut, so that there was no indication for a rescue party till too late, has brought grief and anxious uncertainty to relatives once again. Single bookings at climbing huts should be vetoed.

'It might be contended that to concentrate attention on such incidents may upset climbing confidence and even induce nervousness in a climber. I am quite sure that this is not true, the effect is rather to put a finer point on technique generally. For climbers early in their apprenticeship on hills, actual experience in the rescue of a serious casualty should have a salutary influence. On the other hand, I feel that to call on a climber repeatedly to help in melancholy rescue scenes is not advisable. Rescue work, where a fellow climber can be helped, saved from pain and shock and got down to allow surgery to get him fit to climb again can, on the other hand, be one of the greatest satisfactions.

'The knowledge required for this is not at all difficult

to acquire. Although expert first aid can do more good than in any other kind of accident, a very few first principles are all that the experienced mountaineer need add to his armamentarium. He need not worry about tourniquets for bleeding, for a clean pad on the wound with a bandage tightened over it will stop any bleeding likely to be met with on hills. A possible fracture or dislocation of arm, collarbone or ribs is put at rest when the hand is placed near the opposite shoulder and the injured limb bandaged firmly to the chest with scarf or handkerchiefs. A possible fracture of the leg may be treated by binding it firmly to its fellow, if it is very important because of exposure to get the patient down quickly; otherwise, and especially if it is an open fracture (broken bone coming through a wound), it may be better to await the arrival of the Thomas splint which will come up with the first aid rucksacks and stretcher. Always, the first thing to think about is making the patient comfortable and warm with all available extra clothing or the eiderdown wrap quickly got up from below. He must be kept from cold, wet ground with bracken or grass, heather, rope coils or ground-sheet. The directions in the first aid rucksack for the giving of morphia or the putting on of a Thomas splint are very clear.

'Giving morphine, however, worries some potential first aiders. There should be no fear about giving the full dose, plunging the needle boldly through the skin of the forearm. The dose may be repeated if pain demands this. A proportionately smaller dose is given to children.

'Frostbite is another subject which may seem difficult. It happens not infrequently, though in minor degree, on Scottish hills in winter, most often affecting one or two fingertips, where they have been allowed to come in contact with the bare metal of an ice axe head at high, cold altitudes. There is at first merely a not unusual numbness, usually overlooked, as it progresses to a cold, dead whiteness of skin and even of the underlying tissues. When the process has gone beyond the first stage it is quite wrong to do as the books advise, ie. to rub the part with snow or try to thaw out with warmth. This would do harm. Circulation must be restored very slowly and gradually, the thawing out process taking place as naturally as possible over a long period while the person affected descends to the less Arctic temperatures of lower slopes.

'The building of a windbreak of stones or snow, if it is necessary to wait for a stretcher party, will occupy waiting time very profitably. I have not known of any case in Britain where the ability to build an igloo has saved life, but it is quite conceivable that the necessity may arise, for example in the Cairngorms. I have found it fairly easy to make one, and they are surprisingly warm. Mr Malavielle describes how two climbers were able to live for twenty days in igloos built on Mont Blanc though the weather was bad. With sufficient practice, he says, an igloo of eight feet base, four feet high, can be built in about an hour.

'All mountaineers should know how to make a rope stretcher and also an ice axe stretcher, for this simple knowledge may easily prove life-saving. In wintry or wet weather it will nearly always be best to get the patient down with all despatch to the comfort of civilisation, and if there is even a small party available, the rope or ice axe stretcher should be used. There is an understandable tendency for the layman, unfamiliar with modern surgery, to feel diffident about taking any responsibility for a seriously injured patient, and especially where head, chest or abdomen is involved. Generally speaking, the only good treatment in these cases is a surgical operation in hospital, and the more quickly the patient can be got down the better his chance of survival. To await the arrival of skilled help from the nearest centre may result in death from internal haemorrhage, or from shock which might well have been avoided. To wait, for example, in one of the Glencoe coires for the arrival of a doctor from Ballachulish might mean a delay of an extra four or five hours compared with the time spent if a rope stretcher could be made and used by a mountaineering party. At least four bearers are required to carry a rope stretcher. The simple details of its making will be found in the Penguin 'Climbing in Britain'. An even simpler knot will suffice.

'There are some important considerations in regard to the organisation of rescue parties. There must be a recognised leader who should have all possible information about the resources of manpower, equipment, routes and methods of evacuation. The whole party must keep together; individuals or small parties must be careful to inform the leader of their actions and proposals so that the whole party can act as a co-ordinated unit. It will be difficult at times for all to keep in touch, especially on dark nights in bad weather. A system of signalling is a necessity, and a knowledge of Morse is most valuable. Bright and distinctive articles of clothing, eg. a yellow scarf and white headgear, may help in daylight. Individuals should, I think, be responsible for their own rationing, and will give careful thought to clothing if there is any chance of an all-night search. Usually the call out will come late in the evening and, frequently, it will be best not to bring the whole rescue party out in long dark nights of winter. It will always be essential, however, if the position of the casualty is known, that two men should go up as quickly as possibly, carrying the No 1 rucksack. The patient can then be made warm and comfortable, and that will be half the battle won. The waterproof sheet and warm eiderdown will be put snugly round him, simple first aid effected, morphine given and possibly a tin of self-heating soup, if available. Then, with the first satisfactory light the main party will arrive with the sledge stretcher.

'For a long rough descent the party should number at least twelve. At times it may be necessary to get the casualty from a difficult position on a ledge or in a gully. The triple looped bowline knot – bosun's chair – may be used, but generally it will be best to take the sledge stretcher and the Thomas splint (if required) to where the patient is lying, putting on a Thomas splint for any kind of fractured leg before the patient is moved. The sledge stretcher will facilitate raising and lowering (even vertically), not too uncomfortably, to a safe place where stretcher-bearers, perhaps less experienced in rock work, can take over. Knowledge of the bilgeri and prusik sling methods of raising a man from the depths of a crack are not often required, though we had one such recovery from a bergschrund on Ben Nevis this summer.

'It will be worth while to detail the men for each of the carrying parties – a certain rivalry will not be a disadvantage – and sizing off will make a difference to their comfort and endurance. A little discipline is needed, for it is not unknown for individuals or groups to straggle or take alternative by-paths and so throw more strain on a conscientious and devoted few. Parties of six each will change over about every quarter mile, and it may be found convenient, especially in windy weather, when the voice does not carry, to have a whistle blast as the signal for the change over. They should change, too, from side to side and from front to back of the stretcher, so as to put the stress on difference muscles all the time. They should hold themselves well up and not crouch as they walk. On every possible occasion the stretcher should be drawn as a sledge with bearers ready to check on steeper slopes. Carrying should be reduced to a minimum, and may only be necessary on particularly rough, boulder-strewn ground. In cases where there is an inadequate party with four bearers only may the stretcher be carried on the shoulders – and then only on level ground. The method is used in the Alps, but I know of two deaths, apparently due to falls when tipped off stretchers carried in this way. In the Services the instruction to stretcher bearers is to walk with bent knees, and breaking the step so that there is no rhythmic jolting. Where one has as many as six bearers on a rough hillside this injunction will not apply, but it may be well to remember it when a party comes to a not too strong wooden bridge over a swollen stream, as in Glencoe, where a careful crossing with reduction of the load to two bearers only is necessary.

'The estimation of the time of the descent is difficult, but it is important to give the ambulance a time and a meeting point as accurate as it can be made. The patient should not be kept waiting on the roadside, but neither should an ambulance, liable to emergency calls, be kept for many hours, as I have known in Glencoe, owing to insufficient forethought. If there are plenty of bearers, one may be sent ahead to phone the ambulance when the party is about halfway down.

'And so we hope to get our patient safely to hospital for due rehabilitation as a wiser and better climber, but always let us remember the mighty Whymper's expression of his own unfortunate experience:

'There have been joys too great to be described in words, and there have been griefs upon which I have not dared to dwell; and with these in mind I say: Climb if you will, but remember that courage and strength are nought without prudence, and that a momentary negligence may destroy the happiness of a lifetime. Do nothing in haste; look well to each step; and from the beginning think well what may be the end.'

PHOTO: BOB SHARP

Looking down the Lost Valley in Glencoe, in Donald Duff territory

chapter three

CO-ORDINATION AND CO-OPERATION

The hills are shadows and they flow,
From form to form and nothing stands,
They melt like mist, the solid lands,
Like clouds they shape themselves and go.
Alfred Lord Tennyson

Mountain rescue in the UK is provided free of charge to the casualty. Mountain rescuers expect no payment for their efforts. They voluntarily give up their free time – and often a good deal of their working (and sleeping) time – to help others temporarily less fortunate than themselves. But why? According to the dictionary, to volunteer is to spontaneously undertake a task. The thing about mountain rescue is that spontaneity isn't really the name of the game. Spontaneity implies individual activity on the spur of the moment, rather than the carefully considered teamwork actually involved. Yet, look up the word spontaneous and, several semi-colons down the page you find 'instinctive, automatic' and, more to the point, 'prompted by no motive'. And there we have it - mountain rescue team members, in general, appear to do what they do because they enjoy doing it. That's it. Sure, there may be the odd discount to be had with

manufacturers or retailers, the odd free supper in exchange for delivering a slide show, but more often than not they find themselves out of pocket – what with wear and tear on their own vehicles (in large operational areas it can be quite a drive to team headquarters or rendezvous points), fuel, clothing, equipment, footwear. And, of course, besides the financial cost, there's the domestic side of things – behind many a mountain rescuer stands an extremely long-suffering spouse!

The voluntary ethic is as strong today as it was in those early days of five barred gates and the principle of 'helping your own'. If someone was injured in the mountains it was up to those around at the time – friends, fellow climbers, countryside workers – to organise the rescue. They had to do the job since the emergency services simply did not have the capability. It mattered not whether the injured person was unknown to those around. The

PHOTO: ANDY SIMPSON

instinct and desire to help them to safety, even if it meant placing the rescuers at some risk, was very strong. That instinct bred a philosophy of self-sufficiency, teamwork, initiative and giving to others that remains at the heart of mountain rescue. The sense that you can assist someone in distress – where no one else can – is a powerful motivator, its only reward the intense satisfaction of a successful outcome. Knowing you may have saved a life, found a lost person or reduced the pain of an injured casualty brings rewards that cannot be quantified or measured in financial terms. The small inconvenience of temporary personal discomfort, damaged equipment, loss of earnings or a few cross words with those left at home, is more than outweighed by the saving of a life, human or animal.

So this principle of voluntarism, of relying on voluntary action rather than compulsion, is key to the whole service. Yet, while team members receive no financial remuneration for their work, they operate on an entirely professional basis. Mountain rescue teams are rarely found wanting. They always 'deliver the goods', be it finding a lost walker, recovering an injured climber or solving any number of unusual or difficult problems. The fact is that the modern rescue team is effective and efficient in what it does and achieves. This has to be testimony to the quality of training, absolute regard for safety, and the strength of teamwork, reinforced by a willingness to share ideas across the wider community.

That's it in general terms. What would the individual mountain rescuer reckon were his or her motives for joining a team? Question an entire team of forty or so members and the chances are you would come up with forty or so perfectly feasible reasons! Whilst being interviewed about the Crib y Ddysgl incident in the first chapter, one team member asked the question of his assembled colleagues from the Llanberis and Ogwen Valley teams. The answers were instinctive, heartfelt and various – every call out is an adventure, a challenge, each situation a test of ability, the satisfaction of working together as a team, the ever so slight frisson of being on the hill at a time you wouldn't normally ever dream of (late at night, pitch black, disgusting weather conditions). A recent survey carried out in Scotland suggests there are a few common themes.

For the vast majority, helping people in distress, being able to 'make a difference' sits high on the agenda. Team members seem to value the opportunity to help their fellow hillgoers – and others – in situations where the emergency services cannot assist for whatever reason. Perhaps it's best described as community spirit.

Many placed great store in the voluntary nature of mountain rescue work and the pleasure – we could almost say thrill – in working towards a common goal alongside the statutory emergency services. In fact, the integrated manner in which the voluntary and statutory agencies work together is arguably its greatest strength. There are very few instances in daily life where this happens. Of course, some of this may be down to that fact that when the chips are down everyone involved – whatever their station – pulls together. True team work.

The survey identified a number of factors related to working within a team situation. Many said they enjoyed being able to use their specific skills for a good cause. In some cases it offered a unique opportunity to display talents and expertise that otherwise went unnoticed. One person commented that the mountain rescue environment allowed him to use his fundraising skills in a way that actually went unnoticed in his daily life as a professional fundraiser! He had the freedom to contact individuals and organisations of his own choice, rather than following a prescribed plan, and the money raised

Lomond team members training at night in the use of flares

66

could always be attributed to his own efforts. Another team member admitted that mountain rescue had awakened a deep interest in first aid, which had developed to such a high level it resulted in a career change. Yet another respondent, a hard rock climber, suggested that mountain rescue offered an opportunity not only to fine tune and practice his own technical skills, but also to use them to good effect when required by a rescue situation.

Many people comment that they simply enjoy being part of a larger team of individuals, each with a common goal and similar interests in walking and mountaineering. For some, there is a sense of pride and self-fulfilment. Sometimes, if the rescue is high profile and attracts a lot of media attention there is a strong feeling of public achievement. This occasionally brings fulfilment in more tangible external rewards – many long serving members have received a Queen's Honour for their work in mountain rescue. Others who have made a special contribution at local and/or national levels have been awarded the Distinguished Service Award of the Mountain Rescue Council or Mountain Rescue Committee of Scotland. In Scotland, those who have made a special contribution within their own team may receive the so called 'merit badge'. Some actually say that being part of a mountain rescue team is a kind of advance payment for their own rescue! We don't think they were joking!

So, here we are with three thousand willing individuals, primed and ready to forsake the comforts of whatever they happened to be absorbed in at the time, to pick up their rucksacks and ropes at a moment's notice. For what may be a half hour job with a 'snatch' team – picking up an injured person at a known location inaccessible to a regular ambulance but perfectly within the reach of a handful of team members equipped with stretcher and four wheel drive – or a protracted search covering many hours (even days), and involving

multi-agency co-operation. How does all that voluntary energy become mobilised and directed to the task in hand?

Mountain rescue teams are called out through the police via the 999 system. According to the *Search & Rescue Framework for the UK and Northern Ireland*, published in June 2002, 'the police service, through its command infrastructure, co-ordinates land based and inland waters search and rescue operations, including all those that originate at sea or in the air, and provides co-ordination of all emergency services and other authorities where appropriate.' Co-ordination is the key word here. Whilst the police have a statutory responsibility to uphold the 'three Ps' – Preserve Life, Protect Property and Prevent Crime – they have no such responsibility to provide a search and rescue service and no declared assets for the purpose. However, they have assumed a 'primary responsibility for co-ordinating the role of other agencies including specialist support provided by voluntary organisations.' In the case of major incidents where there may be fatalities involved, the police would ensure the implementation of any special arrangements such as identifying or removing deceased persons, overseeing criminal investigations or facilitating enquiries by accident investigation agencies.

In effect, they call in whatever agencies they deem appropriate to the incident in hand. Mountain rescue is just one of a variety of resources available. Of course, teams are not obliged to turn out at all. It may be seeming to labour a point but – contrary to a belief often expressed by members of the public – teams and their members do not work for the police, but with them.

In most cases it is impossible to route a call directly to a rescue team. Rather it will be routed to the police control room in the area of the incident. It may also, depending on information given by the caller, be routed to another emergency service. If the

999 call centre is not in an area adjacent to the incident, the operator may not even be aware of the existence of a mountain rescue resource. Clearly, in an emergency situation, time is of the essence. But consider this – if the caller doesn't make it clear that the casualty is lying in a remote position, then an ambulance might be dispatched. Once the crew have made their way to the spot, sussed out what has happened and realised the need for mountain rescue assistance and contacted Ambulance Control to request the assistance of team members, valuable time has been lost. The recommended procedure, should you find yourself in trouble in the mountains, is to call 999, ask for the police and explain you need mountain rescue.

mobile phone. Gone are the days when someone would run off the hill to flag down a passing motorist! Once the police realise the incident is mountain related, they call the team leader, either by

Rescue teams work alongside the statutory services as an additional resource and are frequently called to multi-agency incidents

When a call comes through requesting emergency assistance, the police control room takes the details – type of incident, location etc – and the caller's number, in case further information is required. They will request the assistance of mountain rescue if they deem it appropriate. But how? There is no single, national protocol for mobilising mountain rescue – arrangements between police authorities and teams vary across the UK.

In Scotland, a variety of call out procedures exist, but essentially a two phase approach is adopted – police contact the team leader, then the team leader contacts the team members. A call out is invariably initiated by someone on the hill via

telephone or pager. In some cases, several people are contacted simultaneously using a 'group pager'. In the case of Lomond MRT, three people are alerted – the team leader and his two deputies – in the expectation that at least one will receive the message. Once alerted, the leader will discuss the incident with the police and decide on a course of action – whether the team will respond or not, how they will respond, what other services are required, and so on. This established, the team leader will contact team members. Some teams use 'area co-ordinators' or 'call girls' whose job is to telephone each member in turn with the relevant information. Some use a secondary pager system to alert

MRC of Scotland new SARCOM vehicle on the right. New Land Rover given to Glenmore Lodge MRT on the left. RAF 202 Squadron Sea King from RAF Lossiemouth hovering in centre stage.

members with the relevant information, such as the nature of the incident, rendezvous point, at what time. Others use mobile phones to send text messages to group lists. With the forthcoming demise of paging systems, it's likely that mobile phones and text messaging, or the use of commercial emergency communication services, will become more common. Whatever the method, team members are then expected to indicate their availability so the police and team leader can deploy the resources appropriately. Teams have different policies on who they mobilise for a call out. Sometimes all team members are called, whatever the nature of the incident. At other times, only selected people are called, depending on their skills and proximity to the incident.

Aside from a few local variations, the procedure for teams in England and Wales is pretty much the same. But what would you do if there were seven teams and five police authorities covering one tight knit patch? How would you work out which team to call? Teams in the Peak District dealt with exactly that problem by appointing team members as Mountain Rescue Incident Controllers. The controller's job, as the first point of contact for the police, is to advise on the best course of action. He or she uses their experience and local knowledge to identify the most suitable rendezvous point and which of the teams to call. Team members can then be called out in the normal way.

Of course, picking up or rescuing casualties paints only half of the picture. In the event of missing persons, the police will often seek the advice of a team leader or search manager and pursue preliminary lines of enquiry before initiating a full team call out. But once involved, they become just one cog in the emergency services wheel. During an incident, the statutory services follow a long established command structure of Gold, Silver and Bronze. Systems and personnel are set up so that all the available resources can work together within a flexible framework and the levels, incidentally, are unrelated to rank.

The Gold Commander is the individual, typically a senior police officer, in overall command of the incident. He (or she) gathers the resources, chairs the strategic co-ordinating group in the event of multi-agency response and sets, reviews and updates strategy. He must also maintain an audit trail. To support him, he has organisational structures such as radio operators, media support and inter-agency representatives. Gold resources might include mapping systems, air support links, telephones and IT support.

The Silver Commander is responsible for developing and co-ordinating the tactical plan in order to achieve the strategy set by the Gold Commander and provides a pivotal link between the Gold and Bronze. He is responsible for ensuring all staff are fully briefed. If there are linked events in remote locations, there may be more than one Silver Command. Silver Support is the 'command post' with a similar list of potential resources and personnel to Gold. Bronze Commander looks to implement the Silver Commander's plan by the use of appropriate tactics within their geographical or functional area. Bronze Support may include an aide de camp, tactical adviser and runner.

Once an incident is set up, communications are key to its success. Radio channels are established – at least one operational, one for command and call signs allocated. Air support provides visual and radio information which will enable tactical decisions and communication links between any 'command vehicle' and the events control room. If a situation arises where, for example, a mountain rescue team leader's wish to search a particular area could take up resources which might be required elsewhere, it is the Gold Commander's job to assess the situation to best achieve the desired outcome.

The other statutory organisations involved in land based search and rescue are the Fire and Rescue Service, the Ambulance Service and the Ministry of Defence.

The Fire and Rescue Service is used primarily for fire fighting but also has resources to assist with incidents involving chemicals, road traffic accidents and rescues. Its role in mountain search and rescue is minimal, but it occasionally assists in off-road situations where a person or animal is stranded on a steep crag. The Ambulance Service, on the other hand, works in conjunction with the mountain rescue service on a regular basis. Their core role is patient treatment and transport. Paramedics and emergency medical technicians are trained to use a wide range of skills, techniques and drug protocols in order to preserve life and maximise treatment options within the 'Golden Hour'. But when an accident or illness occurs off road or in a remote location, mountain rescue team members, their equipment and vehicles, are often better placed to deliver immediate first aid help and evacuate the casualty – either to the nearest road head and a waiting ambulance, or direct to A&E. The Ambulance Service also has a Helicopter Emergency Medical Service (HEMS) to complement their ambulance-based operation. HEMS aircraft are small and highly manoeuvrable but are required to land on scene, or in close proximity to an incident, and can only fly at night if they land in designated areas. They do not have a winching capability so their use in the mountain environment is very limited.

The Ministry of Defence has search and rescue assets to cover military operations and training. Where these meet the needs of civil, land-based search and rescue operations they can be deployed to help but military operations always take precedence over civil ones. The assets include Royal Navy and Royal Air Force helicopters (Sea Kings) and RAF mountain rescue teams which are all co-ordinated by the Aeronautical Rescue Co-ordination Centre (ARCC) based at Kinloss in Scotland. If a team wishes the use of a helicopter or RAF team to assist with, say a difficult search operation, then it contacts the police who, in turn, contact the ARCC for assistance.

Besides mountain rescue, of course, there are a number of other voluntary resources available – which are either called to assist police in their own right, for their own particular skills, or work together with mountain rescue teams towards a common goal. One of these is cave rescue. Of the sixteen cave rescue organisations in the British Isles, a small number – such as Cave Rescue Organisation (CRO) based in North Yorkshire – also operate as fell rescue teams. Thousands of people go caving every week without mishap but, when problems do arise, police must rely on the specialist knowledge, equipment and manpower of the local cave rescue team. There are many similarities in the difficulties faced above and below ground, but vertical shafts, constricted passages and squeezes, static or running water, sometimes completely filling the passage, foul air and the potential for rockfall or mudslide – not to mention working in the dark – are uniquely challenging. Cave rescue teams have their own geographical areas of operation, usually confined to the main limestone caving areas. As many as 1500 cave rescuers, some with specialists skills such as underwater diving, carry out around fifty rescues a year and attend many other incidents where their particular skills are required. The British Cave Rescue Council, formed in 1967, acts as a representative body for all bona fide volunteer underground search and rescue teams in the British Isles, and is represented on the national mountain rescue committees.

A key resource for any team, and the police, is the search and rescue dog and its handler. These highly trained 'dog teams', whilst required to be members of mountain rescue teams are often called to work alone and many hundreds of miles from their own patch. The Search and Rescue Dog Associations (SARDA) are responsible for the training and deployment of these air scenting dogs to search for missing persons in the mountains and moorlands of Britain as well as the lowland, rural and urban areas. Frequently the dog and its handler are first on scene so they must be proficient in all the skills required to find, treat and recover a casualty – navigation, first aid and communications – and they are also trained in the protection of crime scenes.

There is now a growing number of lowland search and rescue teams. Originally, these were mainly focused in those areas not served by mountain rescue teams – to the south and east of the UK. However, new teams are now springing up in other parts of the country such as Cheshire, prepared to work with their adjacent mountain rescue teams if required. They co-ordinate through the Association of Lowland Search and Rescue (ALSAR).

The auxiliary coastguard service is an organisation of coastguard rescue teams situated at strategic locations around the coast equipped to deal with

PHOTO: BOB SHARP

The Loch Lomond Rescue Boat out on a training exercise with the Lomond team

incidents related to the risks associated with coastal terrain – mud/cliff rescue and coastal searches. There are over four hundred located around the UK coastline. Members tend to live in prominent positions overlooking the coast and, although they are volunteers, are paid a basic rate for hours worked. All the teams have search capability and some have cliff rescue capability. They are mobilised by HM Coastguard through one of several Maritime Rescue Co-ordination Centres – there are two in Scotland, one in Wales and three in England – and co-operate closely with some mountain rescue teams as well as the RNLI and private rescue boats.

An incident which hit the headlines across several days during a hot spell in August of 2003 perfectly demonstrated exactly how the statutory emergency services, government departments, the mountain rescue service and other voluntary organisations work together.

A family of four from the north of England had travelled to Scotland to spend a camping holiday at Ardlui on Loch Lomondside. On the first day of their visit, the fifteen year old son decided he would like to climb a mountain called Cruach across the loch from where they were staying. His father took him across the loch in a rowing boat, planning to return a couple of hours later to pick him up. However, as the expected time approached, the boy was nowhere to be seen. Several hours passed before the alarm was raised but, when the police were alerted, they immediately requested help from members of SARDA. A number of search dogs and their handlers were deployed to search where the boy had planned to walk. They searched throughout the night to no avail.

At first light, the police mobilised four mountain rescue teams – Oban, Arrochar, Lomond and Strathpol. Together they devised a search strategy that extended the search area to higher and more complicated ground. It's stunning scenery – picture postcard stuff – but deceptive. From the pebbled shore at the edge of the gently lapping waters of the lake, the heathered ground rises suddenly and steeply, boulders randomly strewn through the chest-high summer bracken, dense and unforgiving. As temperatures rose to over 80 degrees, movement for the rescuers was extremely laborious. Meanwhile, the Loch Lomond rescue boat was requested to carry out a detailed search of the shoreline and loch as well as the river entering the loch from the north and a police helicopter and Royal Navy Sea King were tasked to search the surface of the loch. Nothing found, all agencies were stood down at nightfall.

At daybreak, mountain rescue team members continued their work, extending the search to adjacent areas and retracing previously covered ground, and a police diving unit was tasked to explore the loch and river. Late in the morning they found the boy's body in the river about a kilometre upstream from the family's campsite.

Throughout the incident, the police managed the search, bringing in different agencies and deploying personnel as the situation required. Over a hundred people were involved across the three day period, each working in partnership with one another, sharing intelligence and playing to their particular strengths.

So, as you can see, teams and their members are, by necessity, organised and safety conscious not least of all to enable collaboration with their emergency service colleagues. One or two are now run as limited companies, and most civilian teams have charitable status. The exceptions are the RAF and the Scottish police teams. As such, they are required to submit copies of their constitution to the Charities Commission and the Inland Revenue, and their accounts are fully open to public scrutiny. Besides the operational side of things, they are each properly constituted with an elected committee and appointed officers – chairman, treasurer, secretary, medical, training, and equipment officers – who effectively become trustees of the charity and are accountable to the team for the work they do. Team accounts are normally audited by an independent person and the annual work of a team – rescues, fundraising, training itinerary and so on – summarised in an annual report. Teams are also required to submit formal incident reports to the national Statistics Officer and training logs and risk assessments to their police force.

In operational terms, teams adopt a strict command structure with personnel deployed according to their competencies, communications systems set in place and leaders appointed as required. In a nutshell, as the UK Search and Rescue Strategic Committee has noted, '...whilst teams are volunteers, their standards are high and the service provided is professional and, as such [the mountain rescue service] is an invaluable addition to the police role in their response to search and rescue and major disasters.'

All teams work within a fairly well defined geographical area. There are no exact rules that determine each operational boundary, more often than not these are defined by features such as rivers and mountain ridges – although, in the absence of such obvious markers, it's not uncommon for boundary lines to become a contentious issue between neighbours! Some teams have a very extensive area, covering many hundreds of square miles, others are small by comparison. For example, Dundonnel MRT in Scotland covers a 2500 square mile stretch which extends from the west to the east coast. By comparison, Keswick MRT in England covers only 180 square miles. And, of course, as adjacent teams frequently work together on incidents, they tend to have a good working knowledge of their neighbouring areas.

Whilst the nitty gritty of mountain rescue, the mud on the boots of teams, is necessarily focused in the immediate locality of the individual teams, there is an increasing desire for teams to work together nationally to secure funding, develop training and equipment and exchange ideas – or simply benefit from the economies of scale enabled by bulk buying. Yet, whilst the aspirations of mountain rescue teams and their members may be very similar wherever they operate, there are distinct differences in the national organisations north and south of Hadrian's Wall.

In England and Wales, teams are first grouped as regions. Just as each individual team is a charity in its own right (as is also the case in Scotland), each regional organisation is run as a separate charity. Representatives from the teams meet on a regular basis to discuss matters applicable to their joint operational areas and how they wish to both contribute to or benefit from the national body. The RAF, SARDA and local cave rescue teams are also involved at regional level. Two representatives from each region – and a number of others who sit on the various specialist sub committees – are then required to attend the twice yearly national meetings of the Mountain Rescue Council. This co-ordinating body – which, in turn, also has charitable status – is administered by a committee comprising chairman, secretary, assistant secretary, treasurer, legal adviser and statistician; and equipment, training, medical, communications, finance and information officers, who chair the relative sub committees. Besides representatives from the regions, SARDA and the RAF, membership also includes the Association of Chief Police Officers (ACPO), British Cave Rescue Council, HM Coastguard and HM Fire Inspectorate.

The MRC acts as a co-ordinating body and represents all its members to liaise with the various government departments in the running of mountain and cave rescue in England and Wales. From the teams' point of view, the council acts as an advisory body, promoting best practice through the distribution of information, training and equipment. It assists communications through negotiating for mountain rescue use of radio channels, undertakes research, development and testing of key items of equipment, arranges accident and public liability insurance for team members when they are training and operational and has established national standards for first aid training. Probably one of the most visible developments of recent years has been the *Mountain Rescue* magazine, which is published quarterly. What began life as a simple newsletter geared to improve internal communications, has

you don't see many mountains around here...

Those teams who operate on lower ground than their loftier colleagues grow used to meeting scepticism on tin shakes. But not all problems begin on steep ground. And, even on steeper ground, not every incident involves a mountaineer.

PHOTO: ARCHIE ROY

The Lomond team was called one Sunday afternoon, midway through a training exercise. The driver of a fast sports car had crashed through a wall, which served as a boundary between the road and a deep loch, coming to rest on the shore. The driver, probably suffering from concussion and unaware of what he was doing, entered the water and started to swim across the loch. The accident was witnessed by a canoeist who paddled quickly towards the badly injured man and dragged him back to the shore before going to summon help.

Leaving the driver lying on the grass, he went to a house to call for an ambulance. At that moment, the casualty appeared to have a violent fit and rushed off at great speed into the adjacent woods. It was at this point that the rescue team were alerted. They made their way to the scene, about a mile from their training venue, and immediately began a thorough search of the shoreline houses and wooded area. One search team was deployed higher up the hillside and began to sweep a complicated area of ground amongst some steep crags. Within thirty minutes, a call was received from this group that the man had been found by one of the search dogs. Unfortunately, he'd fallen about 60 feet over one of the crags to his death.

Team members gathered at the scene, covered the man with jackets and waited for a police officer to arrive. Then, paperwork done, the body was stretchered down to the roadside where a waiting doctor confirmed death.

But not all problems begin on steep ground. And, even on steeper ground, not every incident involves a mountaineer.

flourished into a full colour magazine with a much broader appeal.

In Scotland, there are no regional divisions and teams are represented directly at the national meetings. The Mountain Rescue Committee of Scotland liaises with all departments, authorities and providers of search and rescue services in mountainous terrain. Through the Scottish Executive Health Department, it maintains a series of mountain rescue posts at strategic locations throughout Scotland. It provides grant aid to teams in respect of training and equipment by acting as a central focus for charitable donations – for many years working closely with the Order of St John, which has funded vehicles for all the teams, as well as posts for those in need. Recent years have also seen the revival of Scotland's own in-house magazine, *Casbag*.

The make up of Scotland's Executive Committee is pretty much the same as in England and Wales, with the addition of representatives from ACPO (Scotland) and the Aeronautical Rescue Co-ordination Centre (ARCC) at Kinloss. It has the authority to co-opt additional members. At the time of writing these included Mountain Leader Training (Scotland), Mountain Rescue (England & Wales), the Mountaineering Council of Scotland and the Scottish Mountain Safety Forum. The Executive meets bi-annually and reports to the General Committee, which also meets twice a year. This larger committee comprises representatives from the 28 Scottish teams – including civilian, police and RAF – and SARDA, alongside other organisations including the eight police forces, the RAF, the Royal Navy, HM Coastguard, Bristows Helicopters, Mountain Rescue (England & Wales), the Mountaineering Council of Scotland, the Scottish Mountain Safety Forum, the Scottish Ambulance Service and sportscotland.

One of the key functions of both the national bodies is to collate and analyse mountain incident information, published in the form of their respective annual incident reports. The Scottish report – listing every single incident – is published in the *Scottish Mountaineering Club Journal*. In England and Wales, the report doesn't list each individual rescue but takes the form of statistical analysis and comment. It is sent to the British Mountaineering Council and published on the MRC website.

An area in which Scotland has seen particular success is in securing funding for its teams. In the last few years, substantial donations have enabled the development of the new stretcher and a radical revision of its communications systems. A major gain, however, has been the significant funding from the Scottish Executive to replace essential hardware, as well as a pledge of four million pounds over three years to be distributed amongst all the teams. As we write, England and Wales are in the process of lobbying for similar recognition from Whitehall. Watch this space.

People hear about government funding such as this, witness the professional way in which all teams work with the police, ambulance and fire services, and mistakenly assume that mountain rescue is simply another emergency service, its members on a regular payroll. Or they read of their local team securing Community Fund backing for the building of a new base and query the need for team members to spend a precious Saturday morning outside a supermarket clutching a collection box. The truth is, the figures which hit the headlines might sound substantial and, indeed they are. But the gifts they bring – be it new radios for individual team members or a shiny new stretcher for each team – only form part of the picture. Teams still have to look to the bottom line and meet their everyday operational costs. The notion of the 'mixed economy' is central to every team's survival. It costs money to train people, to buy equipment and clothing, maintain and run vehicles and rescue posts, keep the team headquarters functioning and warm, telephones

...but then we do have a lot of water...

Rivers and lochs often cause problems for people not engaged in mountaineering and the mountain rescue service is often called to help. In August 1999,

PHOTO: ARCHIE ROY

the Braemar and Grampian Police teams were called to find a young man who had gone missing whilst fishing on the River Dee in Aberdeenshire. John and Peter (we've changed their names), both gamekeepers, had decided to go fishing about 10.00pm in the evening. Peter was properly equipped, wearing chest-high waders but John wore only canvas trousers, walking boots and a walking jacket. Peter crossed the river at the shallowest section, noting the current at thigh level was very strong. On reaching the other side, he heard cries for help and turned to see his friend struggling in the deep, fast flowing water. He searched for twenty minutes, swimming on the surface and under the water, to no avail. The police were called and rescue teams dispatched to search the river and both banks, in vain. At about 3.00am the search was discontinued, John's body was eventually recovered by Grampian Police diving team later that morning.

In the summer of 1996, two boys camping with their families at the head of Loch Lomond in Central Scotland decided to leave the comfort of their tents and sail across the loch in a stolen dinghy. The loch at this point is about 600 feet deep and two miles wide. Halfway across they decided to abandon the boat and swim back to shore. One made it successfully but discovered his friend was no longer with him. The police were called and Lomond MRT and the Loch Lomond rescue boat alerted. The boat's crew deployed team members on either side of the loch, who then started a shoreline search. The boat began to sweep the loch in a systematic fashion back and forth across the loch. The search continued throughout the night and well into the following day. To this day, the boy's body has not been found.

About five years earlier, the same team and rescue boat had been involved in another combined search, for two overdue fishermen. The two men had left the previous night to go fishing in the middle of the loch for salmon and sea trout. The weather was appalling – gale force winds and driving rain and sleet. Both men had been seen in the pub earlier and, according to the landlord, were well over the limit. It was known that neither could swim, nor did they wear life jackets. When they failed to arrive home around midnight, the rescue teams were called out. The body of one man was found almost immediately on the shore next to the marina. The rescue team was divided into several units and taken by the rescue boat to some of the adjacent islands in the hope that the other fisherman had survived the water and been blown by the wind to one of the islands. By the next day, there was still no sign and the search was stopped, continuing at intervals over the next few weeks in the hope of finding him. It was six months later before a passing canoeist found his decomposed body trapped in a bed of reeds.

connected and purchase insurance for members. Then there's the hidden, and virtually unquantifiable, cost to each and every team member – their own fuel and vehicle costs to and from rescues, their own equipment and clothing, not to mention the private telephone bills, correspondence, the odd stamp here and there, and the huge amounts of unsung time spent administering the team, cleaning and brewing up, attending meetings... We'll probably never know the real cost of running an efficient mountain rescue service because those involved give so much of their time, and put their hands in their pockets so frequently to fund their 'hobby', it's impossible to assess.

All this comes at no charge to those who need the rescue service, unlike many other countries in the world. In the French Alps, where the service is provided by full time professionals, the full cost is charged to those who are rescued. This is why those who walk or climb in the Alps are advised to take out full insurance to cover the risks and avoid the high cost of rescue – particularly if a helicopter is involved. In the UK, the 'no charge' principle is mirrored by the voluntary nature of the service.

It's been argued that everyone who takes to the hills and mountains should be insured against the need for rescue. But there are insuperable problems with this. First, how do you define the areas where insurance might be required? Whilst most mountain areas are well defined, many rescues take place in non-mountainous situations. When does a mountain become a hill, or a hill become a moor, a moor become a field? And so on. Where do you draw the line? And, in the unlikely event that someone, somewhere does manage to draw those lines, will that same someone be responsible for checking that hillgoers (should anyone wish to continue hillgoing within such draconian bounds) have fully paid up policies, with adequate cover for the area at hand? What would be the penalties for those not insured?

What about those who cycle or hang glide in the mountains or take their dog for a walk or go for a picnic? Would they have to be insured too?

The single most important argument against insurance is that the teams themselves wish the service to remain free. The minute it becomes a paid service, the whole concept of volunteering disappears. So how do teams raise sufficient money to operate? This will vary from team to team – and there are differences between Scotland and the rest of the UK as we've seen – but there are some common features. Traditionally income arises through donations – often from casualties and their families, or legacies – fundraising through tin shakes or events, government grants, the national mountain rescue committees and sponsorship.

Donations often represent a significant part of a team's income. Clearly, this sort of income is extremely variable and unpredictable. There are lean years and there are good years and the busier teams are more likely to benefit through their higher profile. Of course, any donations are gratefully received and work hard for their keep, but we must stress there is no expectation that the casualty will 'pay' for their rescue.

Fundraising is a central feature of mountain rescue work. There are very many ways to raise money – and, unfortunately very many organisations vying for the penny in your pocket. Many thousands of new charities come on line every year. In a climate of endemic charity fatigue, teams must take advantage of local resources and contacts to generate funds. Some have highly successful annual events. The Cairngorm team organises its own bi-annual sponsored walk through the Cairngorm mountains which generates thousands of pounds each year. On a lighter note, the Oldham team undergoes an annual Beer Walk – or should that be stagger – through fifteen miles of Saddleworth villages, taking in about ten pubs and a drink in each one. Difference is they've been known to do this in the style of Little Bo Peep and her nursery friends – the farmer, his dog, a mobile sheep pen and a tiny flock of fluffy white sheep. Or to be more precise, a bunch of willing team members suitably attired in cotton wool studded white suits. There are sponsored walks, sponsored abseils from city centre tower blocks, sponsored tandem sky dives; endurance events, wine tastings, hot pot suppers, barbecues, spring fairs, Christmas fairs, kit sales and open days, safety covers, tin shakes and collection boxes; gift aided donations, legacies, tombolas and raffles... it's a long list. And all these events work on two levels – generating income and raising the profile of rescue work within the community. In some cases, they can also promote safe practice in the mountains.

PHOTO: BILL SEVILLE

Oldham team members, all dressed up and off to the pub...

It's interesting that, whilst fundraising is central to the ethos of mountain rescue, it has aroused much internal debate. At national level, the English and Welsh teams have chosen to adopt a national fundraising strategy, intended to complement any fundraising done by teams at local level – though there have been concerns that a national focus might detract from this ability. Scotland, despite benefiting hugely from government money, has rather confusingly, rejected national fundraising. It is also true that some teams actively oppose any fundraising initiatives, believing they detract from training and operational work.

The Scottish Executive announced in 2003 that it would provide funds for Scottish mountain rescue on a guaranteed annual basis. The money is given to the police forces for them to disperse to the teams, on the basis of incident workload. Prior to this, it was left to the individual police authorities to support teams as they thought appropriate. This meant that some teams received significant funding and others nothing. Besides this money, all first aid equipment such as stretchers, oxygen and splints, is paid for through the Scottish Executive Health Department. Yet, far from coming with strings attached, the government places no conditions or restrictions on funding. As long as funds are used wisely for bona fide purposes, no questions are asked.

In England and Wales, the situation is quite different. The various regions receive a small amount of funding from sportengland but there is nothing large scale. Teams receive some funding from the ambulance service, although this has been cut in the last couple of years, and local police authorities service and license radio equipment.

The national committees are almost entirely dependent on donations to carry out their work and cover their administrative costs. They too receive donations from walkers and climbers, or their relatives, who have benefited from the service. Others who wish to support the cause of mountain rescue make donations knowing the money will help several or all teams. Once administration costs have been met, any money is given back to the members to support training or equipment needs.

Over the years, many teams have established sponsorship deals with various companies and organisations wishing to be associated with mountain rescue. These arrangements tend to work in healthy symbiosis – team members benefit from discounted clothing and equipment and the retailer or manufacturer uses the mountain rescue connection as a marketing tool.

Given the huge commitment asked of any team member, not just in terms of a theoretical twenty four hour availability for call outs and ongoing training, but in the seemingly constant requirement to come up with newer, more imaginative ways to win public sympathy, it's remarkable anyone ever actually volunteers in the first place. But they do. New recruits soon discover how much mountain rescue pervades their lives. And there's no room for those seeking glory or kudos alone. Occasionally, people talk their way into a team on false pretences, or without a clear understanding of what might be asked of them, but they are soon identified and rejected, or fall by the wayside. Team members in general must be competent mountaineers in all weather conditions and at all times of the year. They must be prepared to share their expertise with colleagues and also learn new skills. It almost goes without saying they must have a caring nature and wish to help those in distress.

Different teams adopt different policies in the way they recruit. In one or two, membership is by invitation only. This might be because the team's operational work is so hazardous, in relation to the nature of the terrain, that only those who can demonstrate competence through their technical climbing ability or experience in other teams are considered for membership. But, in the greater majority of teams, those who show interest in a team's work will be considered by that team. There will usually be a set of critical requirements such as fitness or special skills which have to be met. Individuals who meet the criteria, sometimes established through an interview and questionnaire, will join as trainees or probationers. For a period of time – anything from six months to two years and more – the new recruits will take part in team training alongside other team members. This probationary period works both ways, by offering the individual a chance to determine the extent of their commitment and interest in rescue work and their fellow team members the opportunity to see if the person meets the requirements. At a given point, trainees are either accepted onto the operational call out list as full team members or required to continue as trainees for a further period. Sometimes they are rejected if they fail to meet the technical criteria or fail to demonstrate team qualities. Some teams include non-operational members who recognise the ethos of rescue work but play a key role in other ways such as fundraising or administration. Many teams have honorary membership which gives recognition to those who have given outstanding service over many years – these members may or may not help with a team's operational or administration activities.

Vital for any team is the appropriate balance between experience and youth; between the older generation, with their wisdom, local knowledge and established links with the key people and agencies relevant to training and rescue work, and the younger blood, with their sense of vitality and enthusiasm.

So here we are with a diverse, enthusiastic mountain rescue service, which holds within its ranks a broad range of skill, age and experience, trained and willing to cope with just about any eventuality on the hill. And the sort of incident most likely to warrant their response? Just a simple slip.

**Lake District Search
& Rescue (LDSAMRA)**
Cockermouth MRT
Coniston MRT
COMRU (Mines Rescue)
Duddon & Furness MRT
Kendal MRT
Keswick MRT
Kirkby Stephen MRT
Langdale/Ambleside MRT
Patterdale MRT
Penrith MRT
Wasdale MRT
SARDA (Lakes)

**Mid Pennine Search
& Rescue Organisation
(MPSRO)**
Bolton MRT
Bowland Pennine MRT
Calder Valley SRT
Cave Rescue Organisation
Holme Valley MRT
Rossendale & Pendle MRT
SARDA (England)

**North East Search
& Rescue Association
(NESRA)**
Cleveland SRT
North of Tyne SRT
Northumberland NPSRT
RAF Leeming MRT
Scarborough
& District SRT
Swaledale FRO
Teesdale & Weardale SRT
SARDA (England)

**North Wales Mountain
Rescue Association
(NWMRA)**
Aberglaslyn MRT
Llanberis MRT
North East Wales SRT
North Wales CRO
Ogwen Valley MRO
Outward Bound
Wales SRT
SARDA (Wales)
Snowdonia National Park
South Snowdonia SRT
HM Coastguard MRT 83
RAF Valley MRT

**Peak District Mountain
Rescue Organisation
(PDMRO)**
Buxton MRT
Derbyshire CRO
Derby MRT
Edale MRT
Glossop MRT
Kinder MRT
Oldham MRT
Woodhead MRT
SARDA (England)

**South Wales Search
& Rescue Association
(SWSRA)**
Brecon MRT
Central Beacons MRT
Gwent CRT
Longtown MRT
West Brecon CRT
Western Beacons MSRT
SARDA South Wales

**South West England
Rescue Association
(SWERA)**
Avon & Somerset CRT
Cornwall Mine Rescue
Organisation
Dartmoor Rescue Group
Devon CRO
Exmoor SRT
Gloucestershire CRG
Mendip Rescue
Organisation
Severn Area RA
Cornwall Rescue Group
SARDA

**Yorkshire Dales Rescue
Panel (YDRP)**
Upper Wharfedale FRA
RAF Leeming MRT
Cave Rescue Organisation

scotland

Aberdeen MRT
Arran MRT
Arrochar MRT
Assynt MRT
Borders SAR Unit
Braemar MRA
Cairngorm MRT
Dundonnell MRT
Galloway MRT
Glencoe MRT
Glenelg MRT
Glenmore Lodge MRT
Killin MRT
Kintail MRT
Lochaber MRT
Lomond MRT
Moffat MRT
Oban MRT

Ochils MRT
Skye MRT
Tayside MRT
Torridon MRT
Tweed Valley MRT
Scottish CRO
SARDA (Southern Scotland)
Sarda (Scotland)

Police Teams
Grampian Police MRT
Strathclyde Police MRT
Tayside Police SAR

RAF Teams
RAF Kinloss MRT
RAF Leuchars MRT

PHOTO: IAN DAWSON

**Team members are on call
24 hours a day, 365 days each year
whatever the weather.**

some key principles

■ All team members are volunteers and the voluntary ethic is held very strongly by team members. There is no compulsion on anyone to join a mountain rescue team.

■ Team members are not paid for their work. Many teams are sponsored by various organisations which helps to reduce the cost burden. However, all members give their time freely.

■ Mountain rescue teams operate to professional standards. By training regularly and to agreed standards, operational work is efficient and effective.

■ Team members are 'on call' 24 hours a day, 365 days each year, whatever the weather. Incidents can take place at any time of the day or year so team members must be ready to act at any time.

■ Teams would never knowingly place their lives at risk in order to effect a rescue but assess the risks and act within their capability.

■ Mountain rescue teams operate independently, as registered charities, responsible for raising the funds necessary to maintain their service. At the time of writing, there are still considerable discrepancies across the UK, and north and south of Hadrian's Wall. Scottish teams benefit from substantial aid from the Scottish Executive and teams in England and Wales have begun lobbying government for similar recognition of their work. In some areas, police forces have contributed to the provision of radios and insurance. Many teams have received lottery funding to build new headquarters, but this is by no means the norm.

■ All MRTs are properly constituted and elect officers and others according to accepted rules.

■ Team members come from all walks of life and backgrounds and not all are required to be professional mountaineers or qualified instructors. Indeed, degrees of mountaineering skill will vary amongst teams depending on the demands of their geographical area.

■ Teams work in close partnership with many other voluntary and statutory emergency services. Mountain rescue is just one of several assets to be mobilised by the police for search and rescue purposes.

■ Teams are called out through the 999 system and may respond to requests for help from the police, ambulance and fire services. Occasionally, if they witness an accident then they would act immediately and inform police as soon as possible.

■ MRTs' members are insured by the police for training and operational work undertaken on their behalf.

chapter four

THERE'S MANY A SLIP...

Climb if you will, but remember that courage and strength are naught without prudence, and that a momentary negligence may destroy the happiness of a lifetime. Do nothing in haste; look well to each step; and from the beginning think what may be the end.
Edward Whymper

'Accidents on the British hills are usually due to over-ambition, lack of care, or ignorance of the elementary principles of sound mountaineering,' thundered the Mountain & Cave Rescue Handbook – priced one shilling and six 'd' in old money – in 1966. (Can't you just see the stiff upper lip and tweed jacket bristling?) Fine words. Asserted, no doubt, with the utmost conviction and perfectly correct for the times. Mountaineering was still a relatively narrow pastime, enjoyed in the main by graduates of the scout and guide movement or university climbing clubs. It was generally expected that those who chose to stride off into the hills should, and would, know what they were doing. And anyway, besides being a lot of fun, it was hard work. No cosy, thermal, breathable, waterproof high street clothing – just woolly jumpers, draughty wax jackets and leaky anoraks. No GPS tucked in the rucksack or strapped conveniently to the wrist – just a crumpled, weather-beaten old map and stubby old HB pencil. Without the luxury of central heating and tumble dryers

(believe it or not, there was such a time), find yourself caught in a downpour and – if you were very lucky – your heavy, sodden kit might just have ceased steaming by the following weekend. Taking a walk involved checking out public transport, co-ordinating bus and train timetables and, probably, setting off (and coming back) fully kitted up in boots and woollies. As well as all the other stuff such as route planning, slicing the Spam for the butties, filling the thermos and actually doing the walk. Not for the fainthearted!

'To say,' the Handbook continues, 'that mountaineering is the art of going safely in dangerous places may start the beginner off with the right idea if it leads him to study and practise the techniques and precautions which other men's experience has shown to be necessary.' But the countryside is so much closer now, no longer the preserve of the hardy. Most of us have at least one fleece and a smattering of Goretex® tucked away in the closet and more free time on our hands to

PHOTO: SANDY SEABROOK

indulge in a little exploration and adventure. So, how many mountain accidents are actually down to 'the beginner'?

It might surprise you, but often it's the more

PHOTO: ALEX GILLESPIE

Summit of Ben Nevis

experienced who come to grief. According to Davy Gunn of Glencoe MRT '...not only the ill-equipped and ill-prepared, the foolish and the heedless get into trouble... many of the casualties on the mountains are skilled, practiced and level headed. They know the rules and follow them and yet they end up injured or, if luck runs out, dead.' And all it takes is a simple slip.

Ask Dan Hudson. He and his friend Warren had been planning to climb Ben Nevis for a long time. They travelled up from Kendal one day in late March and stayed overnight at a local bed and breakfast, setting off to climb the mountain at around ten o'clock the next morning. Their plan was to follow the tourist path from Achintree to Lochan an t-Suidhe and then towards the CIC hut high up in Coire Leis. From here, they would follow a steep line to the summit of Carn Mor Dearg. They then walked along the fabled Carn Mor Dearg Arête arriving at the summit of the Ben around 4.45pm.

The weather wasn't good – visibility was down to ten metres and it was beginning to snow. They waited a short while before leaving just after 5.00pm, then set off along the main route, intending to follow it all the way back to Achintee. Conscious of the route-finding difficulties in navigating off the summit in bad weather, they set their compasses to the desired bearing and headed off into the mist. They'd walked just 100 metres when Dan slipped.

'My recollections of the events of that day were cold, wet weather throughout, a short break in the weather on the top of Cam Mor Dearg which prompted an ill-advised continuation over the arête, an exhausting snow slog up from the end of the arête and relief and relaxation on reaching the top. We set off on what we thought would be an easy return march back down to Fort William before hitting a small patch of sloping wind-blown ice. The crampons were buried deep in my rucksack and the angle seemed gentle. We were on a bearing and reluctant to change course. The inevitable happened. I slipped and fell. I arrested with my axe and found myself on a steepening ice slope hanging onto my axe. The ground was rock hard. My legs were exhausted. I kicked at the ice with no effect whatsoever. I couldn't release the axe to cut steps without slipping further. Eventually with all the thrashing around, I let go of the axe and slid down the slope.

'The minor slip now became a serious incident. I felt the sudden accelerating tug of the steepening slope. I thought of the thousands of times I must have read warnings about Five Finger Gully and waited for the inevitable. I remember hurtling uncontrollably downward waiting for the killer blow. Then it stopped. I opened my eyes. A sudden exhilaration went through me, 'Christ I'm still alive.'

'Then I looked to one side. I was flat on my back. My left arm appeared to have acquired a second elbow. There was a smear of blood on the snow from the sleeve. 'I realised that I could feel nothing below the shoulder. My glasses had gone. My gloves had gone. I looked at my other arm, which had also stiffened. I could see a red tinge at the top of my vision. I didn't know what had happened to Warren. I realised that I couldn't raise myself to a walking position or reach any of the supplies in my rucksack. I looked across at a patch of bright sunlight over the Mamores and thought that it would be the last thing I would ever see and drifted into unconsciousness.

'I woke up shivering with a horrible gasping cough. I suddenly realised that I could hear a helicopter. It then hit me that I might just get out of this after all. I thought of people on desert islands waving at passing planes, which saw nothing. The helicopter sound grew louder and now I saw it landing in the coire. I saw the flashlights, eerily brightened by my hypothermia, fanning out over the

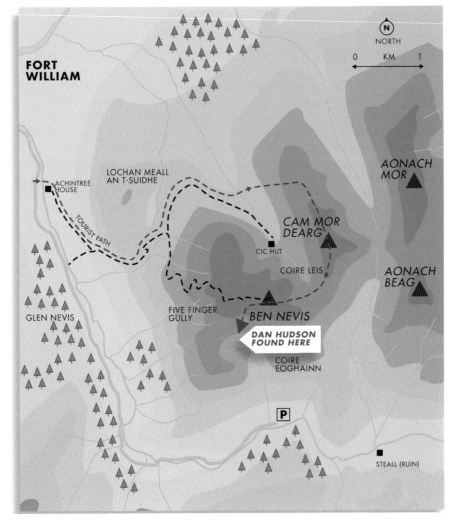

land. In my delirious state I sat there watching the beautiful sight of the lights in the snow like an Alpine festival. Then it dawned on me that they were several hundred feet below and that they would never find me in the dark up here. I gritted my teeth and dragged myself down the snowslope towards them. Suddenly I felt a burning cold sensation. I had landed in a stream and couldn't get out. I shouted for help... nothing. Then I saw a flashlight close by. I shouted. He shouted back. Then six figures in red had converged on me. Someone called my name. I mumbled something about my arms being broken and my legs being OK and passed out.

'My injuries were much less severe than they might have been. The left arm was a mess of fragments. The right arm escaped with a dislocated elbow. The head wounds were superficial. By November, I was fully recovered and I have since been back on the hills although I now find myself putting the crampons on for the most innocent looking ice and hard snow patches. I have yet to go back to the Ben however.'

After Dan had fallen, Warren decided to head down the mountain to raise the alarm. Lochaber MRT responded by sending three search parties up the mountain – one into Five Finger Gully, one into Coire Eoghainn from above and the third group into the Coire from below. It was this latter group that eventually found Dan. The RAF helicopter managed

It's sobering to learn from the statistics that the chief cost of accidents on the hill is a simple slip, slide or trip. Depending on the terrain, the consequences can range from an awkward wrench to sudden death
Davy Gunn
Glencoe MRT

to uplift him in very difficult conditions – dark, misty, high winds and awkward terrain – and take him to the hospital in Fort William. Within minutes he was being treated for his injuries and hypothermia.

Fully recovered from his ordeal, Dan was unequivocal. 'The fact that all of these people went to the extremes of their abilities saved my life. Had any one of these factors been different, I might not have lived to tell the tale.'

In fact, 'the simple slip' is the most common cause of mountain accidents – accounting for over 40%. Of course, it's well documented that slips, trips and tumbles are exceptionally common, not only in the mountains, but in the home and workplace. Alarmingly so.

According to the Health & Safety Executive, one million people every year attend a hospital accident and emergency department as a result of a slip, stumble or fall in the home. That's an awful lot of hours spent sitting on plastic chairs waiting for x-ray, when you really could be better employed back at home finishing the pile of ironing or clipping the hedge. Not to mention the one billion pounds cost to society repairing the hurt. But then, sitting in Casualty would be a better option for the 2000 or so unfortunate souls who die every year as a result of a domestic slip or fall. It's by far the largest cause of death in the home – far more risky than poisoning, fire or drugs.

Back in the mountains, casualties inevitably refer to having slipped, suddenly and unexpectedly. Sometimes, in the manner of the more bizarre insurance claims, the terrain itself conspires to ruin the day. Trees jump out from the shadows to impale foreheads and large boulders pivot backwards tearing Achilles tendons. But... we shouldn't make light. This is actually a very serious issue.

Even team members, out on a shout, can fall victim to the simple slip. Lomond team member Archie Roy was out searching for a group of walkers when he slipped and fell through a snow bridge. He had been walking along the route of a well-worn footpath which was snow covered and, unknown to him, undermined by melt water. As he placed his weight on the snow layer it gave way and collapsed. His leg went down the hole but his upper body continued forward with the momentum of the heavy rusksack on his back, wrenching his knee joint backwards and doing serious damage to the tendons, muscles and ligaments. Which stacked up to six months off work, a full year to recover and quite some time before he made it back to the call-out list!

Women are also more likely to slip than men – especially older women. Co-ordination and speed of reaction decrease with age, but this tends to be more rapid in women than men, especially post-menopause, when osteoporosis becomes an important factor. So, perhaps the increased incidence of slips amongst women can be explained in physiological terms – something that can't be controlled.

Physiotherapist Angie Jackson had first hand experience when she became a statistic herself. 'Two years ago I was walking the Coledale Horseshoe in the Lakes when I slipped and badly fractured my ankle. The weather had started good – warm with light drizzle. Near the top, we stopped to add clothing. The mist came down and the rain increased. The path was quite wide and the easiest I had done in a long time to accommodate friends who were less experienced. By the halfway point, we were walking in mist and drizzle. I was ahead of the other three and turned to listen to one of the group explaining how to make a stretcher out of waterproofs and ski poles! I was feeling fit and was not tired, but must have had a small concentration lapse. That was it. I slipped sideways on a mud-covered stone, caught the inside of my foot on a smaller stone and, in the process, landed on my leg. The result – a lower limb in lots of pieces. Technically, I suffered several oblique fractures of the fibula and a comminuted fracture of the medial malleolus. I couldn't believe it had happened so quickly. Friends went for help and found a fell runner who alerted mountain rescue.

'I was rescued by wonderful people – the Keswick team and the crew of the rescue helicopter. Carlisle Infirmary put my ankle back together and made a good job out of a bad one. It was a traumatic time and resulted in one of the group having terrible nightmares and flashbacks. I had a tough six months trying to rehabilitate my ankle. As a physiotherapist I knew what had to be done. Flashbacks were a great problem to me too.

'I have continued my walking, doing most of the high peaks last year, but in lots of pain downhill. It has been difficult to get back to running and tennis is also out. I've decided reluctantly to have further surgery to remove all of the metal work, to see if it reduces the pain and swelling. The accident had a positive side as it highlighted the following – always walk with someone else; carry lightweight first aid stuff including foil wraps and a bivvy bag; always tell someone the route you are taking, estimated time and where the car will be left.

'It's not something I wish to repeat again. Just one little slip and life can take a big turn.'

Then there's the terrain to consider – poised and ready to trip the unsuspecting at any moment. John Rogers reckons the dividing line between trouble and safety is finely drawn. 'In my own limited experience I have had one or two small reminders. Coming down from the top of Stob Coire nan Lochan in Glencoe, chattering with a friend, on the steep grassy ground above the lochans, I slipped on a wet stone and broke my ankle. I spent several painful hours getting off the hill, even shuffling on my bottom over the difficult bits. But suppose the simple mishap had occurred in winter when I was alone – as I often am – and in bad weather? Suppose the break had been enough to immobilise me?'

A very high proportion of slips happen on rocky ground – both John Rogers and Angie Johnson slipped on wet rock but many slips occur on scree – loose rocks and stones, usually at a steep angle, often found below steep crags and cliffs or where a path is well worn. Negotiating your route over scree is, at best exhilarating but quite likely nerve-wracking as the ground beneath you takes on a life of its own, loose debris clattering and skittering down the hill ahead of you.

Every year, people die in the mountains of England, Wales and Scotland because they slip or stumble and fall a long way. The majority of these occur during the summer not, as you might imagine, during the ice, sleet and snow of winter. In 2003, Lake District teams categorised nine fatalities as 'summer hillwalking' and only one as 'winter hillwalking', with none at all recorded as snow and ice climbing. It was a similar story the previous year, with seven in summer and one in winter. The majority of those who venture into the winter mountains take care to wear crampons – spiked metal plates which attach to the soles of the boots to make foot placement more secure.

But people aren't always properly equipped, as Richard Hartland found out to his cost. It was February, in Scotland. The conditions were perfect for winter climbing – ice sheets everywhere. Richard and his brother were on their annual winter climbing holiday. Heavily laden with climbing hardware, clothing and food for a week, tent and sleeping bags, their walk into the coire took them along a path that is very well trodden and popular with summer walkers and climbers.

'While we were en route, we encountered a particularly large ice sheet across the path. As on previous occasions that day, we decided against donning crampons to negotiate the ice sheet. My brother crossed easily. I, however, stepped onto the ice and instantly started to slide down the slope to my right. Without crampons or ice axe handy, I was unable to stop the slide nor could I control it. Slowly, inexorably, I slid towards a small but steep drop. I cannot remember very much, but I do recall stretching my arms to break my fall. I also remember my feet continuing to slide when they hit the ground at the bottom of the drop. This had the effect of concentrating all my weight and that of my rucksack through my left shoulder. I screamed apparently. My shoulder hurt a lot at this point and I could barely move it. My brother had to remove my rucksack and help me into a kneeling position so I could start to recover. He then put his crampons on, but in the process he nudged me causing me to topple gently to one side. I instinctively put out my arm to support myself and, even with virtually no weight, my arm dislocated from the shoulder socket. I screamed again, and put it back into the socket.

'At this point we did not believe all was lost. I had dislocated my shoulder and probably caused some bruising and minor damage to the muscles and tendons, but in a couple of days could probably climb again. So we carried on (after I had recovered, and my brother had helped me get my rucksack back on). We camped out the night but the continued pain in the morning and poor night's sleep persuaded us to retreat from the mountain and salvage some Munro bagging from the week. I went to the hospital that evening, and it's just as well I did, because I had broken the socket of the shoulder. When I returned home, I was admitted to my local hospital for an operation to pin the bone back in place.

'All this happened at the end of February. I was off work for two weeks, couldn't drive for three months and still haven't started climbing again. My shoulder is back to about 90% movement and the strength is returning so I hope to climb by mid June. All this from a simple slip that could have been prevented by my putting my crampons on.'

Richard was fortunate – many walkers and climbers have lost their lives because they slipped without wearing crampons. James Long and Richard Bell were descending Ben Lawers in Central

Scotland when they slipped simultaneously on a patch of ice and fell about 300 feet down an icy, rocky slope. They were lucky not to have fallen another 1000 feet to the bottom of the coire. Both suffered multiple abrasions and lacerations including suspected spinal injuries. An RAF helicopter landed on scene to give emergency first aid before transporting them to hospital. Neither walker was equipped with an ice axe or crampons and both were wearing light summer walking boots totally inappropriate for winter mountaineering.

Perhaps we should point out – before you become carried away by the notion that accidents befall only the more adventurous (nay, foolhardy) individuals amongst us – that about a quarter of all slips take place on footpaths. Sometimes they occur in the casualty's own back garden. As one unfortunate chap discovered one fine August evening in Lancashire, as he set about mowing his lawn – and slipped twelve feet into the river Ribble! He only sustained minor injuries but it took the fire service and several rescue team members to extricate him from the river.

Another incident, just a small stone's throw from a suburban main road left a forty one year old Manchester man fighting for his life in a hospital for several weeks. At a popular beauty spot, people who probably wouldn't dream of trekking up a mountain with boots and walking poles, rusksack strapped to their backs, can park the car, let their dog out on a lead and, within a few short paces, be under the trees, stepping through bluebells or buttercups, away from the hum of traffic. In one corner of a field is a stile leading to a narrow path with steep drops alongside. It was never clear exactly what happened – perhaps because everything happened so quickly – but it would seem that as they crossed the stile the dog slipped over the path edge, dragging his owner with him - straight down a sixty foot drop. On life support for four long weeks, Ian had no memory of the accident, in which he sustained a punctured lung, broken ribs and suspected liver damage. Surgeons removed part of his lung and used a massive 36 units of blood in the course of the treatment. It was an accident that could so easily have happened to anybody. In fact, the previous year, a young cub scout had fallen to his death at the very same spot. Ian's recovery was a slow process but he survived to tell the tale. Sadly, his dog died in the fall.

So, having established that slips and tumbles can happen anywhere – to almost anyone – how important is the weather? The answer is – very. But the most significant weather factor is not snow or rain, as you might expect, but wind. Probably because winds, especially gusts, can so easily knock you off balance. And the other problem with wind is that it can force you along just a wee bit too fast for comfort, which can be pretty hairy on very steep ground or close to an edge. High winds played a large part in a serious accident witnessed by Manus Graham. Manus was walking in the Cairngorms one day in February. He had walked in to Coire an Sneachda and was facing a cliff popular with winter climbers. He noticed a party descending the 'Goat Track' – a steep route often used for descent. The lower part of the slope is strewn with large boulders and in winter it is invariably covered in hard ice and snow. One member of the group, Gary, had a rolled camping mat positioned on top of his rucksack. Manus remembers thinking it resembled the wing on a Formula One car. As the climber reversed down the slope, facing inwards, his feet appeared to be obscured by spindrift blasted down the slope. He looked very unsteady. Sporadic gusts of wind were catching the rolled mat, almost lifting him off his feet. Eventually he slipped, went over backwards and began to accelerate head first down the slope so rapidly that he couldn't stop.

'He took off over a sort of ramp caused by a boulder and, on landing, started to spin rapidly on his

long axis with such force that gloves and other bits flew off with centrifugal force. He stopped just short of the boulder field. When we got to him he was sore but okay. We made a makeshift stretcher from skis and carried him out of the coire where a helicopter picked him up. The hospital diagnosed a broken foot which, strangely, was probably the best protected part of him!'

Over 60% of those who slip or stumble suffer limb injuries such as twisted ankles, broken legs or dislocated shoulders, but a significant proportion suffer multiple or fatal injuries. It's a sobering thought but, if you slip in the mountains and your accident is serious enough to require outside help, there's a one in ten chance that you won't survive to tell the tale!

When Bob Sparkes survived fractures to his shoulder, hand and spine in a serious hill-walking accident, his story was later filmed for the Discovery Channel and entitled *The Longest Search*. Bob had spent the night on the summit of a mountain following a twenty mile trip the previous day. An early breakfast on the top under his belt, he had begun to ascend a 45 degree slope of heather and rocks when he stumbled and banged his head on a rock. He staggered and tumbled 500 feet down a gully, coming to rest on a ledge a few feet from a 70 foot drop. For three days and nights

he lay unconscious on the ledge. When he came to, he tried to inch his way out of the gully but fell again and fractured his spine. Mountain rescue teams were alerted and he was eventually found, four days

'The Goat Track' (Coire an t-Sneachda) in the Cairngorm, popular with winter climbers. The path angles down from the top right of the picture.

later, by a helicopter. With the benefit of hindsight, he concedes it was a mistake to go walking alone. Nowadays when he takes off on his own, he always wears a helmet.

It's been observed many times, by returning mountaineers reflecting on the difficulties they faced on whichever mountain – that, however exhilarating it might be, however much of an achievement, battling the elements, conquering your own particular odds, touching the summit, breathing in the magnificence

– when you actually reach that tingling moment of achievement, you're only halfway done. There's only one way to go now. And that's down.

Many slips and trips occur as people descend. And you don't have to be descending K2 for the problem to apply. The more tired you are, the more anxious to avoid the home-going traffic jams, make it back to the pub for last orders, find a decent loo to sit on, or pitch a tent before nightfall (indeed, any number of perfectly feasible and suddenly urgent reasons) the more likely you are to stumble. Take the story of John Usher and his friend, Munro-bagging in the Southern Highlands.

'The forecast was for a pleasant late summer's day, so my mate and I set off for a Munro (mountain above 3000 feet) called Meall Glas in Perthshire. It's not high or wild enough to attract the hordes. The ascent was straightforward and we met just one couple on the way. They complained bitterly about the lack of paths, which we thought was hilarious. After gaining the summit, we started our descent with the day getting muggy and cloudy. Our route took us a slightly different line from the ascent and involved hummocky grass, which was too lumpy to make easy progress. We decided to stop for a break (no pun intended) at roughly 2000 feet. It was here, in a split second, that everything changed.

'As soon as we sat down, the midges descended on us so badly that eating was out of the question. I stood up, swatting them away, put my walking poles under my arm and tried to take a bite out of my apple. If I remember rightly, John and I began a discussion about some philosophical conundrum like should you have red wine with chicken. As I stepped forward my right foot slipped away and then stopped. A combination of body angle and absence of poles meant I went forward and my foot turned inward, making a dull crack. It wasn't painful, just different.

'I sat down with my foot in the air and was attacked instantly by the midges. I had to do something because I'd be a skeleton if I stayed where I was! I took off my boot and found I could move the joint well but, as soon as I touched the outside of the ankle, I realised that I'd either torn a tendon or broken a bone.

'John had an ankle support with him, as well as paracetamol. They were used to good effect, then I put my boots back on and tied the laces really tightly. Using the poles now as crutches I began to make my way down. Luckily, the ground further down was spongy and helped to cushion the force of my steps. I very nearly went over on the other ankle at one point and that may well have been the time when we would call a halt. I've always maintained that I would never call out mountain rescue unless it was life threatening.

'The further we descended, the more painful my foot became. To help relieve the pain, we played our own version of Desert Island Discs. John later sent me a compilation of the selection called 'Songs for Broken Ankles'! We actually made very good progress and were well off the hill before dark. I soon realised on reaching the metalled road that I could go no further and John went on to collect the car. When he returned, for some bizarre reason, I decided to drive. I knew that I would be in A&E for some time, so decided to drop John off at his home

Reasons why people slip

- Misjudged foot placement
- Lack of concentration
- Fatigue
- Distracted
- Walking too fast
- Not wearing crampons
- Poor footwear
- Inadequate fitness
- Felt unwell
- Clogged (footwear) treads

whilst I went to the hospital in Edinburgh. Driving was fine as long as my foot didn't touch the floor. In hindsight, I was probably in shock.

'At A&E, I was diagnosed with having a fractured lateral malleolus without complications. I was in plaster for three weeks and off work for two months, back on the hills seven months later, without too much ill effect other than having to cope with the extra weight I'd put on. While in plaster I reviewed what went wrong and what went right with the first injury suffered in thirty years of walking in the wildest country in Britain, the Alps and the Himalayas. The right things were responding quickly to the break, strapping the ankle, taking pain relief and keeping a cool head.

'The wrong things will take a bit longer! Underestimating the terrain, not using walking poles, doing more than one thing at once, driving back to Edinburgh! To cap it all, on my return, I noticed that the heel cup on my boots was in poor shape and allowed far too much movement. A sturdier pair of boots would have probably prevented my foot going over so much and I should have really spotted this before going. It may well be that my next Desert Island Discs will begin with 'These boots are made for walking'!'

Footwear can be a major factor, although it features way down the 'cause' list. Today's boots are designed with comfort, safety and environmental protection in mind. That so few slips can be attributed to poor footwear shows how effective they are.

Walking poles, however, are beginning to loom larger in the incident reports – for better and for worse! Simon Jones was walking on Dartmoor and descending a fairly steep heather-covered slope to the roadside when his foot stuck in a hole and he lost his balance, falling forwards at an awkward angle. Unfortunately, his boot remained in the hole and his lower leg snapped. He reported later that had he been using walking poles his accident would

Caught out in an electrical storm – what do you do?

You will know a storm is approaching because you'll see the threatening clouds and, probably, distant lightning. There may be a stillness in the air. Some people report hearing a humming noise or hair standing on end. Make your way off the tops and avoid high ground, especially summits, peaks and ridges.

But don't seek shelter in overhangs or water-filled gullies as these tend to channel electricity from a strike and – if you are in the way – through you! The best plan is to sit on something dry and make as few points of contact with the ground as possible. Don't lie down as this merely increases the area of contact with the ground.

probably not have happened.

Dave Paine had a similar experience in Scotland. He and his friend were backpacking in a remote part of the Northwest Highlands and were walking from a bothy called Carnmore to another called Shenavall. The two bothies are about eight miles apart and the path between the two, rises to a height of around 1500 feet.

'I think I must have twisted my knee on the rough terrain near Carnmore and over the course of the next few miles made it worse by continuing to walk carrying a heavy rucksack. I'd slept badly at Carnmore but decided to carry on at Shenavall, as it was nearer than returning to our starting point in Kinlochewe. I hoped I could walk it off.

'My leg got much worse over the top to Shenavall. In fact, it took me one and a half hours to

Using walking poles correctly

1. If you want to take full advantage of poles when moving across flat or easy-angled snow covered terrain, they must be used correctly in regard to length, basket size and proper use of wrist loops – check the manufacturer's instructions!

2. Poles should never be used as a substitute for an ice axe. Both help the balance but poles cannot be used to arrest a fall.

3. When approaching snow covered steep ground, poles should be consigned to the rucksack and replaced by an ice axe before there is a chance of a slip. It's vital to make the decision when it is easy to stop and change, prior to the risk of a fall.

4. If a single pole is used in conjunction with an axe when descending steep ground, then the pole's wrist loop should be left free and the axe always kept in the uphill hand. You should practice ditching the pole and using the axe for self arrest early each winter in safe conditions, to ensure it can be done effectively.

walk eight miles. The following morning, I found I couldn't walk at all, so my companion walked out to the road to call mountain rescue. I was expecting a land-based rescue but they sent in an RAF helicopter which airlifted me to Inverness hospital. The doctor told me I'd stopped just in time to avoid serious damage.

'The next year, we went back so I could complete the final stretch – this time with walking poles. I then knew I'd made the right decision the year before – there was no way I could have walked out in the condition I was in. I'd have ended up needing to be rescued from a far more difficult position. If I'd used walking poles the previous year, I could have taken the weight off my knee and would probably have managed to walk all the way out, so I would definitely recommend them for difficult terrain and wading across rivers.'

With the explosion in use over recent years, trekking poles appear to be the new panacea of the walking set. Bad back, dicky knees, dodgy hip? Just plain tired? According to the various manufacturers, using a pair of walking poles will automatically promote correct posture, let you breathe more efficiently, increase your stamina, reduce fatigue, improve balance and stability and save your knees - impressive claims.

It's all down to weight transfer. Descending steeper ground, the weight transfer from the lower to the upper body reduces impact forces inside the knee joint – making the whole experience more comfortable, conserving energy and – hopefully – preventing long term injury. Using poles also provides four handy points of contact which, as anyone who has scrambled over a particularly hairy ridge on all fours will know, is a considerable aid to balance! When scrambling over anything or climbing up a steep snow slope, we hasten to add, we recommend you stick to the four points of contact God gave you and keep the poles firmly strapped to your rucksack.

Although even that can become life threatening. Summer 2004 saw one climber in Scotland killed when a freak bolt of lightning struck his walking pole. Derek Hunter was climbing the 3373 foot peak Beinn Oss near Tyndrum with his brother-in-law. The two were near the summit. A sudden violent electrical storm appeared from nowhere. Derek had just commented about the lightning before he was struck. One of his walking poles was burned through in three places and there was also a burn mark on the handle where he had been holding it. Help was delayed because the storm had knocked out the mobile phone mast. Eventually, a Royal Navy Sea King from Prestwick was alerted along with the Killin rescue team. The team, however, was faced with a dilemma, since they considered they would also be at risk with their radio antennae. Eventually, the storm passed, leaving the Sea King to uplift Derek. Unfortunately, despite attempts to revive him, he died in the helicopter.

Undoubtedly, this was a freak of nature which wrought tragic results but the fact remains that a number of serious incidents appear to be connected with the inappropriate use of walking poles. There was the walker, apparently using a single pole as a replacement for her ice axe, who fell over 1000 feet to her death. In another fatal fall, the climber was using an ice axe in one hand and a trekking pole in the other – making it impossible to arrest a fall. Using an ice axe effectively requires both hands. It's been suggested that walking poles give a false sense of security on steep ground because they generate levels of confidence not always matched by skill and they're certainly no substitute for an ice axe when moving over steep, snow-covered terrain.

So, if slips and trips are so common, can anything be done to prevent the risk? Perhaps not. The majority of mountain rescue teams undertake talks and slide shows in their local community as part of their fundraising activities. Amusing tales and dramatic photography subtly demonstrate the hazards and reinforce the safety message. Fine, but how much can entertaining the local Mother's Union or Rotary group really make a difference to those who take to the hills for fun? It's a tricky one. In the USA and Canada, the mountain rescue service is far more hands-on in terms of prevention than in the UK. The 'Lost in the Woods – Hug a Tree' programme delivered to schools, scout groups, churches and other groups of kids, encourages them to stay in one place when they become lost, not run in a blind panic. They are encouraged to see the tree as a 'friend'. One which provides shelter and shade – and serves as a marker to the searchers. In Iceland, where the whole process is approached with a 'cradle to grave' philosophy, mountain rescue teams run youth groups so the safety message is learnt at an early age. The point being that the education and dissemination of information begins early and involves the whole community.

Edward Whymper's oft-quoted advice: to do nothing in haste and look well to each step, always thinking from the beginning what may be the end, still rings true. As leader of the ill-fated attempt on the Matterhorn, which resulted in the death of three companions in 1868, he knew a thing or two about slips and tumbles. It's a piece of advice one particular elderly walker would have been wise to heed, as Bob Sharp relates.

'The weather was uncharacteristic for midwinter. The day had been dry, very still with no wind and quite warm. In fact, conditions were very spring like, although that was to change. The next two months saw a crop of mountain accidents, with over twenty fatalities in just three months – the worst record in history – in which the weather was considered a major factor. This particular day, however, promised good walking and probably encouraged many walkers on to the hills who, ordinarily, would not have ventured far from the warmth of home.

'The team received the call around 5 o'clock in the afternoon. The police had difficulty raising some key people at this time of the day but, in the event, it didn't matter because only a few were required to manage the incident. Team members gathered quickly and began to make their way up the steep sided hill in the direction of the accident site. As we moved away from the noise of the roadside, our mood was sombre, heightened by the still night. A couple of hours earlier, two walkers had seen a man slip on wet grass, fall about 400 feet from the summit of Dumgoyne and then tumble a long way over cliffs to land amongst rocks below. One of the onlookers, a nurse, was able to lend expert help immediately.

PHOTO: BOB SHARP

Dumgoyne

When looking for people lost in the hills, there's the task of deciding where they may be and the strategic planning involved in deploying personnel efficiently. Searching at night adds elements of navigation and teamwork. Other rescues involve retrieving people whose location is known, but who may have fallen in awkward places – rope work, first aid and team skills play a prominent role. With many rescues, there's a buoyancy amongst team members as they work towards a goal which has a positive and satisfying outcome. But, in this case, there were no such challenges. We all knew our arrival at the accident site would not be pleasant.

'The hill steepened in the dark, its outline casting a threatening profile against the sky. Fatigue, coupled with a certain lack of urgency, made for slow progress. We climbed together in silence. After about an hour, the slope relented and we made our way to one side of the hill, aiming for a point below the crags where the walker had fallen. We soon met up with the nurse who had seen the walker fall. She'd left the body and been replaced by a police officer who had started up the hill before the team. Within minutes, the ground levelled out. We could see a person sitting amongst the rocks some twenty metres ahead. The dark shape silhouetted behind him told a grim story. Few people – apart from the medical fraternity – face death during their

Unfortunately, the walker had sustained fatal injuries and was beyond assistance. One of the walkers made his way down to the roadside to raise the alarm from a local house, whilst the other stayed with the deceased. Later evidence confirmed the walker was experienced and well equipped but, as he stood admiring the views from an exposed vantage point just below the summit, he failed to notice the wet grass underfoot. As he adjusted his position to return he slipped and fell to his death.

'Many rescues are exciting because there's typically an element of challenge or uncertainty.

PHOTO: JOHN PAUL PHOTOGRAPHY

lifetime. When I first joined the rescue team many years ago, it never entered my thoughts but, over the past twenty five years I've had to deal with fatal accidents on many occasions. I probably react in the same way as others – as detached and objective as possible. In one sense, it isn't difficult to do this. There are always jobs to do which have to be carried out in a proper and timely manner. The stretcher has to be unpacked and assembled, safety ropes located, people deployed and advance instructions passed on to police, ambulance crews and so on.

'We held back for a while, planning our actions, before a small number of us moved forward to attend the fallen walker. One of the team medics went through the meticulous and necessary procedure to confirm death, whilst we watched in silence. Within a few minutes we were on our way down the hill to pick up a Land Rover track and transport. The thick heather didn't make for easy progress but we all thought to take great care with the stretcher. Conversation picked up as we saw the lights of a waiting ambulance. We transferred the stretcher smoothly and the ambulance trundled down the track and out of sight into the glen. Another rescue was over. Most of us chose to walk back around the side of the hill to our starting point rather than be uplifted by waiting vehicles.

'The sky was clear and full of stars. We took our time, stopping frequently to observe the constellations and shooting stars – and also to pause for thought. Life is so fragile and so very short. The experiences of the evening had once again brought this into sharp focus.'

RAF crew tend an injured girl on the Ben Nevis path

chapter five

LOST AND FOUND

Support your local mountain rescue team. Get lost!
Anon

Get lost! Now there's an emotive phrase. Easy enough to say, but just how easy is it to do? A glance at the number of searches undertaken every year, the length and breadth of the UK, to find people who are lost or overdue – the subjects themselves often blissfully unaware that they are so (but we'll come to that) – suggests that, actually, yes it is very easy. Next to slips and tumbles, more incidents involve lost people or groups than any other kind.

But how can you ever really be lost? If being lost means losing a sense of where you are, relative to where you think you should be, it's probably an everyday occurrence – whether it's negotiating your way round another traffic diversion or rediscovering where the supermarket put the sugar. A couple of deep breaths, the odd well chosen cuss and a moment's orientation, and there you are. Unlost. If there were such a word.

However, getting unlost in the mountains is altogether more difficult. No helpful yellow and black-arrowed signs guiding you back onto your route. No clever merchandising teasing you round to the sugar. More than likely nothing even vaguely helpful – no recognisable landmarks and no genial staff around to point you in the right direction. Add to that poor visibility, deteriorating weather conditions, cold, wet and fatigue, and being lost quickly conjures up all sorts of emotions – fear, loneliness, depression, apprehension, anger, embarrassment. In fact, being lost in itself isn't really the problem. The problem is the fear of what happens next. Might I have to spend the night, cold and lonely, in this godforsaken place? Will anyone miss me? Will I die? What do I do next?

Perhaps there should be a few more signs about the hills – strategically placed to warn people of the dangers? Or would they simply ignore them? Bob Sparkes – a hillwalking casualty who we'll come back to later in this chapter – asked the question one sunny day in the Cairngorm mountains.

'Last May I went up the Chalamain Gap path, onto Lurcher's Crag and up onto the plateau. A

PHOTO: TOM GRATY

shower approached, so I togged up and made lots of calculations about getting to Cairn Lochan, programming my GPS accordingly. Then, a blizzard hit with a complete white out, so I took the opportunity to continue on GPS alone as I was anxious to see if it worked and it was ideal conditions for doing this. After about half an hour, I arrived at Cairn Lochan, just as the blizzard ceased and the mist cleared. I was elated with the success of my venture.

Just then, two people approached, running from the area of Ben Macdui, yelling and waving. When they arrived, the girl was in tears and they both pleaded for me to tell them where they were. They'd walked up the road to the restaurant and, on a lovely sunny day, had 'gone for a walk'. By then, the mist had cleared so I could point to Cairngorm and Aviemore and send them on their way. Neither had a map or compass, nor even waterproofs! If the blizzard had lasted much longer, they'd be dead. Should there be warning signs on all approaches to popular hills warning people of the dangers?'

Weather conditions, only a few hundred metres above sea level, can be notoriously fickle. It's not uncommon for people to 'go for a walk' up a hill, confident in their own safety, only to become extremely disorientated by a sudden change, as a family in Lancashire discovered one late February afternoon. The father had set off with his three young children – aged between two and seven – and the family dog, to place a flag with their names on it on top of Pendle Hill. The afternoon was clear. They were having fun. What could possibly go wrong?

Several hours later, as the hours ticked by to darkness and they still hadn't returned, the alarm was raised. Two rescue teams were involved in the search. By this time, there was thick fog on the hill and temperatures were plummeting, so rescuers were increasingly worried for the family's safety. When they were eventually found, at ten o'clock – by a dog handler, incidentally, on his first ever shout – they were shivering and cold, but safe, huddled together in a gully, sheltering from the worst of the wind.

Around one third of all reported mountain incidents are down to poor navigation. A good deal more folk probably get lost on the hill – or temporarily mislaid – either through navigation error, poor planning or inattention, but eventually they sort things out for themselves. The cloud lifts so they can see where they are or they use their navigational

a typical tale...

A group of sixth form girls and their teacher, from a school in Birmingham, were lost during a mountain trek in the Brecon Beacons – an area the school had visited many times before. The pupils, aged 16 and 17, were on a practice Duke of Edinburgh expedition for the Gold Award. They had set off in good weather in the morning. However, the mist came down in the early afternoon when the group was on a plateau, making navigation very difficult. Conditions were made more difficult with driving rain and hailstorms. Somewhat confused, they descended into the wrong valley, where they found their path blocked by steep ground and a fast flowing river. At this point, they wisely decided to stay put, put on their warm clothes and survival bags, and called for help.

The alarm was raised by a teacher, who contacted police for help at 7.30pm. Almost 30 personnel were involved in the rescue, including a helicopter from RAF Chivenor in North Devon. It was the helicopter crew who spotted light from the girls' torches in worsening weather conditions, just before midnight. The girls were extremely wet and cold from the heavy rain and strong winds, although they didn't require hospital treatment.

skills to backtrack to a known position, or they descend to a position they can identify on the map. They might end up in the wrong valley or looking at the wrong side of the mountain and need to walk a long way back, but at least they've sorted the problem and, hopefully, learned a lesson.

Mick James was climbing with his friend on Ben Nevis. They had completed the climb in perfect conditions but were aware that a storm had been forecast.

'Within ten minutes, the weather had changed to being near impossible, resulting in a four hour crawl off the summit. For us, we pushed the day a bit too far and should have abseiled back from the Tower Gap, rather than go for a perfect day and a top out. Discretion is the better part of valour as they say! That aside, we found the navigation nearly impossible off the top. We roped up and crawled on a bearing but were being picked up and blown around by the wind. We went south too far and then bore back, but ended up in Five Finger Gully. Here, it seems like you're on the descent path but once the fall line becomes obvious (takes a while when visibility is only five metres!) you are quite clearly 90 degrees off your bearing. The lesson is to trust your compass, no matter what and slog back out – not an inviting prospect when cold and tired, and blinded by snow. But I think this lesson is vital. I'm sure loads of folk die in Five Fingers because they're knackered and hoping their compass is bust – if they're looking at it at all. You think that because you are going down at last, you must be on the right path.'

At least Mick and his friend were aware of the weather and had bothered to examine the forecast before starting their climb. With hindsight, he readily admits the potential pitfalls – navigational problems, not believing the compass and over-ambitious plans. Jane Clark, an active mountaineering club member, has some clear ideas why people make mistakes.

'Key areas of weakness in people's skills are map reading and navigation, especially in adverse or winter conditions when you can't see your destination. I'm pretty sure if you dropped in on one of our walks and asked each member to give you a six figure grid reference of where we were, you would get some surprising results – mostly poor. In my opinion, it is down to lack of knowledge, laziness and lack of confidence. In winter, over-estimating what can be done in daylight hours and generally working out how long things take, are problems. I have not really been involved in any serious incidents but have had some examples of poor navigation leading to lengthy detours or poor route selection, giving some hairy moments. I tend to turn back rather than persist on getting to the top in adverse conditions.

'You need to practice and do it for yourself and not rely on someone else leading the way and taking the decisions. There is a special need to be self-reliant and self-confident, an emphasis on hands-on practical training, not just talking about what to do.'

Hmmm... the problems seem to be building up! Navigation errors, lack of confidence, poor planning, over-estimation, lack of knowledge. But people are not always to blame for being overdue. Sometimes a combination of circumstances creates a situation where no amount of skill, planning or preparation can help, as was the case with Peter Deacon. Peter had been planning a Scottish winter walking trip for some years. He had attended a winter skills training course to sharpen up his navigational skills and appreciation of avalanche risk assessment, snow-holing and winter survival. He knew the Scottish mountains in winter could be especially harsh and unpredictable and demanded to be treated with respect but what happened to Peter could not have been foreseen.

First Day – Saturday 26 January. 'I reached the Linn of Dee car park around 8.30am. Half an hour later, fully geared up, I set off northwards into Glen

Derry, and Derry Lodge. The rescue post there happened to be full of mountain rescue team members – we exchanged nods and greetings as I walked past. I did think for a second about having a chat, but felt very confident I knew what to expect and where I was going. I later wished I had spoken to them as it may have altered my plans – although, at the time, the weather was still good and there was no indication of what was to come.

'My planned route was to have taken me from Derry Lodge, along Glen Luibeg, then up the Carn a Mhaim ridge and via the Allt Clach nan Taillear up onto the summit of Ben Macdui. From there, I would descend into the Coire Etchachan to approach the Hutchison Memorial Hut from the west for the first night. However, although the weather was calm, mild and dry, the cloud base was well down on the summits so I opted to stay in the valley bottoms and follow Glen Derry all the way to Coire Etchachan and approach the hut from the east instead.

'I reached the hut at about 1.30pm. I spent the remainder of Saturday chatting to Nicholas – a Frenchman, staying there as part of a University Mountaineering Club ice-climbing expedition – drinking tea, pitching my tent and enjoying the views of the coire walls. The weather was good, a bit windy for a while but nothing remarkable and not particularly cold. I got plenty of sleep, waking only once at about 3.30am for a pee and to tension the side of the tent. It was a crystal clear night with pin-point bright stars.'

Second Day – Sunday 27 January. 'The weather was calm again, the cloud base higher with one or two breaks. As I set off walking at 10.00am towards Loch Etchachan, it seemed set for another fine day. My every step broke through thin, hard crust on top of soft pack – very tiring and difficult to keep any kind

View looking south west along Loch Avon from 'The Saddle'

of walking rhythm. So I turned north west and picked my way down the very awkward, broken and steep terrain towards the Shelter Stone, arriving at 12.30am.

'The wind had freshened but visibility was good. With 5km to cover to the Fords of Avon refuge, I decided to stick to the northern shore – an estimated one and a half hours – then ford the river, if safe to do so, and head south for Glen Derry and another night in the Hutchison Hut.

'After lunch, I left the Shelter Stone to cross the Feith Buidhe burn at the top of Loch Avon. I felt in good form and, with only a short and apparently easy walk ahead of me, I made for the loch to pick up the northern shore footpath. As I surveyed the ground ahead from a small knoll, I remember thinking, 'So where's the damn path?' Whoever had penned that dotted line on the OS map had made a mistake. There was nothing on the mountainside which remotely resembled a path of any description. But my desire to press on was quite strong, so I headed in the general direction of where I thought the path must be. It was 1.00pm – the beginning of probably the most unpleasant five hours I have ever spent in any mountain range during a thirty year walking career. I never did find the 'path'. The going was terrible with deep, soft, sugary snow embedded between thigh-high gullies and boulders. It was impossible to take more than two steps without one leg or the other disappearing up to the knee or, occasionally, the waist. I completely collapsed once or twice, as my pack was well loaded and the snow and terrain conspired to unbalance me totally. Gradually, I moved along the side of the loch until I judged I was about half way along it. The refuge was ahead of me and I had no desire to retrace my steps across such awful ground.

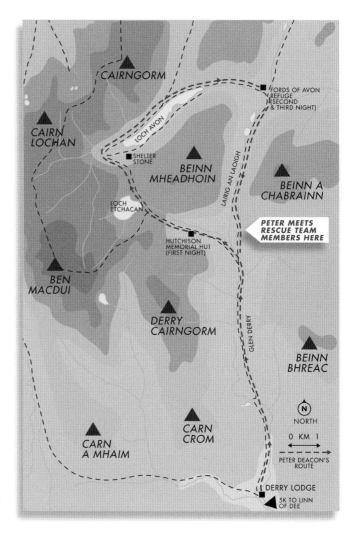

'The weather was quickly turning from unpleasant to serious – lowering cloud base, gusty winds and rain turning to sleet – and it was growing dark. I left the loch behind me at about 5.00pm with 1.5km still to cover. I knew if I didn't find the refuge soon, I might not find it at all – ever – and for a while I contemplated my own demise. Finally, at around

6.30pm, there it was. With a huge surge of relief, I pulled back the bolt, dumped my rucksack and prepared for the long night ahead, hopeful the storm would blow itself out and I could head back down Glen Derry to the Linn of Dee by late afternoon and ring my wife as arranged.'

Third Day – Monday 28 January. 'I knew immediately there was no chance of leaving – the wind was blowing the heavy snowfall horizontally with great force. Tuning in to Radio Scotland, I was amazed to hear reports of death, destruction and disruption all around Scotland and the Borders. The storm force winds were expected to continue for several hours more. Still, at least I was alive, uninjured, warm and dry and my temporary abode was in good shape. But, as the day wore on, I realised I would be spending another night in the refuge, and my wife would become increasingly concerned as the hours went by without contact. I turned the phone on several times but no signal. I felt frustrated and angry with myself for being in this situation, knowing the police and others would now become involved. On the other hand, it was comforting to know professional search and rescue personnel would, by now, be alerted and taking steps to find me. I was no longer the only person trying to extricate myself from this situation. I went to sleep planning to assess the forecast again in the morning, then make a decision whether to go for it.'

Fourth Day – Tuesday 29 January. 'I woke at dawn and realised the blizzard had passed. Visibility still wasn't tremendous, but I could see about half a kilometre to the head of the Lairig an Laoigh, my route back to Glen Derry. Slowly and methodically, I packed my gear and said thank you to the refuge, not entirely sure I was doing the right thing – had I stayed, the mountain rescue teams would eventually find me – but I didn't want to spend another night there. I made my way down to the river and mentally prepared myself for the crossing and long walk out.

The water flowing past seemed swift and forceful, knee and thigh deep in some places. I lengthened my walking poles so I could use them to balance myself and began picking my way carefully across, using the larger of the submerged rocks. Then, a brief glance back to the refuge that had been my life support system before I faced into the wind and headed along a track in a steady striding rhythm, snow still swirling. But, as I dropped down into upper Glen Derry, the visibility improved markedly. I lengthened my gait to begin eating up the distance back to the car so I could, at last, make that telephone call to my wife.

'As I drew alongside the opening to the hanging valley west of Glen Derry that leads up to Loch Etchachan and the Hutchison Memorial Hut, I finally saw three mountaineers ascending towards me. I knew immediately they had to be part of a mountain rescue team.'

'You wouldn't be looking for me by any chance?' I asked.

'If you're Peter Deacon, then yes,' he replied, holding out his hand to shake mine.

'A handshake hardly seemed sufficient so I gave him a hug. Members of the Aberdeen MRT, they were heading to the Fords of Avon refuge to look for me. A radio call was made to the Braemar Rescue Centre to confirm I'd been found, safe and well and to notify my wife. I remember feeling relief and some satisfaction at the thought that I had at least done everything I could to hasten my location and recovery and had, therefore, shortened the period of uncertainty for my wife and others.

'As soon as it was clear I was okay, and fit to continue, we set off down Glen Derry at a good pace. I was keen to know about the rescue effort and extremely grateful for, and apologetic about, the involvement of so many good people – all strangers. The team members were curious to know what route, decisions and actions I had taken before and after the bad weather closed in. I wanted to know more about the weather conditions and events across Scotland. Without exception, they were friendly, supportive, humorous and professional. I greatly enjoyed their company and was grateful for their positive comments. I had expected to be criticised and condemned for having caused so much trouble and expense but there was no hint of this from any of the team members or police officers.

'Back at the rescue post, I was greeted with a hot cup of tea and a sit down, while team members warmed themselves in front of a huge stove and chatted about the incident. I asked the team leader if I could just avoid the press altogether and sneak away in my car, but he felt if I tried to do this, they'd keep pursuing me until they got the story somehow. He then

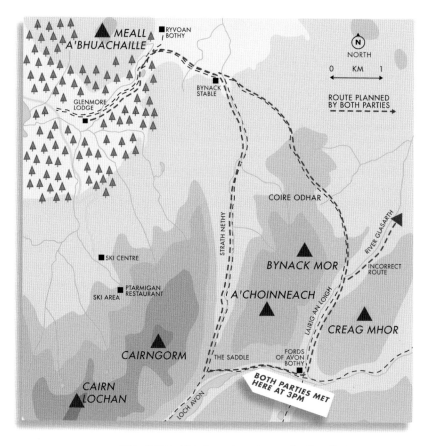

made it clear that he was satisfied I had done everything I could to ensure my safe return from the mountains – I'd left a clear route plan with my wife, marking on it all the bothies I would access; I was a reasonably experienced walker, well equipped for several days walking and camping in the mountains; I had intended to telephone at a pre-arranged time and when this did not happen, my wife had done entirely the right thing by contacting Braemar police; and I'd stayed put in the refuge when the weather turned foul.

'In front of several cameramen and journalists, I explained as clearly as I could what had happened to me during the four days I was in the Cairngorms. After several minutes of questioning, it was time to call it a day and make my exit. Some of the team members had kindly brought my car from the Linn of Dee car park to the rear of some shops in Braemar. Finally, I set off home, arriving just after midnight on Wednesday 30 January.'

Peter was well prepared and organised. He acted in a responsible manner. The same could hardly be said for two people from the East Midlands, set on a New Year's day out in the same remote spot. They had planned to leave Glenmore and follow the route to Ryvoan, Strath Nethy, The

Saddle, Loch Avon, Fords of Avon Bothy and return via the Lairig an Laoigh track and the shoulder of Bynack More. A second group of friends planned the same route in reverse. Both parties left at 9.00am meeting up six hours later at the east end of Loch Avon. The pair said they felt fit and well. The weather was reasonable with only a few blustery showers but, with only an hour of daylight left and a long journey ahead of them, they should have quit there and then to return with their friend, but they didn't. Big mistake.

Quickly benighted, with only a single torch between them, they chose to follow the footsteps in the snow left by the other group, rather than use a map. Consequently, they missed the route north into Coire Odhar and, instead, followed the river Glasarth north east. As they lost the footsteps, the weather worsened with high winds and heavy showers of sleet and snow.

When they realised they were completely lost, they formed a snow shelter for the night. They were wet, cold and miserable, with no equipment, spare clothing or food. Just before midnight, their friends raised the alarm. Members of the Cairngorm team and a search and rescue dog handler made their way onto the plateau of Bynack More. A request for a helicopter was turned down because the windy weather was too severe for safe flying. But, by first light, as members of the Braemar team swept up Glen Derry from the south, Kinloss team members were being helicoptered in to the Fords of Avon Refuge, to retrace the route in both directions. Weather conditions finally permitted the RAF helicopter to search the area and find the walkers at 11.30am, making their way to the refuge from the north. Both were very wet and cold and taken immediately to Glenmore.

So what went wrong? Neither of the two had any experience of winter mountaineering, nor were they carrying ice axe or crampons. They admitted to

An unusual benefit of mobile phones

The following took place on a cloudy night, with two MRTs and an RAF helicopter involved in the search. The helicopter crew were using NVG (Night Vision Goggles) which enhance low light vision.

'We knew the missing group was on the moss and they told us, via their mobile phone, they could see the helicopter searching for them. But, as they didn't know where they were, they had no way of describing their position. We explained this to the helicopter crew who asked me to tell the group to switch on their mobile phone and point it in the direction of the aircraft. Within minutes, the crew had seen the backlight and were on their way to the missing group. A few minutes later, they were uplifted and returned to base. Without the use of the mobile phone's backlight, it might have been another hour or so before the troops on the hill located the missing group.'

Willie Miller Team Leader, Ochils MRT

severely underestimating the length of the route and not using their map and compass at critical points but – worse – they had expected to use 'proper tracks' that were easy to follow! The entire incident took well over one thousand man hours, involving search dogs, four rescue teams and the helicopter.

It's often said a party should never divide into smaller groups. But how true is this and why? Well, first of all, there are no hard and fast rules about it. If members of a group wish to divide in order to carry out different objectives, then fine, just as long as the new groups each have the skills and equipment to succeed and be safe. Perhaps the reason for the advice is evidential.

A group of seven middle-aged men had climbed Helvellyn, in the Lake District, in late September, arriving at the summit at 2.00pm before heading down towards Striding Edge. About one kilometre along the ridge, one member split with the group complaining that the rest were going the wrong way. The group continued down the ridge, arriving back at their cars as planned to wait for their colleague. When he failed to turn up, they left and alerted the police. Three mountain rescue teams, plus dog handlers and the RAF helicopter searched throughout the following day to no avail. Later that day, the police received a message saying the missing walker was safe at home. He had, apparently, made his way back to the starting point but, when he found his friends had departed, decided to camp overnight, then make his way back home by hitching a lift, oblivious to 480 hours of mountain rescue search effort.

At least his friends bothered to report his disappearance. In another incident, in Grasmere, Langdale/Ambleside team members were asked to launch a search when a man phoned to say he had become separated from his companions while crossing Greenup Edge. Despite trying, he couldn't find his way down and was now sitting in snow on a north west facing slope. He was eventually found descending with another party. It appeared his friends (one wonders for how much longer!) had climbed into a cab in Grasmere and continued to Patterdale without him. As the team's annual report reflects, 'At what time they would have reported him missing is anybody's guess!'

So now we know how easy it is to be temporarily mislaid, in some cases, without actually being lost. More often than not, the person is reported missing by those back home, concerned for their loved one's welfare. But, once the call comes through, how do mountain rescue teams go about finding missing people? How do they know where to look and how to deploy members?

Let's imagine a weary walker, overtaken by nightfall en route down the mountain, calls 999 and asks for mountain rescue. His torch battery has gone and he's unsure of the path. But he does have a rough idea of his position – rather like our man in Grasmere, perched in the snow on a north west facing slope. A handful of team members are easily dispatched up the hill to find and escort him down. If communication on the mobile is good, they might even be able to 'talk him down' without leaving base.

Or maybe an entire group is overdue, reported missing by a diligent hotel owner, concerned at his unusually empty dining room. The only available information might be, 'They set off to Glenridding just after breakfast.' Sometimes, people leave word of their intended journey but then change their plans without informing anyone. Or there's the economy of style approach – 'I'm off to Wales for a few days walking.' Away from the hills, an increasing number of incidents involve people who are depressed, psychotic, suicidal or suffering from Alzheimer's – they just disappear with little or no indication where they might be. How does mountain rescue deal with these problems?

The most common approach is the Six Step Process or Incident Response Process, which originated in the US. This systematic and logical method enables those in charge (incident controllers or search managers) to make rapid decisions on tactics and deployment of resources. As the incident evolves, and more information becomes available, the six steps are repeated in a continuous cycle. If you'll pardon us waxing a little academic for a moment, we'll explain but, in a nutshell, the police and team leaders will size up the situation, identify the contingencies, determine the objectives, identify the required resources, build a plan and structure – and then take action!

● Step One. Sizing up the situation involves gathering a whole heap of information which may or may not be relevant, in order to build a profile of the missing person and an incident history. Specifically, this will look at the nature of the incident, any hazards present, weather and terrain, nature of any potential injuries and method of evacuation, what resources are available, how large an area is involved and how urgent the required response. Possibly the most significant piece of information will be the Initial Planning Point (IPP). This will either be the Point Last Seen (PLS) or the Last Known Position (LKP). The PLS will be a positive, identified sighting of the missing person. The LKP indicates that the person was not actually seen, but that some item, identified as theirs, has been found – a parked car, perhaps, or distinctive item of clothing. Experience shows that when a child, elderly person or despondent goes missing, they will often be found within 300 metres of the PLS. Family members, friends, local people, even work mates may be interviewed in an effort to paint as detailed a picture as possible. At this stage, an organisational structure will also be established.

● Step Two. What happened to cause the situation? Why has the person gone missing? Is there anything that could make the situation worse, such as onset of darkness or approaching thunderstorm? If the missing person is sick or suicidal, or suffering from Alzheimer's – are they on any medication? Do they have this with them? What are the consequences if they don't? Do they have money with them? Has there been a family row? Identifying the contingencies involves assessing all the factors behind an incident. There is a huge amount of data available on 'Lost Person' behaviour which shows that different types of people behave in different ways. Often, they'll tend to follow some kind

Hunt the 'doughnut'

The longer a person is missing, the greater the potential distance travelled from the last known point. Given that they are unlikely to walk in a straight line, the potential search area grows exponentially. Imagine, though, that they do walk in a straight line for an hour, straight out from the LKP marked on a map – that line now forms the radius of a small circle with the start point as the centre. Now imagine them walking on for another hour – still, miraculously, in a straight line – and you have a second radius and a slightly larger circle. Superimpose both those circles onto your map and – hey presto! – it's a doughnut! This area is the 25% zone of probability of a find – in other words, four out of sixteen searches may be successful.

Experience shows that many lost people detour dramatically as they try to find features and locations with which they are familiar. By referring to 'Lost Person' data, the search manager can establish a median distance of travel. According to the laws of probability, more lost people will be found closer to the median distance than any other point. If two circles are drawn encompassing the four closest cases adjacent to the median distance, with the last known point at the centre of both circles, they present a good start point for a search area.

of route. They meet features on the terrain such as paths, streams, walls and forest edges that cause them to change direction and certain features act as 'magnets', places of safety as darkness falls or the world closes in – the lights of a building at night, a familiar place from the past, or simply shelter from a storm. All this information helps teams develop

lost person behaviour

When people get lost, they tend to behave in particular ways. The analysis of this typical behaviour started in the US, back in the 1970s, and has now developed extensively in the UK. Consequently, there is a huge raft of data available to help searchers. Here are a few examples...

Small Children 1-6 Years

Up to aged 3

- No concept of being lost
- No navigational skills
- Tend to wander aimlessly
- Do not respond to calls and whistles

Aged 3-6

- Have a developed concept of being lost, so they will attempt to return home or to a familiar place
- Consequently, may panic and become further lost in an attempt to 'find themselves'!
- More mobile than children 1-3 years old
- Attracted by random events such as a tunnel, path or an animal or group of older children

Both categories will usually be found sleeping (anywhere – against a rock, under a bush, under a picnic table). They are difficult to detect and rarely walk out by themselves.

Fifty per cent of lost children are found within half a mile of where they were last seen. Strategies to find them involve the use of search and rescue dogs and searching high priority areas close to that previous known location.

Alzheimer's

- Poor short term memory
- Loss occurs when the person leaves nursing home, possibly with last sighting on a road
- Often oriented to the past – may be on their way 'home' to a childhood home, or other familiar place
- Impaired ability to make sense of their surroundings or recognise potential hazards
- Hallucinations or perceptual distortions
- Coexisting medical problems which limit mobility
- Previous history of going walkabout
- Will not cry out for help or respond to shouts
- Will not leave many physical clues

Fifty per cent of Alzheimer's patients who go walkabouts are found within 0.6 miles of the IPP, ninety six per cent within 1.5 miles, usually a short distance from the road and often caught in bushes or brambles. Often they will be close to – if not actually inside – an old home or place of work.

search areas and boundaries. Walkers, children (1-6 years), children (7-12 years), youths (13-15 years), despondents, walkaways (people with dementia and mental illness), psychotics, climbers, skiers... they all have their own group characteristics and a natural inclination to seek out a particular place.

● Step Three. What are the major steps required to meet the ultimate objective – finding the missing person? At this stage, decisions will be made about searching particular areas or deploying people to confine an area (such as positioning someone at the bottom of a path so they don't slip out of the search area undetected!) Often, each objective will contain a number of secondary objectives or practical tasks. The objective to clear a small hill may involve carrying out a broad sweep of the entire area, as well as a detailed exploration of the rivers running down the flanks and a small wooded area near the bottom. Of course, with all these potential tasks, the important thing is to prioritise – more often than not there will be insufficient resources to attend to everything straight away. Each task might be given a 'likelihood' rating to help decide which resources to assign first. So, if it is known that a missing group had planned to cross a river swollen with heavy rain, it might make sense to deploy people to search the area of land on the nearside of the river before the far side is covered.

● Step Four. Every task defined in Step Three demands resources. Step Four is about deciding what resources are required (including any special resources such as technical or medical), how they are obtained and how long they will take to acquire. And, turning that on its head, whether or not particular resources are available may well determine the approach adopted. Search dogs are often used in the initial response to avoid any contamination of scent from other walkers. They are best deployed when nobody else is on the hill. Another person, acting as navigator, will often

THE SIX STEP PROCESS
Managing a search for a missing person

accompany the dog handler, freeing the handler to concentrate on the search itself. If a helicopter is available, it can provide massive cover in a short time, although the crew's ability to spot people is severely limited in poor weather and at night. RAF helicopters are now fitted with 'Forward-Looking Infra Red' (FLIR) capability, similar to that used by the police helicopters when chasing criminals at night time. This, together with 'Night Vision Goggles' (NVGs), makes the crew's task a whole lot more effective. In fact, while we're on the subject, here's an interesting nugget for you (next time you're stuck overnight on a mountain) which has already proved useful on more than one occasion – we're told the backlight on a mobile phone can, in good conditions, be seen several kilometres away in the dark. But don't forget – your battery must be charged!

Lost Person Behaviour may give an indication of

the kind of resources needed. Each resource, with a note of where they are coming from and when they are expected to arrive, is fully documented using special pro-formas or specially developed computer programmes.

● Step Five is all about giving responsibilities to individuals or agencies, assigning resources to the tasks that have been prioritised, establishing a chain of command and co-ordinating the whole operation. This involves setting up a Control Centre and the support facilities which go with it, positioned to facilitate good communications with everyone involved in the search. Many teams have a dedicated incident control unit – such as a trailer or minibus – specially kitted out with communications equipment, computer and GPS facility, seating, exterior floodlighting, and other key items – not least of all the ability to make a brew! A few teams are able to manage operations from their rescue headquarters. It is usual for the person(s) in charge to be free of 'doing things' – their role to supervise, direct, plan and evaluate. Others are given subordinate roles so that a well defined and effective chain of command – from search manager to individual searcher – is established.

● Step Six... and action! But, first, comes the briefing – vital to the entire proceedings – clear and unambiguous, for all concerned. How do they reach their search area? What's the timescale? What are the procedures for communication? What do they look for and what do they do if they find a potential clue or find the person – report it and leave it, stay with it, or bring it in? The

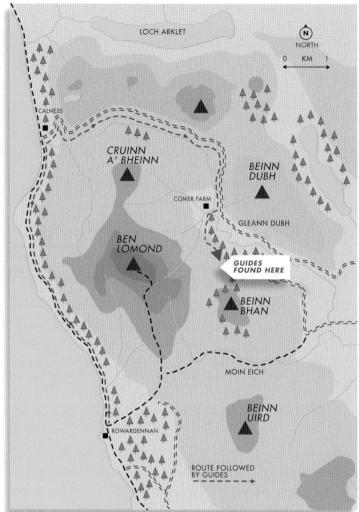

continued collection of information and appraisal of the situation is an important factor. Very few searches unfold exactly as planned. They tend to change and develop as new facts come to light and search information grows. All aspects of the search are recorded and the control centre maintains an ongoing log of events.

When search groups return from their task, it is important they are questioned to determine if their brief has been carried out, in particular that they're able to report with accuracy the ground searched. Increasingly, some teams use GPS receivers to log the route of individual members. On return, their tracks can be downloaded to computer to create an objective picture of the search area.

So that's the theory, but does it really work?

One April day, four girl guides, aged thirteen to fifteen years, decided to climb Ben Lomond, 3100 feet of mountain in Central Scotland. Their plan was to leave the youth hostel at Rowardennan, walk along the West Highland Way to Cailness, then take the forest road round to the farm at Comer. They would then climb to the summit of Ben Lomond via the north east ridge and descend via the south ridge to the forest and back to the hostel, an estimated journey of nine hours – by any stretch of the imagination a challenging and ambitious trip for a group of young, inexperienced walkers.

The youth hostel warden contacted the police when the girls failed to return by 9.00pm. The police alerted the Lomond team, requesting team members rendezvous at the youth hostel. No other agencies were called at this time. Team members duly arrived and were ready to be deployed within the hour.

● Step One. The warden confirmed the girls had left at 9.00am that morning, saying they would be

back around 9.00pm, but he didn't know their route up the hill. They'd never tackled such an expedition before and none were described as 'hill fit'. They had adequate clothing and footwear for an April day, as well as a small tent for emergencies. No injuries or illnesses were recorded. The weather that morning was good – light winds, cloud above the tops and no rain. During the day, it became progressively worse. By late afternoon, it had been raining heavily for several hours and the cloud base was down to about 200 feet above sea level. Winds were still light.

PHOTO: CHRIS BOYLES

Rossendale & Pendle team members assist police with a line search

There was additional information from the farmer at Comer Farm, who told police he had seen the girls passing his house, travelling westerly, in the late afternoon. He couldn't recall the exact time, but thought the girls looked very tired and wet.

● Step Two. It was reasoned the girls were overdue for two reasons. Firstly, they had walked a lot slower than anticipated due to bad weather and

the sector ladder method

Step 3 of the Six Step Process focuses on the possible areas to search and prioritises which ones to cover first. It's all about attaching probabilities to likely areas. One approach is to use the 'Sector Ladder' method, which involves several people looking at the available evidence and quantifying it to come to an overall decision about where to search.

First thing is to divide the area into a number of logical search areas. These are usually based on geographical features so may be linear – such as a good path – or a wide area such as the land contained between two rivers. This done, a small number of people will rank the sectors in terms of search priority. The ranks are then combined to give an overall list of priority sectors. The advantage of this system is it uses the combined experience of several people, rather than leaving the decision to just one or two.

Since we've been on the mountain for some time, let's use Ben Lomond as an example – the diagram shows how the area could be divided into sectors. The method was used to search for someone who was overdue having planned to climb the mountain via the south ridge and descend via the Ptarmigan Ridge (in Sector 3). When the Sector Ladder method was applied, Sector 3 was given first priority, Sector 1 second, and Sector 7 third priority. The missing walker was located in Sector 3, about half way down the mountain.

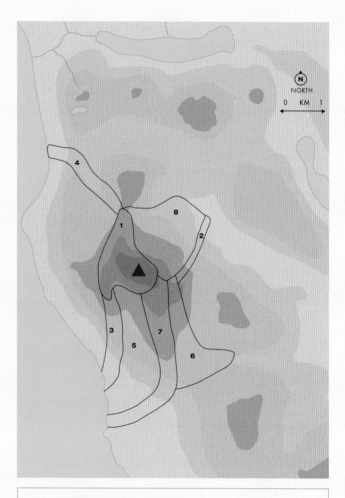

SUMMIT DESCRIPTION

1. SUMMIT PLATEAU
2. NE GULLY
3. MINOR RIDGE
4. NW GULLY
5. MAIN CORRIE
6. MINOR CORRIE
7. POPULAR ROUTE
8. NE COIRE

poor fitness. Secondly, they'd been overtaken by darkness. There was nothing to suggest they'd changed their route plans and, in any case, the scope for doing this was very limited. Appraisal of the Lost Person statistics suggested the girls might not have ventured very far from the route, but were probably way behind schedule. The same statistics also suggested that, if the girls were benighted and had decided not to continue, they would find a landmark or obvious feature such as a forest edge, to give protection from the weather.

⦿ Step Three. Because of the poor weather, it was reasoned the girls would not be found on open ground, but would make their way to shelter of some kind – a forest, wall or old building.

It was decided to deploy several search parties, each with a specific task. One group followed the path from Rowardennan to Cailness, in the event the girls had decided to backtrack. A vehicle drove up Gleann Dubh to Comer Farm. This would confirm if the girls had made a decision to skip Ben Lomond and descend to the main road to the east (off the map section). The vehicle would also carry two additional groups – one headed for the north east ridge, as the girls intended, the other south east from Comer Farm, following the south bank of the river to the forest edge. This second group would then follow the edge in a southerly direction. The vehicle, in the meantime, was tasked to follow the road on to Cailness.

A further two parties were deployed from the youth hostel. One group took the main path along the south ridge, their task to sweep the path in the hope the girls were still on their intended journey, and then serve as a communication link when at the summit of the mountain. The second group set off up the same path but left after two kilometres to sweep over Moin Eich to the forest edge. From here, they were to follow the forest edge to meet the other group ascending from Comer Farm.

All these groups were tasked simultaneously. There were enough team members to cover what was considered to be the main search areas. Groups from the youth hostel were able to start earlier than those travelling across to Comer Farm, a one hour journey.

⦿ Step Four. In order to effect this search plan, various resources were required.

• Group 1 included two persons.

• The vehicle (Police Land Rover) travelling to Comer Farm carried ten people. Two persons remained in the vehicle as it made its way to Comer Farm and then Cailness. Two people comprised Group 2, whose task was to sweep the north east ridge. The remaining party of six comprised Group 3, which swept the river and forest edge.

• Group 4, which took the summit path, included two team members.

• Group 5 included eight.

• A second police vehicle with two officers was tasked to contact all the houses on the road to the east of the mountain. It was decided that additional team members arriving late would be deployed to join Group 5.

⦿ Step Five. A search control centre was established at the youth hostel. Radio call signs were established before each group moved away. It was recognised that the groups departing for Comer farm would be out of communication for a while but would then have to report to control via the link established near the summit of Ben Lomond. Each group had a mobile phone but there was also permission to use the landline in the youth hostel, should communications prove difficult. It was agreed that each group would follow the initial plan and report back to control on a regular basis.

⦿ Step Six. All the groups left the control centre around 10.00pm. Although those travelling to Comer were out of touch for about an hour, Groups 1, 4 and 5 set about their tasks, reporting progress regularly.

A night navigation exercise

The weather remained stable with light winds. A rising cloud base lifted above the high ground at Moin Eich. Around midnight, the Comer groups reported they had begun their searches. Groups 1, 4 and 5 had not seen the girls at this point. At around 1.30am, Group 5 reported seeing faint lights at the forest edge, just beyond Moin Eich. This was reported to Group 4, who were higher up the mountain. When alerted, they too, could see flashing lights at the forest edge. At this point, all groups were advised of the possible sighting, but instructed to continue on their present course. Within about twenty minutes, members of Group 5 had arrived at the forest and located the missing girls, all extremely cold and wet, but otherwise in good spirits.

It transpired that they had arrived at Comer Farm very tired – as the farmer had noted – and decided to follow the forest edge and cross back to the hostel via the lowest point at Moin Eich. But, when one of the girls said she could go no further, they all decided to move into the forest for some protection and sit it out until daybreak. Four weary young ladies were given warm clothing and hot drinks before being escorted to a vehicle, waiting at the head of the track above Blairvockie Farm. They were finally reunited with their parents at 4.00am.

The search – and Step Six –– brought to a successful and happy conclusion, all that remained to be done was to tie up a few administrative ends. Before leaving, each and every team member was checked in and briefed on events. The waiting press had already carried out interviews with the team leader and police representatives and, finally, the police controller called a formal end to the search and everyone was stood down.

Okay, that's probably enough about strategy – what do rescuers actually do when they're on the hill? Frequently team members are deployed to sweep areas in lines although search strategy may negate the need for it. A sweep search is effective where there is a high probability that the target is within a known area and may comprise as few as two or three people, with ten or twelve the optimum (the greater the number, the more difficult it is to manage the line, the less flexible the operation). Team members are lined out at ninety degrees to a given bearing, spaced at close enough intervals that no ground between any two people is missed. Lines are roughly straight – no easy task, as each person must also decide their own route within the line, often across complicated and hazardous terrain, and ensure they don't move too close to their neighbours! All this, at the same time as keeping their eyes peeled for the missing person!

Lines must be managed and usually the person detailed to do this is not part of the line itself. They tend to walk behind or to one side, or watch from higher ground to see what is happening. Communication within the line is critical. If radios are used, then different channels may be used for communication within the line and for incident control. Before the search commences, every person is told exactly what to do – typically decisions are passed down the line from one person to the next but, if everyone has a radio, then information can be transmitted quickly. A daytime sweep is often managed using a system of hand signals and commands. At night, lines are identified by the head torches worn by members or a lightstick, carried on the rucksack.

Another approach – 'Purposeful Wandering' – is a variation on the traditional theme of team members walking the line abreast and shows a very high detection rate over rough ground. In this instance, searchers use their initiative to check out all the likely spots within the area between themselves and searchers on the other side, whilst still maintaining the principle of sweep searching and critical separation.

Once a line is on the move, it's up to individual

members to play their part in keeping it straight and on the move. If a difficulty is encountered – perhaps a particular area needs to be studied in detail or a steep section slows the line down – then word is passed along the line to halt the sweep. Observation by each person has to be structured and disciplined – looking to the front, left, right, behind, underneath, over the top – and bearing in mind that attention can wander very quickly.

A searcher may have to resort to hands and knees if looking through rhododendron bushes, bracken or loose snow – small children or Alzheimer's sufferers will frequently hide under bushes. Conversely, a suicide victim may well be found hanging above head height in a wooded area, out of the normal line of vision. On one search, a fell runner, overdue from his regular evening run, wasn't found despite a search involving many hundreds of people, including search and rescue dogs and a helicopter, which examined the route for several days. A few months later, when the bracken had died down, his body was discovered just metres from a path searched by many sets of eyes! The most obvious places can be overlooked. In another incident, a tourist – who went for a stroll in the woods and fields local to his hotel – was not found for a couple of days. His body was in an outhouse to the hotel, never even considered as a possibility. Incidents such as these only reinforce the fact that, when people do go missing, it is critical for searchers to cover areas very close to the point where the person was last seen.

A recent development with sweep searches is the use of sound and light. With a 'sound line', searchers are spaced out as normal but each blows a whistle on a regular basis. This creates a circle of noise from each member, which radiates out to the surrounding terrain. After the whistle blast, everyone listens intently before moving along a hundred or so metres and repeating the exercise. Hours of fun!

Sound lines work best with groups of two or three – the probability of finding someone is far higher than a search team relying purely on a visual search – and are excellent for checking long features such as paths and routes. The noise does the work by reaching into areas off the side and widening the sweep area. Of course, if our little old lady or potential suicide is crouching under the bracken, intent on remaining hidden, then no amount of bells and whistles will find them.

The 'sound light line' involves each searcher describing a figure of eight with a powerful torch, so the light goes out in a wide and consistent manner to maximise light dispersal. It also helps if the torch is used to reflect light from the underside of trees or clouds as this provides a high point which can be seen by a distant person.

So... to return to our earlier point – and bearing in mind that this clearly applies to missing walkers and climbers, rather than young children or other 'wanderers' – should we have more signs about the place? Strategically placed to help people navigate their way safely across the hills and mountains? It has been said that if navigation is such a critical problem, perhaps there should be guidance – especially in places where an error might have very serious consequences. It would seem a simple solution to a serious problem. But – and it's a big but – the jury is most definitely still out on this one. Do we work towards a landscape scarred and bristling with painted poles and warnings triangles, earnestly advising 'adventurers' which way to go, how far to travel, what to avoid, how far to the top, when to turn back, what time last orders are at the inn? Or should they be left to their own devices – and continue to make mistakes?

Those in favour of waymarking the mountains argue on the basis of precedence, history and safety. There have always been stone walls, cairns, fence posts and paths, so what difference if a few more are added to improve safety? These features – and you could include things like signposts, old farm buildings, disused mining structures and ancient steadings – simply reflect our history and culture. (Of course, there's something infinitely more endearing about a rain-raddled, crumbling reminder of our industrial heritage, than a brightly coloured chunk of 3mm aluminium clipped atop a plastic coated steel tube, however aesthetically considered.)

On the other hand, there's the view that markers (of any kind) go against the principles of self-reliance and responsible risk-taking central to mountaineering; that increasing the number of cairns or markers just encourages inexperienced people to continue onto more hazardous terrain when they would otherwise have returned earlier. In other words, they give a false sense of security. There are practical concerns, too, regarding maintenance – who builds them and what form should they take? Would adding more waymarkers generate even more – 'litter begets litter'? Is education the key to increased safety?

What do you think? Should safety override other concerns, whatever the cost? Or should we support the spirit of self-reliance and consider removing all signs, cairns and markers?

Navigating in white out conditions

time line
of a 'lost person' incident

A vital part of managing an incident is to keep a precise record of all that happens. It's especially important to note how people are deployed and to record key actions and decisions. Some teams are beginning to use bespoke computer software to manage incident recording. This is useful during the course of the incident, but also provides a record for subsequent analysis. Here's an example.

Two lawyers had decided to spend a day in early March climbing a 3500 ft mountain in the Scottish Highlands. The mountain – Beinn a Chlachair – is centred in the Ardverikie Forest, about 6k from the nearest road. The couple left their car by the roadside at 10.00am and cycled about 4k before leaving their bikes and continuing on foot. When they failed to return home the police were called to assist.

23.00 hrs
A friend reported the walkers overdue. The police were given details of their experience and equipment carried. One was a competent winter walker, fully equipped for winter conditions, the other less experienced and equipped. The Cairngorm team leader was alerted.

23.55 hrs
The police reported locating the walkers' car at the bridge near Moy Lodge.

01.00 hrs
A rescue team member reported clear weather on the mountain but a high avalanche risk. A decision was made by the MRT to establish an Incident Control Centre at the bridge and deploy people at 07.00 hrs. The Aeronautical Rescue Co-ordination Centre (ARCC) was contacted and alerted to the situation. The SARDA co-ordinator was also asked for assistance. Access to Ardverikie Estate gates/roads was obtained.

02.45 hrs
The police requested a helicopter and RAF MRT support from the ARCC.

03.10 hrs
The ARCC confirmed that a rescue helicopter from RN Gannet plus fifteen RAF Kinloss MRT members would be at the incident control by 07.30 hrs.

The SARDA controller confirmed that eight dogs and handlers would be at incident control by 07.00 hrs.

07.50 hrs
Both the Cairngorm and Kinloss MRTs assembled at incident control and awaited the helicopter arrival. The weather was noted to be deteriorating with the cloud base descending.

08.11 hrs
The RN helicopter arrived at control. A decision was made to take some Cairngorm MRT members and search at low level, looking for possible avalanche debris. Members of the Kinloss MRT were despatched to search the northern corrie of Beinn A Chlachair. The remaining members of the Cairngorm MRT were detailed to sweep the ridges on the mountain.

08.17 hrs
The helicopter began to search carrying Cairngorm MRT members.

08.40 hrs
A police vehicle found the mountain bikes belonging to the walkers at the end of the track.

09.37 hrs
The helicopter reported locating both walkers safe and well making their way to Ben Alder Lodge.

Postscript

The two walkers had made a serious navigational error on the mountain. As a result, they were forced to spend a night out in sub-zero temperatures. They survived by digging a small scoop in the snow and moving on at first light.

They had left the previous day and cycled up the Land Rover track leaving their bikes at the end of Lochan na Earba. They walked up to the bealach just west of Loch a Bhealaich Leamhain then south west up the ridge to the summit of the mountain, arriving about 3pm. By this time the weather had closed in and become misty and windy. They had considered descending along the north ridge and taking a direct line to their bikes but, instead, decided to backtrack to the bealach. Unfortunately, their compass bearing was 180 degrees out. So instead of walking east, they went west, making their way down the ridge until they came to a path. Assuming this was the path they had climbed up, they turned left expecting to arrive where their bikes were left. Instead, they were actually travelling along An Lairig towards Loch Pattack. As darkness overtook them, they realised they were lost and sought shelter for the night in a snow bank. At daylight, they continued walking and reached Loch Pattack and finally Ben Alder Lodge where they were spotted by the helicopter.

A simple navigation error resulted in an enforced night on the mountain plus the deployment of 22 members of the Cairngorm MRT, 12 members of RAF Kinloss MRT, 6 search dogs and handlers, plus an RN Sea King helicopter from HMS Gannet – a combined total of over 500 man hours invested by the various emergency services in dealing with the incident.

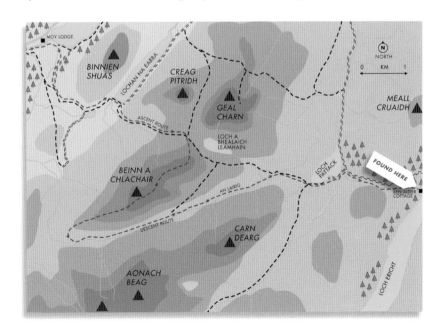

what to do if you're lost...

We would expect everyone who ventures into the hills and mountains to carry with them a compass and, certainly, a map of the area – and to have practiced how to use them. Let's take it you have both. You're on a mountain. A thick mist has silently crept around you and now you don't know which way to go. What can you do? Well first thing – don't panic! Sounds simple enough but it's important to recognise that you're not lost forever! You will find your way off the hill. So, having composed yourself, here's a few tips.

1. Think about backtracking to reverse your route. Consider how long you've been walking from your last known point and how far along the ground you may have travelled. Can you walk back the way you came? You may come across a feature such as a stream or change of vegetation that gives a clue to your whereabouts.

2. Make a decision to walk in a straight line, say 200 metres. Use your compass to give direction and to assess distance, simply count paces. Most adults walk between 60 and 70 double paces for every 100 metres. As you walk, note how the land changes. Then look at the map – can you see the change reflected in the map? If not, walk another 200 metres. You can repeat this a few times – taking care not to walk over a cliff, of course! If it doesn't work, you can at least go back to where you started by reversing direction and counting paces. By the way, it's a very good idea to work out your own rule for pace counting. Measure out a 100 metre length along the ground and walk it a few times. Record your number of double paces and commit it to memory

– you never know when it might come in handy!

3. Rather than walking in a straight line, you could perform a 'box' or 'spiral' search, which also allows you to return to your start point. It works like this. First, estimate the limit of visibility – say it's 20 metres. Use your compass to identify north. Now walk north for 20 metres. Then turn east and walk 30 metres. Now turn south and walk 40 metres. Then turn west and walk 50 metres. Repeat this process adding 10 metres for each turn. In time, you will see a feature that helps you locate your position. This is a good technique for finding the summit on a broad plateau in mist. If you know you are quite close to the actual top, this will guarantee (!) you arrive there during one of the legs. And don't forget to use pace counts.

4. If you are in mist, it helps to lose height. When you drop down below the cloud base, you should see where you are. You must make an informed decision about which way to go. If you're on a slope, then follow a line down the slope. If you're on the flat, think back to what the ground was like before you became lost and judge from this which way to go. It's a good idea to monitor your direction and distance so you can return to your present location. Take care if the ground suddenly steepens. As you descend and the ground changes, this might be a clue to your general position.

5. See if you can match the ground close by to the contours on your map – perhaps the ground rises to your left and falls away to your right. Look at the map to where you think you might be, and see if the contour lines match the ground. Are you on a linear feature such as a forest edge or ridge? If so, take a bearing along it and find the feature on the map using the bearing just taken. For instance, if you've been walking along a ridge running north to south, can you find a ridge on the map which also runs north to south?

6. If all this fails, you could try sitting it out till the cloud lifts (bearing in mind this could take 24 hours – or more!) or you could start walking towards a 'collecting feature'. (A what?) A collecting feature in an obvious feature in the landscape such as a ridge, forest edge, path, road or river that will 'collect' you if you travel towards it. So, look at the map, identify your feature (say the road where you parked your car) and take off towards it. In time, it will 'catch' you. Another couple of useful – and very easy on the pocket – navigation tools are the wind and sun. Can you judge where the sun is in the sky? By noting the time of day, you should be able to make a rough guess about direction. So, if you face the sun at mid-day, you're looking southwards. Is there a wind blowing? From which direction? Did you hear the weather forecast? If you can judge which way the wind is coming from, then you know which way you are walking.

Whatever tactic used, people tend to locate where they are fairly quickly. Of course, if it's dark, then you may be stuck. In this case, do your best to find shelter and sit it out overnight.

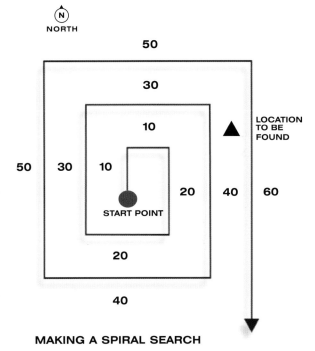

MAKING A SPIRAL SEARCH

- Suppose the limit of visibility is around ten paces.
- Decide to move in a given direction (say North) and then walk ten paces.
- Then turn through 90 degrees and walk another ten paces.
- Continue like this but increase by ten paces every two legs.
- You should find your location.
- If not, you can always backtrack to the start.

chapter six

A STITCH IN TIME

I shall fill my days
But I shall not, cannot forget:
Sleep soft, dear friend,
For while I live you shall not die.
Anon

Winter 2003. Andy Nisbet, one of Scotland's 'gurus' of winter climbing, was guiding two clients up a route called Poacher's Fall on Liathach in the Scottish Highlands. He was leading the third pitch – a chimney, most of which was filled with good ice – when, as he neared the top, he stepped out right, on to the rib of the chimney and fell, his long, spectacular plummet to the bottom of the cliff halted only when an ice screw 25 metres below held fast. As he slammed against the rock, the impact fractured his femur. He has no memory of the exact details but remembers some concern that the ice at this point was unexpectedly brittle and reckons his ice axes popped out when he tried to move up.

Hanging on the rope, it was a few minutes before he regained consciousness and his two clients lowered him the ten metres to their belay. He didn't recall being unconscious and, in the absence of any pain, thought he might rest a short while then climb on. His clients could see otherwise and quickly assured him as much!

Andy looked back up the route and reasoned that a helicopter could winch him away from the cliff face. But first they must raise the alarm – and therein lay a dilemma. Should the three of them abseil off together, his clients slowly, laboriously lowering him alongside themselves? Or should he remain alone on the rockface, leaving his clients free to face the risks unguided? Could they make it on their own and how would he fare, once left? Neither prospect was very appealing. In the event, the two men made sure Andy was safely tied on and abseiled down the cliff to raise the alarm. Andy later clipped himself into a long sling, which allowed him to stand in semi-traction and rest more comfortably. The clients, meanwhile, made their way into the coire below the cliffs only to discover there was no mobile phone reception. Nor was there anyone else around to help. It wasn't until they made their way to Torridon village, three hours after the accident, that they were able to raise the alarm.

Torridon mountain rescue team assembled at

PHOTO: CHRIS BOYLES

...as he neared the top, he stepped out right, on to the rib of the chimney and fell, his long, spectacular plummet to the bottom of the cliff halted only when an ice screw 25 metres below held fast.

7.00pm, but the RAF helicopter had already been engaged on two rescues that day and was forced to go to Broadford in Skye to refuel before a serious rescue attempt could be made. By 9.30pm the RAF Kinloss team had also arrived. Windy conditions meant that the rescue teams could only be dropped at an altitude of 450 metres on the moors under the cliffs. The teams split into two sections, one to access the route from above and the other to prepare evacuation from the steep névé slopes (that's old hard snow) at the foot of the climb.

About four hours after his fall, Andy saw a helicopter appear. It buzzed about the cliff and went away. Several hours later another one arrived, shone its lights a short distance away but not in his direction. This puzzled him, his immediate thought that he wasn't going to be winched. Up to this point, he still had no pain and kept himself adequately warm by swinging his arms. But after a long wait, he realised he was getting colder and unable to warm his finger ends even by arm swinging. He still had partial feeling and probably no frost nip but, towards the end, he felt his temperature was dropping. His spirits beginning to falter.

By 11.00pm the team had managed to climb to the top of the cliff. Andy was still conscious and yelling vigorously. His pain was relatively mild but a deep ache had begun to set in. True to his hardy reputation he protested that after ten hours spent standing on one leg, without analgesics and with a couple of pints of blood sloshing around in the other, he was 'struggling a bit' and not happy! He could see from the torches that some members had climbed above the cliff whilst others were waiting below in the coire. The team had some trouble locating the top of the route – the exit to Andy's route led onto steep slopes of neve and boulder fields which made the logistics of arranging a stretcher lower very time

Liathac in Torridon

consuming. It also made it very difficult to get a stretcher down the correct line of the gully. The urgent priority was to get Andy off the cliff as quickly as possible, so two members were lowered on a 180 metre rope – the intention to put him into a cradle of slings and get him to the stretcher at the bottom. The gully selected for the lower was ten metres to the left of Poacher's route but, by arranging intermediate anchors, the lower put the rescuers five metres to Andy's left from which position a handrail of slings was made to get across to him.

For Andy it was a cruel misfortune that the carrier of the morphine kit was waiting at the bottom of the route! He merely expressed some disappointment that the lower could be made on a few lungsful of Entonox. And, had morphine been available, he might not have felt the need to fend off banging against the ice as he was lowered, potentially exacerbating his injuries. Negotiating the route back across the handrail and into the line of the lower was the most complicated manoeuvre – a substantial pendulum was averted by the controlled release of a short line from the handrail as the threesome swung down. The remainder of the lower went smoothly without any serious jolts, although by now Andy's pain level had risen significantly. He was lowered over 100 metres into the coire. When he was finally put in the stretcher there were just five metres of the rescue rope left! A waiting Coastguard Sea King helicopter picked him up at 4.30am and whisked him to Raigmore Hospital in Inverness.

Hospital examination showed that Andy had suffered a spiral fracture of the femur. The fracture was closed and high up which limited haemorrhaging, but the bone was shattered into seven pieces. He needed two operations and eight weeks in traction and reckoned it took him about a month to fully return to earth, psychologically! He was very lucky to survive at all, waiting so long for help in such extreme cold conditions. Many would not.

Well over half of all mountain rescues in the UK involve someone – like Andy – who needs first aid and subsequent specialist medical treatment. Add this to the fact that most accidents take place in remote

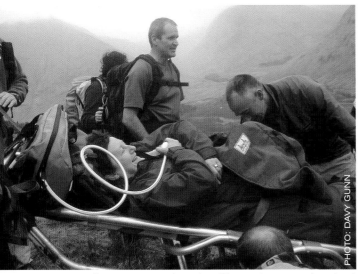

Entonox to ease the pain... Glencoe team members treat casualty with broken ankle on the 'Pap of Glencoe'

PHOTO: DAVY GUNN

locations and 'scoop and run' isn't an option. In theory, the rescue team member first on scene at a traumatic accident must be sufficiently capable – and confident – in delivering not only immediate first aid treatment but, with the help of other team members, in making the casualty comfortable for what might well be a prolonged stretcher carry off the hill. It can make the difference between life and death. Of course, there are levels of capability within teams, and not all team members are trained in advanced casualty care, but the ability to assess basic ABC (Airway, Breathing, Circulation) is a standard requirement. So how do teams respond to this need? What kind of special equipment do they use and how do they train? Are members permitted to carry out life saving procedures normally the

reserve of medical personnel? And what about drugs?

Andy's shattered femur could well have cost him his life. A fracture to this long thigh bone causes considerable blood loss, especially if the femoral artery is involved. This can result in 'shock' diversion of blood away from other organs so as to keep a supply of oxygen to the heart and brain. If a fractured femur is associated with other serious injuries the casualty may die during his evacuation from the hill. The powerful quadriceps muscle contracts like taut elastic bands, causing the bone ends to overlap. The leg becomes distorted and shortened and the thigh more swollen.

Over 40% of injuries involve fractures to the lower leg, by far the most common in mountain rescue terms. Often, the casualty actually hears the bone break or sees it appear through the skin! It can happen with spectacular speed, the damage done all too obvious. The standard first aid treatment for any broken bone is to restore the normal alignment of the limb, then reduce further movement by splinting. Compression of the damaged area reduces pain and prevents further damage. The most effective treatment for Andy's shattered femur would have been to place his leg in a traction splint to stretch the muscles and separate the broken bones – team members are trained to use specially designed splints which allow the leg to be placed under tension and hold it in position – but, unfortunately for him, it was impracticable to do this 2000 feet up a cliff face. His rescuers were obliged to lower him unsplinted to the bottom of the cliff before his fracture could be addressed.

Rescue teams use a variety of special splints to immobilise fractures but they might also employ a number of other very simple procedures. For example, a broken hand, wrist, ribcage or collarbone can be treated by placing the arm in an elevated sling made from a square of material. A broken leg can be strapped to the other leg. A broken jaw can be supported with a hand. And let's not forget the value of kind words. Rescue team members across the UK are renowned for their apparent ability to maintain a constant stream of wit and repartee whilst battling the most inhospitable of elements!

Janet Suchet slipped whilst descending a Lake District fell and broke both her legs. When the rescue team arrived, she was amazed the restorative effect it had on her morale and pain.

'I had been lying in pain for what seemed like days and, with each passing hour, the pain in my legs increased more and more. When I heard voices and the noise of clanking metal I knew the team had arrived. Suddenly, all my worries melted away – and with it the pain. Help was at hand and my body seemed to react normally once again. Everyone seemed to know what to do and there was a friendly banter which lifted me enormously. At one time I even found myself laughing at their quips. I had almost forgotten my shattered legs and the weeks of recuperation ahead.'

Laughter, of course, is a powerful analgesic but then there's the real thing. Thanks to the persistence of Wilson Hey in the early twentieth century, morphine is currently licensed for use by mountain rescue teams. Yet, despite its reputation as the gold standard in pain control, there are many instances when this drug cannot be used, or must only be administered in small doses. It can induce marked nausea and vomiting, can cause drowsiness and may seriously affect breathing. Its use may also mask underlying problems not immediately apparent to the rescuer. Whatever drugs are used, it's vital that the A&E staff know what has been used and take it into account.

The quantities of controlled drugs made available to teams, their storage and use, is strictly controlled and monitored. In Scotland, the Mountain Rescue Committee holds a license for morphine to be administered by any member of an affiliated team. No special certification is required although it is normal practice for a team doctor to train members in its application. In England and Wales, only those team members who hold the MRC Casualty Care Certificate are permitted to administer morphine and team members other than qualified doctors, nurses and paramedics require insurance different from that normally provided by the police.

Team members generally are trained to recognise and provide first aid for a wide variety of problems – asthma, angina, heart attack, hypoglycaemia, anaphylaxis, epilepsy, near drowning, lightning injury, hypothermia. Even, in theory, imminent childbirth! Some teams carry inhalers for asthma suffers and Hypostop® which, when administered under the casualty's tongue, provides energy very quickly. It's useful for someone

The defibrillator, Entonox and oxygen cylinders and Little Dragon warm air breather are standard kit for most UK teams

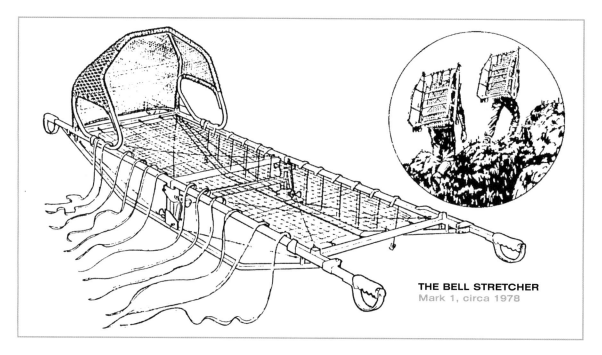

THE BELL STRETCHER
Mark 1, circa 1978

who is exhausted or mildly hypothermic and there are no side effects or special skills required to administer it.

In reality, the majority of team members are unlikely to ever use controlled drugs but many will administer other painkillers such as Entonox. A weak anaesthetic gas – a mixture of 50% oxygen and 50% nitrous oxide – Entonox is an extremely versatile drug and very effective in controlling pain, particularly during procedures such as moving a badly injured person onto a stretcher. The casualty is able to self administer so the dosage depends on their breathing – the less vigorously they breathe, the less they inhale, and vice versa. However, it should not be used in the case of head or chest injuries.

Oxygen is another bottled gas used regularly by teams to great effect, especially in shock or heart attack. Vital though both these gases are, the sheer weight of the heavy steel bottles puts them way down the popularity stakes when it comes to team members carrying kit up the hill. In recent years, however, many teams have been able to switch to lightweight aluminium cylinders. Rumour has it their members now fall over themselves to put them in their sacks!

In fact, there's a point here on which it's worth dwelling. Effecting a rescue in a remote spot is not merely a matter of a few chaps (we use the term loosely as the rescue party might include female members too) throwing on boots and waterproofs, jumping in a team vehicle then walking or climbing, with all possible haste, to the appropriate location. There's a substantial inventory of rescue kit to consider – a trauma sack containing medical equipment such as cervical collars, bandages, drugs and cards to record details of the casualty's history, symptoms and medication; splints, oxygen and Entonox bottles, casbag, vacuum mattress, casualty shelter; possibly a pulse oximeter and defibrillator; and – arguably the most vital piece of equipment on the list – a purpose designed mountain rescue stretcher. Not all of which might be necessary. Frequently, a fast response team – perhaps one or two team members – sets out to reach the casualty armed only with a first aid kit. The theory being that they can deliver immediate first aid treatment, assess the situation and radio back to the incident controller with a required 'kit list', which must then be carried up to the casualty on the backs of team members.

Without doubt, the heaviest item on that kit list will be the stretcher, albeit split into its component parts. Wilson Hey and Eustace Thomas may have produced their definitive mountain rescue stretcher in the 1930s, but the search for the perfect – lighter weight – mountain rescue stretcher has continued to exercise minds ever since – Donald Duff and Hamish MacInnes in Scotland, Peter Bell in the Lake District and, more recently, the MRC of Scotland. Stretchers provide stability and safety for the casualty and enable rescuers to carry an injured person across uneven terrain for long distances. They also provide a safe way to winch someone into a hovering helicopter, although helicopters are only permitted to winch stretchers that have met MOD requirements.

These days, there are many different types of stretcher in use but the two mainstays are the Bell and the MacInnes. Both meet all the relevant criteria for winching and have undergone continuous development over a period of thirty or so years.

The Bell stretcher – used primarily by teams in England and Wales for almost 35 years – was designed, and is still built, by Peter Bell. The two-piece design made of stainless steel with carrying handles at each corner, a tough headguard to protect the casualty and a bed of wire mesh weighs

in at just under 22 kilograms but is very precisely engineered and superbly 'fit for purpose'. It has established a reputation for toughness and rugged durability in the most demanding situations.

In Scotland, the 'definitive mountain rescue stretcher' is the MacInnes, according to Roger Wild, Mountain Safety Adviser with the Mountaineering Council of Scotland, and member of the Lochaber team. Hamish MacInnes's first stretcher dates back over forty years and, like the Bell, comes in two halves. In contrast, the MacInnes is made of lightweight aircraft alloy and is much simpler in its overall construction and assembly. Each half incorporates locking tubular retractable handles and integral skids for use across snow or easy terrain. A double wheel arrangement allows ease of movement over tracks and good paths.

Writing in *The Scotsman*, in January 2004, journalist Jim Gilchrist took a look at how it all started. 'Hamish MacInnes and the rest of the newly formed Glencoe Mountain Rescue Team had been out all night and they found the girl at dawn. The young nurse had fallen off the Aonagh Eagach after losing her way in the mist. She had a fractured spine, broken ankle and head injuries, was still conscious and was lying, miraculously, on a ledge on the south side of the ridge, in what MacInnes describes as 'a kind of cartoon situation', her legs hanging over the drop. 'It was just unbelievable,' the veteran climber recalls, some forty years later. 'We had a great deal of trouble getting the Thomas stretcher up there and I remember thinking at the time that this was ridiculous and that we should do something about it.'

'What he did about it, after they eventually brought the girl down, with difficulty, was to devise the MacInnes folding stretcher. Built by a subsidiary of the De Havilland aircraft company, the Mk 1 came out in 1962 and was immediately in demand. Over the subsequent four decades, he has developed the lightweight aluminium alloy design for use by rescue teams and military units across the world. Now, the Glencoe-based climber, author and mountain rescue pioneer has launched his Mark 7 version, using even lighter, space-age materials.

'While the current Mark 6 model dismantles into

A stretcher lower on snow and ice in Glencoe using the Mk 7 MacInnes stretcher

two halves, carried by two people, the Mark 7 is a folding one-piece which, at 11kg, weighs less than half as much as the Mark 6 and can easily be carried by one person in a special pack frame. Its shell is made from an advanced composite material which, according to MacInnes, is so new it doesn't have a name yet.'

MacInnes lives in Glencoe, the knife-edge crags which first inspired his efforts, still within his sights. Despite a lifetime's association with the mountains, as mountaineer, mountain rescuer, equipment designer, author, film producer and adviser to many a Hollywood climbing epic, he is adamant that no one ever got rich 'inventing life-saving climbing and rescue equipment, no matter how widely adopted'. As he told Jim Gilchrist, 'There are enough people

falling off, but not enough rescue teams,' a sentiment which may well be echoed by others!

Stretchers for mountain use must be extremely robust to withstand the tough environment but also light in weight to be carried over great distances. Both the Bell and MacInnes stretchers continue to undergo development in the quest to balance function with weight. In late 2003, the Mountain Rescue Committee of Scotland, with the help of a substantial bequest, set itself the task of designing a stretcher for the future. The first step was to establish a number of criteria in regard to function, safety, ergonomics, durability, reliability, materials, ease of maintenance, aesthetics and cost. Then, the designers looked at how modern lightweight materials such as carbon fibre and mountain bike technology might be used to construct a stretcher that met these requirements. At the time of writing a prototype is being tested.

Once a casualty is loaded onto a stretcher, their safety, comfort and security has to be assured – it's rather bad news if the casualty slips off the stretcher whilst being lowered down a cliff face! They have to be firmly fastened and safeguarded from the weather and incidental knocks when transported across rough terrain. All stretchers come equipped with straps, which both bind the casualty to the stretcher and limit their movement both up and down. A firm base adds warmth and protection from underneath but also serves to splint anyone with suspected spinal fractures.

Splinting is a critical first aid procedure, particularly with spinal injuries. These injuries – both suspected and confirmed – occur in around three per cent of mountain rescue casualties, usually following a free fall from a height, a tumbling fall or a fall from height where the casualty lands directly on

A Glencoe team member guides a 'Puigilem' stretcher and casualty as they are hauled out of a crevasse in the Alps

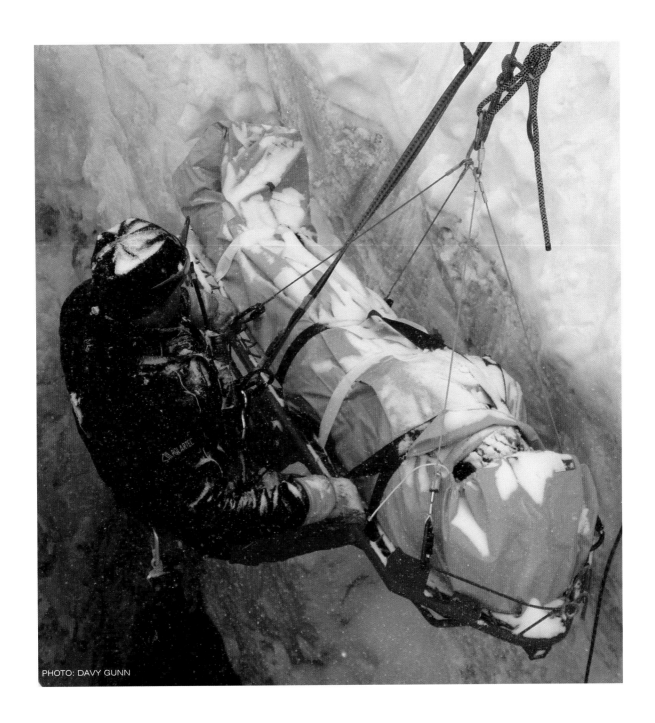

PHOTO: DAVY GUNN

their feet. Not good! In *Casualty Care in Mountain Rescue*, John Ellerton and Stuart Durham state that 'whatever the mechanism of injury, 14% of spinal injuries will have spinal cord damage. Of the cases with spinal cord injury, 40% are in the neck, 10% in the thoracic region, 35% at the junction between the thoracic and lumbar spine and 3% are in the lumbar region.' So the neck and thoracolumbar junction regions are most likely to be affected. The aim of any treatment delivered by the teams is to prevent further damage and reduce the chances of hypoxia or hypotension which might exacerbate the injury. Hypoxia is a deficiency of oxygen in the tissues, hypotension occurs when arterial blood pressure is abnormally low. Any treatment – including the evacuation of the casualty from the hill – must be done with considerable urgency.

To this end, the full spine, from pelvis to head must be immobilised. The accepted practice, both here and abroad, is to immobilise the whole body within a vacuum mattress. The 'vac matt' is basically a flat, airtight beanbag on which the casualty is laid before being wrapped up in it. Once the person is secure, the air inside the bag is pumped out, producing a semi-rigid cocoon in the shape of the casualty. This limits movement and provides a total body splint, which effectively reduces the worsening of any injuries already sustained.

During use, it's common to expel some of the air initially to allow the mattress to be used as a semi-rigid working platform. A casualty with a suspected spinal injury would be fitted with a neck collar and then placed in the correct position on the mattress. The straps are tightened and adjusted to ensure even pressure over all body contact points and the mattress fitted as tightly as possible around the casualty. All gaps and hollows are packed and the air expelled using the pump. Safely cocooned in this rigid shell, both the casualty and mattress are then strapped onto a stretcher for transport off the

Pigott Rope Stretcher
(from the *Mountain Rescue & Cave Rescue Handbook* 1966

'A stretcher can be improvised quickly from a 100 or 120 foot rope. It can be very useful for carrying a man whose injuries permit it, to shelter in the shortest possible time, but it is tiring to carry and uncomfortable to lie on. It must not be used if there is a possibility of spinal injury.

'To make, it leave six yards of rope free, and then make a series of eight loops a hand span's length apart. The loops should all be the same length, say three feet, or the distance from chin to outstretched finger tip, and are made with a simple overhand knot. Leave now enough rope to pass over the shoulder of the end bearer, and then fasten the end of each loop to it in turn, spacing them evenly. Make another shoulder loop at the other end and if the rope is long enough thread the ends back to the middle to make slings to help the carriers at the side. The bed of the stretcher should be well padded.'

mountain. Once in A&E, the casualty can even be left inside his cocoon during X-ray – avoiding further handling until a more accurate assessment and diagnosis can be made.

The cervical collar is another vital piece of equipment. Whenever a casualty has a confirmed or suspected spinal injury, their neck is always immobilised. Collars not only reduce spinal deformity and prevent further damage to the cervical spine but they sometimes improve the function of the airway. So, in the case of say a fallen climber, on arrival at the scene, the team would immediately deploy someone to hold the climber's head firmly to prevent any kind of movement. That person would then remain dedicated to this task and not release hold until the collar was firmly attached to the casualty. Applying a collar is not always an easy operation – particularly if the casualty is lying in an awkward location and severely injured – it requires teamwork and skill, so practice in their use is an important part of team training.

The importance of neck collars was firmly illustrated in the case of a walker who fell whilst scrambling on the Cuillin Ridge in Skye, as one of the hospital consultants at Portree Hospital relates.

'On the morning of Sunday, 12 August 2001, a mountain accident took place in the Black Cuillin on the Isle of Skye which turned out to be much more serious than both the patient or myself had anticipated. The day before, the gentleman, who is a twenty four year old PhD student, had arrived on Skye for a week of walking and climbing. He had planned to do the Cuillin Ridge on that Sunday morning but when he got up early it was much too wet and he decided to go for a walk into Coir a Ghrunnda and check out some of the paths that led higher up. He was alone at the time and not wearing a helmet. Shortly after 7am on one of these paths, a small ledge, suddenly gave way under him and he fell and tumbled between 50 and 100 feet, over

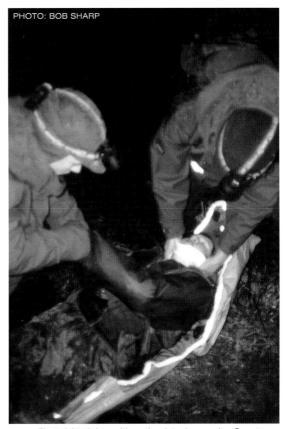

PHOTO: BOB SHARP

First aid training with a simulated casualty. One team member immobilises the casualty's head and neck whilst she is wrapped in the vacuum mattress ready for transfer to stretcher and transport downhill

some scree slopes and small ledges. He did not lose consciousness but picked himself up and described himself as feeling 'banged up all over'. He then walked out of the mountains by himself. He arrived at Glenbrittle campsite at approximately 10.00am and went into the shop to inform the people of his predicament. Two of the campers there brought him in their car to Portree Hospital where I saw him just after 11.00am.

'Examination revealed an alert and orientated

PHOTO: CHRIS BOYLES

gentleman. The obvious findings were a 15cm laceration over his right forehead, an obvious fracture to his left hand and a possible fracture to his right wrist and elbow. He was tender all over but had no specific neck or spine tenderness or swelling. He was fitted with a cervical collar and his wounds cleaned and dressed. He was given morphine analgesia and was helicoptered off to Raigmore in the early afternoon. I phoned later that evening to check how he was and was quite surprised to discover that he actually fractured his sixth cervical vertebra. A CT scan went on to show that this was actually an unstable fracture. Thus, his walk out of the mountains, and indeed his drive up from Glenbrittle itself, could have at any stage resulted in a severed cord and limb paralysis. He was transferred to Glasgow Hospital where he required bone grafting of the unstable fracture and immobilisation of his neck in a brace for several weeks. He has made a good recovery and by the end of September he was out of his neck brace and had returned to work.

'This incident serves as a reminder to all of us that the need for cervical spine immobilisation should be carried out for any history of significant energy transfer. Thus any substantial fall or blow to the body should alert us to the possibility of a cervical fracture, even if the person is fully conscious, has no history of alcohol or drug intoxication and is not complaining of any neck pain or indeed any specific tenderness over the neck. Indeed, the gentleman stated that as the two people drove him out of Glenbrittle, he turned his neck on several occasions to get a last glimpse of the Black Cuillin as he was aware that he probably wouldn't see them for a few weeks. We are all now very much aware of his lucky escape.'

So that's the big stuff. The stretchers, casualty bags and splints, the gas bottles and trauma sacks but what about all the other things we talked of – the pulse oximeters and defibs? Mountain rescue teams have moved a long way from those early days of limited equipment, or gear that was simply too heavy to take on the hill. If the central purpose of mountain rescue is to deliver a casualty to hospital in the best possible condition, with the greatest possible prospect of recovery, then effective medical equipment – and training in its use – has been central to its development and given rise to some of the most significant innovations. Whilst many items have been designed especially for mountain rescue, others have been adapted from ambulance paramedic practice.

In any first aid situation, it is vital to monitor parameters such as heart rate, blood pressure and temperature. To do this, teams use electronic instruments that are portable, simple to use and extremely lightweight, such as the battery-powered tympanic thermometer, which provides a good approximation of core temperature via a probe placed in the casualty's ear canal. A battery pack and digital display can be secured to the casualty's head by a foam pad and elastic strap to allow temperature monitoring during transport. Although, with few teams likely to possess such advanced technology, it is more probable they will monitor a casualty's temperature through repeated use of a good old-fashioned thermometer.

The pulse oximeter, which measures oxygen saturation in the blood is also battery-powered and attached to the casualty's finger for immediate reading. Oxygen saturation is a reliable indicator of an adequate airway and cardio-respiratory function. The read-out is a percentage of the possible total oxygen saturation of the blood. Normal arterial blood is 96% to 98% saturated. Falls to between 90% and 93% indicate that some parts of the body, especially the brain, are becoming short of oxygen.

Other special items include portable blood pressure monitors (wrist mounted) as well as

A brief history of medicine!

2000 BC
'Here, eat this root'.
1000 AD
'That root is heathen. Here, say this prayer'.
1850 AD
'That root is superstition. Here, drink this potion'.
1940 AD
'That potion is snake oil. Here, swallow this pill'.
1985 AD
'That pill is ineffective. Here, take this antibiotic'.
2000 AD
'That antibiotic doesn't work anymore. Here, eat this root'.

programmed defibrillators for use in the treatment of heart attacks. These have reduced in size and weight considerably in recent years. One version is so small it can be held in the palm of one hand. It's been suggested that the combination of use of a mobile phone by the person raising the alarm, administration of cardio-pulmonary resuscitation and use of a defibrillator has greatly enhanced the recovery of heart attack victims on the mountains. A few teams use specialised equipment for the cannulation (injection of fluids) and intubation (insertion of devices to make an airway) of casualties although, in these cases, rescuers must be trained to Emergency Medical Technician level. Modern communications technology even makes it possible to relay pictures of the casualty – in real time – to the A&E unit of a local hospital so that expert guidance can be given to rescuers on the hill. In turn, the doctor is more informed about the casualty once

they are admitted to hospital. Some teams have experimented with this system but it would seem a long way off adoption by mountain rescue in general.

When Andy Nisbet fell on Liathach, it wasn't just a shattered femur threatening his life. He was obliged to suffer some ten hours in temperatures below freezing, 2000 ft up a mountain in the middle of February. Unable to move, he gradually lost heat and began to suffer hypothermia. Today's walkers and climbers typically wear the very best of clothing and footwear. They are far better protected from the elements than used to be the case. As a result, hypothermia is not the problem it used to be although, interestingly, there are more reported cases in the summer months than winter. In England and Wales, hypothermia is recorded in around eight per cent of casualties, but many milder instances probably go unrecorded or unrecognised. The human body is a miracle of nature in many ways, not least in its ability to maintain homeostasis – the physiological process whereby the internal systems such as blood pressure and body temperature are maintained in balance, despite variations in external influences. When those external circumstances are so extreme that the process falters, the body begins to shut down. Anyone who is forced to remain still for a long time on the mountain – perhaps several hours – will lose heat. Their core temperature gradually falls to match the environmental temperature. This is made worse if they are in shock and immobile, and have suffered associated injuries. Hypothermia is defined as a core body temperature of less than 35°C – only two degrees less than normal. There comes a point when core temperature drops to such a level (around 28°C) that the risk of ventricular fibrillation becomes life threatening and the casualty falls into unconsciousness. There are some exceptional cases where people have suffered

MacInnes Mk 5 stretchers – the Superlight and Standard version

PHOTO: BOB SHARP

Casualty safely strapped into the stretcher. At least he's still smiling!

extreme cold and survived with no long-term complications as noted by the *British Medical Journal*.

'A fit young woman was cross country skiing with friends when she fell down a water-filled gully and became trapped beneath an ice sheet. Frantic efforts were made to extract her but, after forty minutes, all movements ceased. Her body was eventually recovered, one hour and nineteen minutes later, through a hole cut in the ice downstream. She was pronounced dead at the scene, but was given cardiopulmonary resuscitation throughout the air ambulance flight back to hospital where her rectal temperature was recorded as

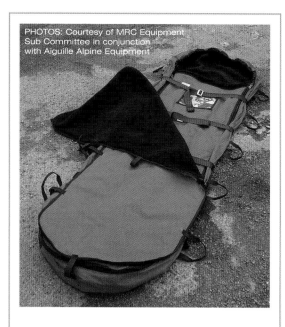

PHOTOS: Courtesy of MRC Equipment Sub Committee in conjunction with Aiguille Alpine Equipment

MRC (England & Wales) casbag

The MRC (England & Wales) spent over a year researching and developing their own casualty bag with the help of Aiguille Alpine Equipment. The new bag has all-round access to the casualty rather than a single zip down the middle, and is slightly longer and wider than usual so the casualty can be secured in a vacuum mattress. It also has an innovative rubber base which reduces

sliding on snow or slippery grass. Once snug inside the casbag, a casualty is well protected from rain, snow and wind.

13.7°C. Her body was rewarmed by means of an extracorporeal membrane oxygenator. After 35 days on a ventilator and a further five months of rehabilitation, she was able to continue her job as a hospital doctor.'

CPR is not part of MRC hypothermia protocol so how do teams respond to someone with hypothermia? Well, firstly, an assumption is always made that anyone who has been on a mountain for an extended period of time, particularly if they are exhausted or injured, will be hypothermic. Once the casualty has been located, team members look for signs and symptoms such as shivering, lack of co-ordination or acting out of character. In cases of extreme hypothermia, there may actually be an absence of shivering despite the cold, and a casualty may begin to remove their clothing. The immediate treatment is to arrange some kind of shelter, insulating them from wind and the ground cold, and to add more clothing. In fact, a 'bivvi bag' is an excellent piece of personal kit for walkers to keep in the rucksack in case of emergency. Two things rescue teams emphatically do not do is rub the casualty's skin or provide comfort in the shape of liberal quantities of alcohol! This merely succeeds in forcing warm blood to the surface of the skin, sending the colder blood from their extremities towards the core - a sure way to worsen the situation!

Some teams use a hot air device called the 'Little Dragon' warm air breather which is designed to insulate the airway to prevent further heat loss in the air breathed in and out. Cool oxygen is fed into the Little Dragon, which warms the air for the casualty to inhale via a facemask. Unfortunately, this device was not around when Jane Thomas died of hypothermia on a treacherously cold December day. It might have saved her life.

Jane, her husband Rob and George McEwan had travelled up from Penrith for a week's climbing holiday. Jane was a mountain rescue team member and all three were experienced mountaineers and qualified outdoor instructors. They left the Cairngorm ski lift car park around 8.30am to complete a climb in one of the northern coires, their plan to do a short route before the expected bad weather settled in. The walk-in took them across easy angled terrain for about two miles to the foot of the cliff face in Coire an t-Sneachda where they intended to tackle an ice climb called 'The Message'. At this point, Rob – who had been ill all week with a virus – felt he wouldn't be able to complete the route so he bowed out and returned to the car park. What he didn't realise was that when he took a last glance at the pair beginning the route, it would be the last time he saw his wife alive. Both climbers were properly dressed for a winter's day on the mountain – Goretex® jackets, thermal underwear, hats and gloves. They also had spare clothing and an emergency plastic survival bag.

Their ascent took several hours. The final pitch was very difficult and required George to abseil down from the top to help Jane. It was a manoeuvre which meant Jane expended vital energy on an unexpected challenge that would have been helpful later on. She'd also had a minor cold the previous week which didn't help. That said, neither could have foretold what was to happen. It was a further two hours before both climbers reached the end of the climb and stood on the plateau. They stopped briefly for a bite to eat but it was now dark and the bad weather had already descended on them some six hours earlier than expected. In fact the weather worsened considerably. Biting winds gusted to over 90 mph, lowering the effective temperature to minus 25 degrees. They struggled towards the ridge that would lead them back to the car park, but the foul

PHOTO: JAMIE KEAN

MRC (Scotland) new stretcher and casbag

The MRC of Scotland was able to develop a new stretcher and casbag thanks to benefactor George Smith whose daughter, Catherine, died of altitude sickness in 1991. On his death, he asked that part of his estate be used by a Scottish charity in pursuit of research into altitude sickness and mountain safety in Scotland. The subsequent £40K donation came with three requirements – that it be used for charitable purposes, was administered in good faith and that the name of Catherine Smith be associated with the development.

The new stretcher – officially called the Catherine Smith Casualty System, but more commonly referred to as the 'Katie' – has a three piece load bed, with a quickly detachable head guard and wheel unit.

The lower half of the load bed is a composite shell structure for drag ability, while the top is a lightweight metal frame structure providing lift and tie-on points. The load bed incorporates storage for gas bottles and casualty insulation. The wheel unit utilises a rubber torsion suspension system, with a cheap and durable wheelbarrow wheel.

Other improvised aids to carrying

(from the *Mountain Rescue & Cave Rescue Handbook* 1966)

'Carrying by hand is practicable only for short distances. The patient can sit on the crossed hands of two people, with a third to take the weight of the legs, or by one person pick-a-back, or by the fireman's lift; the carrier brings the patient's left arm over his right shoulder and passes his left arm between the patient's legs; he has both arms free. A coil of rope can be helpful when carrying pick-a-back. Separate the coils into two and put the arms through the loops, as if wearing a rucksack. If the rope has been coiled so that the loops are of a suitable size the patient can be lifted up and his legs passed through them.

'A frame rucksack can be turned into an effective carrier by cutting slits in the bag for the patient's legs.

'Quite a useful stretcher can be made from one or two pairs of skis with the aid of two or three wooden battens and screws carried ready for the purpose, and ingenuity can make do at a pinch with one pair, across which have been lashed pieces of ski stick broken to a suitable length.'

weather reduced visibility to a few metres and the swirling winds lifted them off their feet throwing them both against the rocks and ice. The terrain was strewn with boulders and they had to wade through deep snowdrifts. They found it hard to breathe and could only communicate by shouting in each other's ear. It was a fight for survival.

Progress was very slow and at times they couldn't make headway at all. But worse was to come. Suddenly, George sensed the ground was sloping the wrong way. They should have been descending when, in fact, they had begun to rise steeply. They had made a navigation error which was taking them in exactly the opposite direction! It's not uncommon – even competent mountaineers make mistakes when the going is so tough. They could do nothing but turn around and begin to fight their way back once more. This time, the wind attacked them from the opposite direction. It wasn't long before Jane began to tire dramatically. She was forced to sit down and rest. The effects of her cold, the energy expended at the top of the climb and now the atrocious weather conditions meant she was almost exhausted. George was tired too but realised they had to keep moving and get out of the weather. He knew the way down, but was held back by their extreme lethargy. He was forced to help Jane by pulling her along but that didn't work for long. Several times, he tried to dig an emergency snow hole but found it impossible as the fresh snow kept collapsing. Each attempt wasted more time and energy.

By now Jane was able only to crawl, George pleading with her to keep moving. Somehow he found the presence of mind to fashion a rope harness, and the energy to drag her for over a mile. But she was lapsing into unconsciousness. Still, he kept moving her along, until finally, he felt he could go no further. He made a shallow scoop in the snow and positioned Jane with her back to the wind with her rucksack for protection. She was unconscious, unresponsive to his shouts and prods. Instinct told him that if he stayed he would also succumb to the elements. The only hope for both of them would be to move forwards and get to the car park for help. He found it very difficult to walk away and leave his good friend, but to stay would have meant certain death for both of them.

Detaching himself from the rope he had tied to Jane, he staggered onwards. He'd lost all sense of time and had begun to hallucinate about friends urging him on. His navigation and knowledge of the mountain paid off. He bumped into a ski tow pylon. Now he could follow a line down to the car park. It was 4.00am, some twenty hours since they'd first set out. Unknown to George, the rescue teams were already on the mountain having been alerted by Rob the previous evening. In a state of shock, George was taken to the rescue centre where he met Rob and, over warm drinks, explained to the rescue controllers where he thought Jane might be. Despite the high avalanche risk, over seventy rescuers struggled against the elements in the search for Jane, along with a number of search and rescue dogs. RAF helicopters couldn't be deployed because of low cloud and high winds. Ten hours after the search commenced, Jane was found – still with a pulse – by Cobra, a police German Shepherd. She was treated at the scene by RAF medical personnel before being airlifted to Raigmore hospital in Inverness with deep hypothermia. Sadly, despite intense efforts by all rescue personnel, attempts to revive her failed and she was pronounced dead on arrival at the hospital.

Jane died not because she was reckless, inexperienced or ill equipped. In the event, her demise was a cruel combination of the unexpected weather, a minor illness and fatigue because of an unexpectedly hard climb. As George commented later, 'When you're operating on the hills you need that little bit of extra stamina and, possibly because of her recent illness, she didn't have it. If Jane had had her full fitness she would have walked out with me. People think accidents happen because of one factor – bad weather, people's inexperience or whatever. But accidents happen because of an accumulation of little things which ultimately add up and tip the scales. I think the illness Jane had the week before, a minor thing, a cold she shrugged off, tipped the scales.'

A fortuitous rescue

Mr Fleming was a poor Scottish farmer. One day, while out working in the fields, he heard a cry for help coming from a nearby bog. He dropped his tools and ran to the bog. There, up to his waist in black muck, was a terrified boy, screaming and struggling to free himself. The farmer saved the lad from what could have been a slow and terrifying death. The next day, a fancy carriage pulled up to the Scotsman's sparse surroundings. An elegantly dressed nobleman stepped out and introduced himself as the father of the boy the farmer had saved. 'I want to repay you,' said the nobleman. 'You saved my son's life'. 'No, I can't accept payment for what I did,' the farmer replied, waving off the offer. At that moment, the farmer's own son came to the door. 'Is that your son?' the nobleman asked. 'Yes,' the farmer replied proudly. 'I'll make you a deal. Let me take him and give him a good education. If the lad is anything like his father, he'll grow to be a man you can be proud of.'

And that he did. In time, the farmer's son graduated from St Mary's Hospital Medical School in London and went on to become known throughout the world as the noted Sir Alexander Fleming, the discoverer of penicillin. Years afterward, the nobleman's son was stricken with pneumonia.

What saved him? Penicillin. The name of the nobleman? Lord Randolph Churchill. And his son's name? Sir Winston Churchill!

PHOTO: BOB SHARP

A moment of sad reflection. Lomond team members pause to catch their breath as they carry a climber's body off a misty Ben Lomond.

You don't have to be several thousand feet up a Scottish mountain, or wading through snow and a swirling white-out, for hypothermia to creep up on you. Back on that aspirant mountain, Pendle Hill, three walkers sparked a six hour rescue operation – and a race against time – one October Sunday evening when one of their party slipped into a stream. Cold, soaking wet and exhausted – not a good combination, as wet clothing leeches heat from the body at an alarming rate – he was fast becoming hypothermic. When they had parked their car at nearby Sabden and set off walking over the hill to Barley, the weather was still fine – a crisp, sunny afternoon. But, as the autumn night drew in, the cloud cover settled round them and a wintry storm set in. They continued to make their way off the hill, but visibility was so poor that by 8.00pm, they had to admit they were lost and called for help on their mobile phone. That in itself proved less than straightforward. In a valley, they were unable to get a signal at first. It was another three hours before rescuers found them, by which time the gentleman who had slipped was deteriorating rapidly. Team members administered the Little Dragon warm air breather and huddled with all three walkers inside casualty shelters for body warmth.

Having found the walkers, it was vital to get them off the hill as quickly as possible before the other two walkers also succumbed to hypothermia. The police helicopter had been called, but was unable to get to the scene thanks to the increasingly dreadful weather conditions. It was a tortuous distance across rough terrain to the nearest road – not an enticing proposition for those team members carrying the stretcher through the dark and dense low cloud. The chances of getting off the hill in a hurry appeared to be slim. At midnight, the RAF helicopter arrived on scene. At least, team members could hear it – but couldn't see it. Then, just as quickly as it had arrived, the muffled sound of the

helicopter tailed away again, leaving those on the ground wondering whether they'd imagined it. It was only later they learned that, unable to see clearly or land, the pilot had decided to return to Leeds/Bradford airport for refuelling, before coming back to resume the search. And this they did. Only now it became obvious the only place to land was on top of Pendle – an uphill stretcher-carry of over a mile, across overflowing becks, hidden hollows and very muddy tussocks. At 3.00am, the rescuers, by now themselves pretty exhausted, loaded the casualty into the helicopter and watched it disappear once more into the early morning mist, leaving them to tramp back down to the team vehicles in the pitch black! Final stand down came at 6.00am, just as Monday morning alarm clocks were buzzing into life. The rescued trio had been suitably dressed for the expected conditions but were caught out by the sudden, unforecast storm. Fortunately, they had sustained no major injuries and their discomfort on the hill was only temporary, soon repaired with warmth and rest. But it could easily have been so much worse had they not been able to rouse help.

It's all well and good having the right medical equipment but team members must also have the skills to match. Most teams have a Medical Officer – often, but not always, a qualified doctor – who oversees and co-ordinates medical matters. In fact, many have a fair share of medical personnel, working as nurses, paramedics or first aiders in their professional lives, though it's by no means obligatory! The nature of mountain rescue means teams cannot always rely on the Medical Officer being first on scene. As we mentioned earlier, not all team members are trained in advanced casualty care, but the ability to do a basic assessment of airway, breathing and circulation and perform CPR is a standard requirement.

In Scotland, there is no standard award or training scheme, but in England and Wales, the MRC

as simple as ABC...

Team members are taught the principle of ABC when dealing with a casualty. Committed to memory, this systematic approach can be applied in any emergency situation, whether on the hill or in the office. But first… whatever the incident, ensure your own safety. Is the surrounding area safe? Are you in danger of falling rocks, running water, electric cables, vehicles, prevailing weather conditions? Look for potential dangers to yourself and your group. Once you know it is safe, you can approach your casualty and begin first aid. Is the casualty alert? Are they responsive? Introduce yourself, ask them if they can hear you. Squeeze their shoulder, pinch their ear.

A AIRWAY

Is the casualty's airway open, clear and unobstructed? There must be a clear passage of air to the lungs. Is the airway fine now but at risk of obstruction through swelling from facial injuries or bleeding? If necessary, open it by a simple chin lift or jaw thrust. Turning the person into a 'recovery position' saves more lives than any other first aid procedure. But not before you have checked breathing…

B BREATHING

Is the casualty breathing? Look, feel and listen for up to ten seconds to determine whether breathing is present or absent. If they are breathing, are they distressed? Assess their breathing rate. The normal respiratory rate at rest is 12-15 breaths per minute. Anxiety and pain increase the rate – below ten and above thirty indicate potential problems. If there's no sign of breathing, commence cardio-pulmonary resuscitation (but only if you have successfully completed the appropriate course to learn this). If breathing is present, then so must a pulse be, so check for major bleeding…

C CIRCULATION

Is the casualty showing signs of shock – pale, sweaty skin, nausea, fainting in the early stages; agitation and obscured vision as the shock progresses? If possible you should check the neck or wrist pulse and monitor over a period of time. However, this might not always be feasible, under stressful circumstances, with cold and poor weather conditions. Are they bleeding profusely? Stop any bleeding from wounds by elevation and direct pressure to wounds or clothing.

Once you have the hang of that, you can go on to D and E…

D DISABILITY/DEFORMITY

Discover the damage. What is the casualty's level of consciousness? Is there evidence of head or spinal injury? Look for bleeding, bruising, pain, loss of function, deformity, swelling. Compare one side of the body with the other. Check pockets, wrists and neck for MediAlerts or clues as to the casualty's medical history, all the time explaining what you are doing!

E EXPOSURE/EXTREMITIES/EXPLAIN

Are the long bones and major joints intact? Is the blood supply to those limbs intact? Is there any likelihood of hypothermia? And – just as important as any first aid treatment or ongoing examination – continue to explain and engage with the casualty – even when they appear unresponsive – giving comfort and reassurance throughout the entire process.

has established a course, which leads to a national Casualty Care Certificate. Teams do their own training but, over the years, they have also relied on organisations such as the St John and St Andrew Ambulance Associations. The British Association of Ski Patrollers (BASP) is well known and most teams in Scotland are locked into its scheme of first aid and safety training designed specifically for outdoor users. All BASP trainers are qualified ski or mountain instructors, emergency medical technicians or paramedics with a wealth of practical mountain first aid and the BASP scheme is nationally recognised by all sporting governing bodies.

None of the courses are quite as radical in their approach as advocated by Squadron Leader Dave Dattner, the officer in charge at RAF Kinloss back in the fifties. He argued that, as doctors were often not available at a rescue, all team members should not only be able to inject morphine but sew up a wound. He was adamant that there had been occasions when casualties might have lived had rescuers been better trained in medical procedures. It seemed to him that, not only were his men horrified at the prospect of approaching a corpse or an open wound – worse – they were afraid at the sight of blood. He determined to change the situation. Team members were obliged to practice using a hypodermic needle, using him as guinea pig, prior to injecting morphine into a casualty. At 'Dattner's Sewing Parties' he would cut himself deliberately, so his men could experience inserting stitches into the wound. And, for the more squeamish, there were trips to the morgue!

The week long course which leads to the EMT qualification is recognised by the Faculty of Pre-Hospital Care of the Royal College of Surgeons and much sought after by team members who wish to develop their first aid skills. Primarily, it's about the care of acutely ill or injured individuals. It's a very practical mix of topics – everything from safe management of the mountain rescue scene, through pre-hospital trauma, basic and advanced life support, paediatric emergencies, climbing and suspension trauma, to the management of general mountain injuries and the search and resuscitation of avalanche victims. One of the most positive spin-offs is that successful students learn a systematic and organised approach to casualty management, which they are able to pass on to their fellow team members. Martin McCallum, of the Lomond team experienced the course first hand.

'I felt like a bit of a swot walking into the lounge in Glenmore Lodge for the opening of the EMT course. I had a thick *Emergency Care for the Paramedic* book under my arm that I had been feverishly reading all summer, well, I'd reached nearly half way. As I walked in and sat down I noticed even thicker books on the floor at people's feet. Some even had multiple books. Suddenly I felt the smugness drain out of the soles of my feet. Perhaps taking the book to the Alps to study hadn't been such a good idea.

'The BASP Emergency Medical Technician course is held once a year, primarily for mountain rescue personnel and ski patrollers who wish to upgrade their first aid skills to an advanced level. It is open to others, providing their CV passes vetting by the BASP board. My course included two teachers and a policeman as well as ten MR and one Ski Patrol member. It was mainly taught by mountain rescue personnel with a huge breadth of experience in the care and treatment of badly injured people, not only on the hill but also in everyday life situations.

'Doing first aid within the normal mountain rescue environment does not prepare you for the course. As we all know, many team members are not eager to treat casualties and often, when they do administer first aid, it's the obvious injury such as a broken ankle or exposure that's dealt with. The whole idea of the course is to instil in you an ability to make fast and accurate assessments of the casualty's overall condition and give them appropriate first aid that will help them to survive to get to a hospital where the 'cure' is waiting. You must be able to do this in adverse weather and under pressure – something the instructors are very adept at providing.

'Shortly after arrival we spent time on basic life support procedure – how to perform CPR and, equally important, the steps involved in assessing firstly your own safety and then the condition of the casualty. Tasks were set and tested such as completing chest compressions and rescue breaths on a manikin linked to a computer, as well as testing on the procedure for approach and casualty assessment. This is very daunting, but very useful as it gets you into the way of following a procedure to repeatedly assess a casualty and administer the first aid they need to survive.

'The course is a mixture of lectures and practicals, with a greater emphasis on practical work towards the end of the course. Lectures cover a wide range of subjects such as pain, shock, medical trauma, triage, and head and neck injuries, and are not confined to during the day. The evenings are also taken up by lectures, some given by guest lecturers.

'The first practical of the week was, as you can guess, a complete comedy. We had no structure, no leadership and the poor casualties were tied up like lambs in Aberdeen. The debrief for this had a very sheepish group of students standing around wondering how on earth we were ever going to pass this course. However, our confidence gradually grew, especially as we came together more as a group, learning each other's strengths and weaknesses. The night exercise really turned us into a team, even though we made several mistakes. It gave us structure and enabled us to recognise those who had good leadership skills and those who were less keen to take charge. The debrief in the bar afterwards was a turning point where we could see we had the skills to get through and apply ourselves. Being part of a team again was very reassuring for those of us from mountain rescue. We no longer felt out of our depth and it also brought those not from MR much more into the team.

'The last day was test day. There was some time for revision first thing in the morning followed by a multiple-choice test. At coffee we were a very nervous group, with the smokers outside chain smoking and the rest of us inside wishing we had some way to calm our nerves. We swapped papers at the end of the test and marked each other's, turning over the name so we did not know whose paper it was. These were then handed back to the instructors while we went for more coffee and/or nicotine. Dave, the course leader, had the unenviable job of informing two of the group that they had failed. It hurt us all to see two people fail. We'd arrived as a very fragmented group, but we had grown into a team. There were a few tears shed as the two bade their farewells.

'It was now time for the practical test. There was no particular order – those whose nerves could stand it better let others go first. The practical involved casualty assessment with one of the instructors as the casualty and the others as bystanders. Once you started, the nerves disappeared as the methods and techniques you had been taught during the week kicked in. After the test we each stood outside the room as the instructors discussed and assessed our individual performance. Time dragged as I relived the test remembering every mistake I made. Fortunately I didn't have to wait long before Dave popped his head round the door and said, "You've passed. Send the next one in, and don't tell anyone what the test was!" We all passed the practical and it was a very relieved group that had a final wrap-up session with the instructors.

'Was it worth it? Definitely. I now feel a

confidence as I approach a casualty on the hill knowing that I can quickly assess what the priorities are, and give the casualty the best care I can to allow them a more comfortable journey to hospital. Have I used it? Yes, less than twenty four hours after returning I was on a callout where I was able to see how I could apply in a real situation what I learned during the week. Did it work? Well, I think so. The casualty made it to the helicopter much more comfortable than when I first got to her, which is more than can be said for the deer fence between the casualty and the helicopter! The course will not suit everyone as it requires a lot of commitment and some degree of leadership skills. You don't have to be the world's best at bandaging or need to be completely medically literate. However, reading and fully understanding the course text *Casualty Care in Mountain Rescue* is essential. The course is about enabling you to use your head in a pressure situation. The techniques and methods taught allow you to apply the best possible first aid to a casualty on the hill, often saving his or her life or preventing further damage. I now understand why having an EMT on the hill greatly increases the casualty's chance of survival and can improve recovery. It also helps the team morale to have someone there who can confidently assess casualties and implement appropriate and knowledgeable first aid.'

Bob Sharp, when not engaged in professional or mountain rescue activities, or busy co-writing this book, occasionally finds time to dispense with the heavy rescue gear. Every year, along with fellow team member and friend, Archie Roy, he treats himself to a couple of days travelling light as 'normal walkers'. That was the plan in early summer 2004, but fate clearly had other ideas, as he became unexpectedly involved in a dramatic mountain incident which demanded all his mountain rescue first aid skills to save someone's life.

'The pair of us, along with Archie's two boys and brother-in-law, were walking on the Cuillin Ridge on the Isle of Skye. Unique in the UK, it offers over seven miles of exposed, unrelenting scrambling amidst majestic mountains steeped in tragedy and climbing history. The extreme exposure and loose rocks make any trip along the ridge a daunting and serious proposition. But, for all the risks, it offers a mountaineering expedition to which many aspire. The classic challenge is to complete the entire ridge and return to the start point (on foot) in less than twenty four hours. A small number achieve this goal whilst many lesser mortals make do with a day trip into one of the high coires.

'One of the popular start points is at the campsite in Glenbrittle. When we left Glenbrittle about 8.00am, the weather wasn't good. In contrast to the forecast, the cloud base was low and thunderstorms threatened. But we moved on up the hill following the well-worn path as it wends its way up into Coire Lagan. About the same time, but unknown to us, Mike McErlean and his friend also left the campsite intending a similar route to our own.

'Our plans were to walk into the coire, then ascend the 'Great Stone Shoot' to the col between Sgurr Alasdair and Sgurr Thearlaich. The stone shoot is a 1500 foot scree slope which steepens to about 45 degrees near the top. It's a wretched climb! Every rock you stand on moves and falling rocks from above constantly threaten life and limb. It took what seemed like an eternity to reach the top but as we stood on the col, we were treated to a break in the sky and the promise of much better weather. Things were looking up – but not for too long. The short 100 foot scramble to the summit of Sgurr Alasdair was straightforward but the one up Sgurr Thearlaich was thwarted by problems. We couldn't decide which way to begin the climb. It looked too steep from every angle. Eventually, we committed ourselves to a sloping gully which turned out to be technically easy but much steeper and more exposed than I

Walker Mike McEarlean on the left, pictured fifteen minutes before his fall

remembered from a previous visit. After about fifty feet, we found ourselves on steep, exposed ground. One slip would have signalled the end. However, there was no turning back. We continued quickly and deliberately until the ground relaxed and the top appeared out of the mist. At least the rock was very dry.

'Those who have been to Skye will know that the prominent rock is gabbro. It's exceedingly coarse and gives excellent grip for hands and feet. But it's also brittle. The entire ridge is very broken. Loose blocks teeter unsteadily and sections are covered in gravel just waiting to unbalance the unwary. A simple slip almost anywhere on the ridge invariably takes the unfortunate person on a one-way trip to oblivion!

'With nerves somewhat frayed, we continued down the ridge to the low point before the next summit – Sgurr Mhic Choinnich. Soon we had all gathered together to discuss how to negotiate the next steep section. As with many other parts of the ridge, there are critical route choices to be made. In the event, we rigged up a couple of small abseils to bypass the impossible bits before arriving at the

base of Sgurr Mhic Choinnich. The next section on the ridge – 'Collies Ledge' – is a well known landmark. The ledge circumvents the peak and is highly exposed and broken. It's not the place to dawdle or meet another group but that's exactly what we did. Dan Carroll, leader of the Kinloss RAF MRT was bringing a party of fellow team members from the other side and we met at the narrowest section. We had a brief chat before continuing, not realising we'd meet again shortly under very different circumstances.

'Eventually, after a further section of intimidating scrambling we descended to the low point before An Stac and the 'Inaccessible Pinnacle'. Our plans had been to climb the 'In Pin', but with time marching on we decided to descend into the coire and retrace our steps back to Glenbrittle. The route into the bowl of the coire is steep and broken and has to follow the line of the Ac Stac screes – another roller coaster of broken, moving blocks similar to the Great Stone Shoot. The best plan is to keep together so that any dislodged rocks don't have time to gather pace before they strike someone. We had dropped about 200 feet when my attention was suddenly drawn to the left. It must have been a scream or the noise of falling rocks. Hurtling through the air was a walker who had fallen from the ridge above. His body cartwheeled with limbs flaying out of control. Every fifty feet or so he made contact with the rocks before bouncing back into the air. I thought he would tumble all the way to the floor of the coire – about 1000 feet, but he came to rest abruptly against a large block. Stuart Roy, one of Archie's sons had seen the whole accident unfold.

'The walker – Mike McErlean – had been descending the ridge behind us but had strayed off line onto very steep ground. This forced him to traverse a steep wall with his back to the coire. As he held a large block for balance, it suddenly gave way and he fell backwards, falling about eighty feet

View along the ridge, showing the kind of terrain encountered. Mike fell down the steep ground in the middle of the picture

vertically before striking the rock with his back. He then bounced and began to cartwheel down the screes for another 400 feet. It was some consolation that the detached block didn't follow him down.

'Mike came to rest a short distance to my left. I realised I'd be the first on scene with about two minutes to rehearse what to do. Conscious of people rushing down I turned back and shouted, 'Slow down!' There was a real danger that not only would Mike and I be bombarded with rocks, but also someone else would fall. I continued towards Mike, pausing in preparation about ten feet away. To my utter disbelief, he was still alive! He was facing downwards and choking on blood and spinal fluid.

The RAF Sea King involved in the rescue

He had to be moved immediately or would certainly asphyxiate. Conscious of exacerbating any spinal injury (which was more than likely in view of the fall) it was paramount to manage Mike's airway. Archie arrived on scene within seconds and held Mike's head steady whilst we manoeuvred him into a flatter position. Almost immediately, his efforts to breath improved remarkably – we'd begun to save his life! However, the steep ground, moving rocks and weight of Mike's body made this an extraordinary effort. We were both totally occupied just stabilising his body and trying our best not to slip further down the slope.

'We waited a few minutes for others to arrive

and during this time had an opportunity to make an initial assessment. Mike was barely conscious but breathing with difficulty. His head and face were badly lacerated and bleeding profusely. But, with hands occupied to support Mike, we couldn't investigate the extent of other injuries.

'Once other people arrived we were able to manage things better. One person secured him with a rope to a large block. Another stabilised his neck by holding his head. Two people made their way down into the coire to raise the alarm using their mobile phone. Archie attended to Mike's obvious head injuries and cleaned his face, whilst I began a detailed overall body examination. All the time we monitored his level of consciousness, which rose slowly over the next hour or so. Even though he couldn't speak we kept reassuring him that things weren't too bad and that help was on its way. His pulse, breathing and capillary refill were acceptable although we noticed a gradual blackening of his eye sockets. This, coupled with the presence of spinal fluid seeping from one ear indicated he had a serious base of skull fracture. He didn't seem to have injured his spine or chest but he did have arm and knee fractures.

'Matters took a significant turn for the better when another walker arrived on scene, pronouncing that he was a doctor - even better, he was a trauma specialist! We exchanged notes before he commenced a further examination. By this time, Mike was slightly more alert but unable to talk. However, his body language told us he wanted to sit up. Conscious of spinal damage, we were forced to hold him down. The doctor confirmed our own diagnosis but there was little else he could do without specialised equipment. At this point, the RAF team arrived on scene. They too had seen Mike fall and raced up from the coire to help. Dan Carroll confirmed that an RAF helicopter was on its way from RAF Lossiemouth. His men moved in to give support and help manage the difficult situation.

'On arrival, the helicopter hovered very close to the crags whilst the winchman was lowered to join us. All winchmen are trained to advanced level casualty care and are highly competent at their work. Duncan Tripp is no exception and he set about treating Mike with specialist equipment. He attached a pulse oximeter to monitor Mike's blood/oxygen levels and set up a cannula to inject a small dose of morphine. We attached a neck collar and splinted Mike's badly deformed right arm and then, with great physical effort, loaded him onto the stretcher. He was winched up and the helicopter departed to the hospital in Fort William.

'The whole episode was highly traumatic for all concerned. One or two people were quite shocked, including Mike's friend who had remained at a distance throughout. It was important to monitor him as we scrambled to easy ground and then back to Glenbrittle. On the walk back, we shared ideas about what we might have done different or better, but our doctor friend was absolutely confident our first aid had been absolutely right. For the first time in my life I had been faced with the classic dilemma of treating someone who has probable spinal injuries but has to be moved quickly to help them breathe. You know that moving them will restore breathing, but it may break their spinal cord. In the event there was no debate, Mike's airway had to be restored. Mike was fortunate in that two of us were available to stabilise him as we moved him to a recovery position. He was also fortunate in that within a few minutes of falling he had a couple of qualified first aiders on hand and then soon afterwards, a doctor and rescue team.

'The prognosis for Mike was not good. He'd shown signs of improvement but definitely had skull fractures, possible spinal damage and internal injuries. During the helicopter flight, he had come close to death on a couple of occasions. The following day, I learned that after a brief visit to

PHOTO: CHRIS BOYLES

Come on up! A casualty's eye view as they're winched into an RAF Sea King

Accident & Emergency for stabilisation he was transferred to a special accident unit in Glasgow. He remained on full life support for several days and was in a coma for a week. He then began to recover slowly and left hospital four weeks later.'

And what was Mike's recollection of the whole incident?

'My memory of that late afternoon in May – and my lengthy fall – and the following five days until I woke up, is non-existent. Some say just as well. I remember when I finally left hospital after treatment for my skull and arm fractures, I quickly wanted to resume life where I left off before the accident. Foolish I know - injuries and energy reserves would

not permit. As the weeks have passed I've learned more about the events of 29th May and, far from wanting to resume life as it was, I am just glad to be alive and here with my family. At present I am living a quiet life and allowing my body to get on with the work of recovery. The recovery seems to be going well and my body seems to be returning to as close to normal as possible – but I think I'll give the Tour de France a miss this year!'

The full-time emergency services such as the fire brigade and the ambulance service are used to dealing with tragic accidents and helping people with life threatening injuries. They are often forced to confront horrific sights, but are better able to cope with these experiences through training, peer support and regular experience. In contrast, most rescue teams are less accustomed to coping with some of the awful sights seen by other professionals. But their effect on the individual rescuer, when it does occur, can be quite traumatic. So how do team members cope?

Well, it's remarkable how people do handle these situations. Quite simply, you have to cope. Rescuers tackle an incident as 'a job to be done'. Emotions take a back seat whilst the technicalities of the rescue are undertaken without hindrance. This works well, but there is often a payback after the event when a team member suffers some kind of post-traumatic stress. The tried and tested way to deal with this is to talk about it with fellow rescuers – be it down the pub, nursing a pint and a packet of pork scratchings, or the local burger bar – wherever. Some teams have a more structured strategy of reviewing an incident and its possible effects on individuals immediately afterwards. Sitting down and being open about the emotions of a particularly traumatic incident can go a long way to releasing tensions and reducing the risk of long-term effects.

Very useful support is provided by some police forces. One we know has a comprehensive post-incident procedure called Critical Incident Stress Management, which is available to serving police officers as well as rescuers. A four-stage process covers the period from the beginning of an incident right through to a point several weeks after it, the main aim being to support the individuals involved.

Stage 1 is the period where people are engaged in, or at the periphery of an incident normally of a serious or major nature. This stage ensures the provision of adequate facilities, equipment, rotation and rest periods and continual briefings where the incident is major or prolonged. It gives those involved the opportunity to discuss and share their experiences with colleagues. Rescue personnel are monitored with regard to their psychological and emotional well being and appropriate action is taken where necessary. An area is established where the Critical Incident Stress Management team is based. Most important, the area serves as a transition area away from any trauma in order to reduce the immediate stress reactions before returning to routine.

Stage 2 follows immediately after the incident and takes the form of a structured meeting involving a supervisor and those involved in the incident. The aim is to provide early support, information and guidance to ensure the welfare of those involved and to encourage effective coping and restoration of adequate functioning. It also allows supervisors to assess the impact of the incident and to decide on the necessity for further support.

Stage 3 takes place two or three days after the incident. It's a prearranged meeting of those who were involved, with the intention of enabling them to share experiences, access group support and address feelings of uniqueness. This enables the team to offer emotional and practical support, education and 'anticipatory guidance'.

Stage 4 is a longer-term follow-up where the Team makes individual contact by letter with all of those who attended the debriefing and requests they complete a standard questionnaire. Completed questionnaires are returned to the trauma treatment centre in order to assess any residual issues and, if necessary, offer appropriate therapy.

This sort of disciplined approach is typical of the organisation and procedures within the statutory services. Whilst the degree of internal structure within the volunteer mountain rescue teams might vary, in the RAF teams, such structure and discipline are essential features of daily life.

chapter seven

FLYING HIGH

As the stars descend from heaven and our highest symbols pale,
As the sway of nature falters and our trust in reason fails.
As we bend our knee to days gone by and our tears become a flood;
Remember then what common bonds were forged in fresh spilt blood.
Brian McManus.

The vast majority of people involved in mountain rescue are mountaineers – in the broadest sense of the word. We all love the mountains and enjoy the pleasures and challenges they provide. That makes sense and seems obvious. In fact, we take part in the same activities and subject ourselves to the same risks, as those we rescue. But, that said, we're all involved at different levels and in different ways. Where some will be hotshot rock climbers accustomed to dangling from a precipitous face, empty space beneath their feet, there are a great many more who are well-seasoned walkers, orienteers, fell runners or simply ramblers. Many spend their working days on the mountains as park rangers, access workers, foresters, mountain instructors and guides. A great number of team members venture into the winter mountains – at home and abroad – to test their own physical abilities and technical skills to the limit. But a very small

Royal Navy winchman winches casualty on a MacInnes Superlight stretcher

PHOTO: BOB SHARP

PHOTO: RAF MRS

Lucky thirteen – the first Single Service Expedition to Everest, May 2001

group venture to the very limit of human endeavour.

On 21 May 2001, Chief Technician Dan Carroll and Corporal Richard 'Rusty' Bale made RAF history when they stood on the highest point in the world – the summit of Mount Everest – in the first ever single service attempt on the mountain. Dan, from Lossiemouth, and Richard, from Kinloss made it to the top at 6.25 BST, returning to base camp at 17,300 feet two days later. The rest of their team, including expedition leader Flight Lieutenant Ted Atkins were beaten back by the weather. Ted wrote this report on his return:

PHOTO: WG CDR BRIAN KIRKPATRICK

Flt Lt Ted Atkins climbing the North col

an altitude of 5200 metres and, even better, equipment can then be transported by yaks to advance base camp at 6400 metres. Each one of these hairy bovines can carry a load of forty kilos over the rough, moraine tracks, thus removing much of the personal drudgery of heavy load carrying.

'Preparation to climb a mountain such as Everest must be meticulous and exacting. Proper acclimatisation to altitude is vital. For example, if you were suddenly transported from ground level to the summit of Mount Everest, you would die within thirty minutes without the use of supplementary oxygen. At such altitudes, two-thirds of the world's oxygen is beneath your feet! The weather can also be severe and unpredictable, and there are only a few days when an attempt on the summit is feasible. So, the problem is simple, all you have to do is guess when the weather is going to be right, make sure you have all the equipment in the right place, and then have a fit and acclimatised team ready to go! Oh, I didn't mention that your Chinese entry visa is only valid for fifty six days, so obviously it all has to happen within this time frame.

'In March 2001, thirteen of us left for Tibet via Nepal. We had selected the North Ridge route as the line that we would take to climb Everest. The North Ridge is a difficult and more technically demanding route than the normal route from Nepal. The great advantage of tackling the mountain from the north side, in Tibet, is that the team and equipment can easily be transported by truck to the base camp at

'Life at high altitudes is about as uncomfortable as it gets. At base camp it is freezing cold, hot, wet, windy and dry and a fine dust permeates everywhere. At first, we all suffered from the altitude – shortness of breath and dizzy spells when you bend over. It sometimes seems as if the world is against you as another bout of 'Kathmandu Quickstep' sends you rushing for the toilet tent in a blizzard, in the middle of the night. On a good night you make it to the tent before events overtake you! One night we were even 'called out' to rescue a climber from another expedition who had failed to return. We found him in the early hours of the morning, critically ill, and carried him back to base camp on a stretcher in a blizzard. There, we administered drugs and oxygen, and nursed him through the night until he was stable enough to be evacuated.

'Time at base camp was well spent, however. We could recharge our batteries and relax in our unique shed while the blizzards raged outside. Between acclimatisation sorties we were able to eat well, drink the occasional dram and, most of all, banter to our hearts content while we made up ridiculous words and cheated at scrabble.

'From base camp to the summit is about twenty six kilometres, with a height gain of 3600 metres. Twenty-six kilometres is not a great distance for a mountain rescue day out in Scotland but on Everest, at altitudes over 5000 metres, it is not a case of packing a flask and a few sandwiches. The strategy is to take on the mountain in bite-sized chunks, to gradually acclimatise because, in essence, that is all you can manage. Every day spent above base camp caused us to be in physiological decline, yet this was where we had do the bulk of our work. By using a system of camps established up the mountain we were able to leap frog up the mountain, gain fitness and acclimatisation, then back to base to rest.

'Our first objective was to walk to the half way transit camp and spend one night there before returning to base camp. After a rest at base camp, and when the weather permitted, we returned to the transit camp for another night before moving up to advance base camp, where we spent one night before returning to base camp in one journey. At this stage of the climb the team split into small groups climbing up and down to the various camps to acclimatise to the conditions, thus 'leap frogging' up the mountain. It was on one of these acclimatisation trips that I came across a party of Chinese scientists who were descending with a stretcher. This is always a serious event in these regions and it was immediately obvious that the casualty was dying. We had all been well trained to recognise the symptoms of high altitude pulmonary oedema, an extremely dangerous condition, which causes the lungs to fill with fluid. In our first aid kits we each carried one tablet of a drug called Nifedipine, for personal use. I gave my drug to buy extra time while we organised the stretcher party to carry him to a lower altitude to receive oxygen and expert medical help. Thankfully, the man lived and made a full recovery. It was a classic illustration of what can and does go wrong if you fail to acclimatise properly.

'The climb above advance base camp, to Camp 1, on the North Col at 7000 metres, was the first serious climbing undertaken. Even with the use of fixed ropes (to aid climbing and security) this was not a place to dawdle. The chance of a fall was minimal due to the ropes, but we had to spend time under the ominous shadow of unstable hanging ice blocks called seracs. Whenever I thought that I could go no further without resting I would look up and then find the energy for a few more steps to get clear of a potential serac fall line. It was a long steep haul to Camp 1 and, whilst the route to Camp 2 at 7700 metres was neither terribly steep nor technically demanding, it was the highest climbing that we planned to undertake without supplementary oxygen – and it hurt. Camp 2 was on the exposed North Ridge, constantly battered by high winds charged with ice crystals that would remove bare skin. In

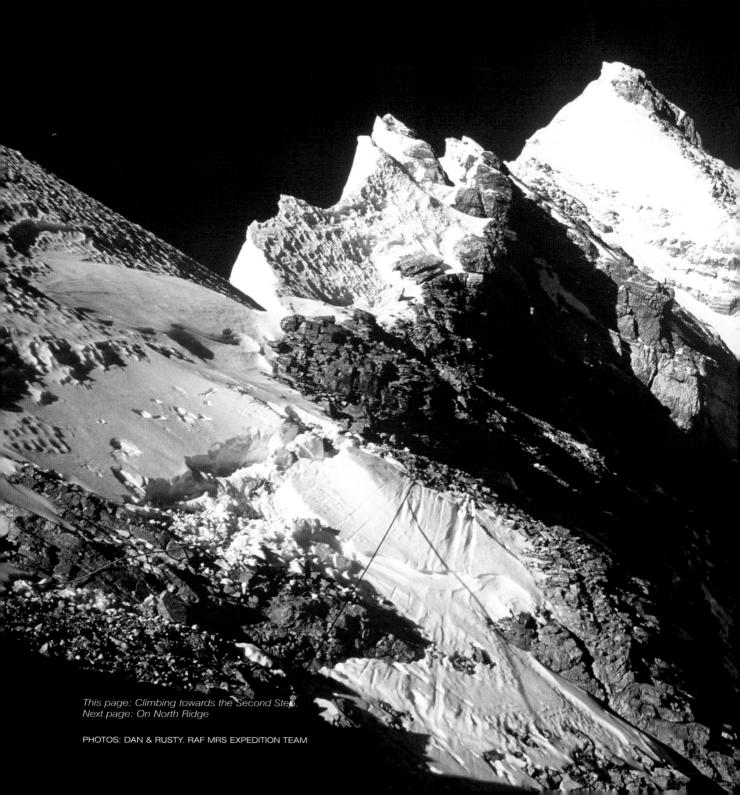

This page: Climbing towards the Second Step.
Next page: On North Ridge

PHOTOS: DAN & RUSTY. RAF MRS EXPEDITION TEAM

Before we left the mountain two climbers from other expeditions died around us, while others were severely injured. Climbing Everest is an outstanding feat that only the fittest and most determined survive.

order to stop the tents blowing away we covered them with cargo nets anchored to the rock. The climbing up to Camp 3, using oxygen, was up the steep ridge then the North Face, which offered little purchase for crampons or an ice axe (try to imagine climbing a steep slate roof in hobnail boots and you begin to get the idea) then out onto the exposed North Face at 8300 metres. The camp was established on a system of narrow ledges built from rock and snow – very uncomfortable – one slip and it would be the end! But what a place, it seemed as if I could see half the world from here and the ambiance of the mountain was simply stunning. I looked across the North Face to the end of the West Ridge where as a twenty-something-year-old member of a Joint Service Team destined to fail, I had looked at the North Ridge and decided that if I was ever to lead a team on Everest, that I would choose to climb the very line that I was standing on. Everest was personal for me.

'I was at Camp 3 with Corporal Jim Groark and Wing Commander Brian Kirkpatrick to make an attempt on the summit. Because this is the longest stage of the route, normally taking up to sixteen hours, it meant leaving at midnight. This would enable us to tackle the greatest difficulties higher up the mountain in daylight, and be able to return in daylight when every advantage is needed to overcome the perils of mind numbing fatigue. Some new snow fell during our preparations in the afternoon, prior to our planned assault and, as this was not forecast, it caused some concern but not enough to dampen our spirits.

'It takes three hours to get 'booted, spurred' and ready to go, constantly brewing and drinking as much as possible. The massive boots make it seem as if your feet belong to someone else. Then the layers of clothing are put on before the down suit. I felt like a spaceman but the worst was yet to come. Fitting crampons can only be undertaken outside of the tent and the effort of bending over to do this made me feel dizzy. The last and worst part was lifting my rucksack containing two oxygen cylinders, while keeping the delivery tubes and regulator clear for use. And so, down mitts over gloves, hood up, oxygen mask fitted, goggles over my eyes – there must be no exposed skin anywhere for it would be frostbitten in minutes – headtorch on and into the snowy blackness. The snow had become worse, making each step more difficult as we climbed solo (it was dangerous to be roped together because if one of us slipped we would all be pulled off) towards the sections of buried anchor ropes that mark the route to the summit. The anchored ropes had all been fixed at various stages up the mountain by different teams in previous seasons, usually in daylight and in good weather conditions. We finally managed to find the buried fixed rope that we had seen in daylight the day before and the three of us began to climb up the mountain towards our dream.

'All too soon the rope ended, leaving us to go back to free climbing around the face to locate the next section and the next anchor rope. This was the most difficult and dangerous climbing I have ever undertaken. There were no second chances; the first slip meant a one-way trip to the bottom of the North Face! We could not find the rope and we were wasting vital oxygen and sapping our strength climbing unprotected on steep and lethal ground. So, after a heartbreaking search of three hours, I had to pull the plug. I drew my hand across my throat and pointed back to camp. There was still tomorrow.

'After stripping off my ice encrusted equipment I discovered that my feet, despite the best equipment available, were frozen and I prayed that they would be okay for our next attempt. Daybreak came. It was

An Australian climber, rescued by the team two miles along the glacier from Base Camp, suffering from a respiratory tract infection. He eventually made a full recovery.

still snowing, but anxious to carry on with our attempt, we tried to find the missing section of rope, this time in daylight. We quickly found our original route again and as we neared the top I found a second section of rope hanging down and decided to use this, as it is inadvisable to have everyone on one section, just in case it should become overloaded. As I pulled the slack rope from the snow it just kept coming free. Eventually I was horrified to discover that it was in fact the other end of the rope that we had all climbed the night before, and it was not fastened to anything! Only the weight of snow on top of it kept it fastened to the surface. Brian and Jim were now only connected to me and not the mountain as I held the loose end! I shouted down not to rely on the rope and to free climb once again until I could find a secure anchor rope.

'I managed to find another rope and we climbed on for 200 metres until the route seemed clear ahead and above for our next section. The weather began to get much worse; now snowing harder than ever. It became too dangerous to continue; even simple things like taking a drink of water became difficult. At such high altitudes, because you are breathing so quickly, you lose a lot of body fluid through your breath and it is imperative to remain properly hydrated. If hydration levels drop, the blood thickens and does not circulate so well – a prime cause of frostbite at altitude. However, the ambient temperature is so low that water bottles will freeze even when placed next to the body inside a down suit! I think I realised that Everest was not to be for us this time and I made the decision to turn back – again! Back at Camp 3 we watched our tracks being quickly buried in new snow and I finally had to say the cruellest words that I have ever to had to say, 'It's time to go back down.' Both the other members of my team were with me. It was the only way. To go up might not be a return trip.

'Normally, an expedition leader has to face the dilemma of whom to choose to make the attempts on the summit, but in our case the prospective 'summiteers' were self-selected in that they would be the ones, who were fully acclimatised, fit and in the right place, with the right weather conditions, when the opportunity arose. It takes five days to get from base camp up to Camp 3 in order to make a summit bid. My group had got the timing wrong and we realised that there was not enough time left for us to go down to rest and make another attempt. It was this element that the very experienced team of Dan and Richard got so right. The route from Camp 3 to the summit is the steepest and most technically demanding part of the climb. Therefore, the condition of the mountain and the weather needs to be at least fair or better, as you can expect to climb for between twelve and sixteen hours to reach the summit and return to camp. Back at advance base camp we watched Dan and Richard anxiously through binoculars. The team goal is far more important than personal ambition and the whole team was right behind them. We were glued to our radios and every crackle caused our blood to race.

'Dan called me on the morning of 22 May to tell me that they had reached the base of the summit pyramid. While this was a tantalisingly close point, metres are measured in minutes at these altitudes and it was several fraught hours before we got the final fantastic message to say that they were on the top. It was an incredibly emotional moment for me. After nine years dreaming and four years of planning we had accomplished the mountaineer's ultimate challenge. Come what may now, we had succeeded. But what would success have been worth if Dan and Richard had not come safely home? Before we left the mountain two climbers from other expeditions died around us, while others were severely injured. Climbing Everest is an outstanding feat that only the fittest and most determined survive. We defied the terrible accident statistics of Everest to return home, fit, healthy, and as a happy, cohesive team of friends.

'In terms of Service expeditions, this is the only military team to have placed non-Special Forces personnel on the summit. The success is a great credit to both the RAF and its Mountain Rescue Service, in that it was able to produce the calibre of person to undertake and successfully complete this great challenge. Eleven individual summit bids were made and eight members climbed above an altitude of 8000 metres. We would have placed more people on the top but for one of our team becoming ill on a summit attempt. That illness cost the summit ambitions of four hopefuls, who selflessly sacrificed their personal ambitions to ensure the safe recovery of a colleague. Looking back on our Everest adventure, it is wonderful to have been a part of the effort that created this first for the RAF. If I were to say that I would not go back to the Himalaya again without a team as good as this one, then I would be condemning myself never to return there again.'

In May 2004, Ted Atkins finally achieved his lifetime ambition and climbed to the summit of Mount Everest. He is still involved in military mountain rescue. The RAF Mountain Rescue Service has come a long way since its early days of rubber boots and battledress. Today, the four teams are based at Kinloss in Moray, Leuchars in Fife, Leeming in North Yorkshire, Valley in Anglesey – each comprising seven permanent members, with up to as many as thirty volunteers who have regular 'eight to five' jobs within the RAF, available 24 hours a day at one hour's notice. Their primary aim is to render assistance in military and civilian aviation incidents but they have additional responsibility for missing and injured military personnel. The great majority of their time is devoted to assisting the police, civilian mountain rescue teams and HM Coastguard in civilian search and rescue operations. RAF MRS headquarters staff are co-sited with the MRT at Valley.

Each team is equipped with several 4x4 vehicles including communications, command and control (C3) vehicles with a comprehensive communications suite that allows two-way capability with the Aeronautical Rescue Co-ordination Centre at RAF Kinloss (ARCC Kinloss), search and rescue aircraft, emergency services helicopters, both service and civilian mountain rescue teams, the police and HM Coastguard. Teams are also equipped with satellite communications and mobile phones. Team members train in the hills every weekend, throughout the UK, including immediate first aid and emergency care – often to an advanced standard, similar to search and rescue helicopter crewmen. The equipment they carry is comparable with that of the helicopters and all protocols are NHS-approved.

It is by law that the RAF MRS take the lead whenever an aircraft crashes, largely for reasons of safety and expertise. Effectively, the RAF teams are another vital link in the emergency services chain yet, although occasionally seen in uniform, their standards and practices are compatible with those of the civilian teams. In other words, they think and act, in the main, in exactly the same way as civilian mountain rescue teams, their mission to render the best possible assistance to the casualty by the most effective method available. Besides the standard mountain rescue gear, they carry additional facilities and equipment – such as ordnance, pyrotechnics and fuel – for dealing with the specific hazards associated with aviation incidents. For the first twenty four hours following a crash, team members will frequently be tasked to mount a guard at the crash site. When an aircraft goes down, they will work hand in hand with the military search and rescue helicopters to provide a rapid response. Their resources and experience are particularly invaluable in areas of inhospitable terrain. However, in spring 2001, even they were put to the test, when two American F-15C Eagle jets went missing somewhere in the Cairngorm mountains.

in the beginning...

'Montrose, a nice quiet, grey-stone town on the Scottish east coast was wrapped in mist early on that Saturday morning in 1938. The mist swirled across the airfield as the corporal went from billet to billet. LAC Jack Drummond, flight mechanic, was woken out of a deep sleep by a shout and an urgent hand shaking his shoulder. Someone was standing by his bed. 'Come on airman!' said the corporal, 'we've got to look for a crashed aircraft. Get dressed.'

'Others were being roused as well. He looked at his watch, and groaned. It was five o'clock. He and many others had been out the previous evening and were hungover. Outside the billet was a three ton truck and they piled in, still bleary. They were told that they were on their way to Cairn o' Mount to look for a Hawker Audax, which had crashed round there somewhere. The lorry, in the cold mist of the Montrose dawn, turned out of the gates of RAF Montrose and towards the hills.

'There was then no RAF Mountain Rescue Service. There was scarcely a civilian mountain rescue service. Drummond and his mates went up into the hills with no climbing gear and, for the most part, no climbing experience. But Drummond's incident, which he remembers vividly after fifty five years, was exactly the sort for which the Mountain Rescue Service was formed, five years later, in the intense aerial activity of the Second World War.

'A young Royal Auxiliary Air Force Spitfire pilot, Flight Lieutenant Sandy Johnstone, was also roped in to form a scratch team. In 1939, before World War II broke out, he was an instructor at Prestwick. An Avro Anson crashed in the Rhinns of Kells, west of the Galloway to Ayr road. For a whole day the aircraft remained missing. Johnstone and his fellow flyers conducted continuous aerial searches, without success. At eight the next morning, a shepherd, William McCubbin, left his cottage as usual. From his door he could see Meikle Millyea, and this morning his attention was caught by a wisp of smoke rising from the side of it. Curious, he called his dogs and started walking.

'He reached the spot after an hour, to find a horrifying scene. The Anson had totally burnt out. Three of the crew had been thrown out and were dead. The nearest cottage was some distance away but, on the way there, McCubbin met the postman, Robert Dalziel, doing his rounds in his car. Dalziel turned the car round and went to the police station. Sergeant Hutchinson was just about to go out with a search party, so instead telephoned Prestwick to give the Air Force the news, then started organising the recovery party.

'A stretcher party of forty, including Sandy Johnstone – still weary after a day's continuous flying – was assembled. The party met McCubbin and he guided them to the wreck. Those few words make it sound so easy. In fact, for a party of non-climbers (except for the leader) without proper clothing or equipment, it was a dreadful night. Temperatures were below zero and Sandy Johnstone remembers vividly his breath freezing and ice forming on his clothes. These consisted of a Sidcot flying suit over flannel trousers and a sports jacket, with ordinary brogues without studs. He remembers also having to wade waist-deep through icy streams. Each of the party was issued with a pork pie and a hurricane lamp. Johnstone lost the *former and broke the latter when he fell down a steep slope in the pitch darkness.*

'Reaching the scene at nightfall, they decided it was not practical to do a stretcher carry over the terrain in the dark. What added to the almost bizarre aspects of this episode was that nearby was another crashed aircraft, a civilian Tiger Moth. The pilot, Hugh Barrow, had spotted the Anson and gone down to have a closer look. Then he had been caught in an air pocket and completely lost control. The aeroplane ended up nose-down in a bog; luckily Barrrow and his passenger were able to crawl out unscathed. They found Mrs McCubbin in the cottage. She gave them tea and sympathy and set them on their way.

'Overnight, a few of the stretcher party found room in the tiny McCubbin cottage and others slept, frozen, in a nearby barn. They were the lucky ones, for the barn was only small and some had to sleep in the open with only topcoats over them. At the McCubbin cottage in the morning, things started to look better. Somehow, Mrs McCubbin found enough tea and eggs for forty men. Then they brought the bodies down carrying the stretchers three miles over the rough terrain before they even reached a track of any sort and eventually the main road. One man by this stage was in a piteous state; he had fallen in a bog during the night. His wet clothes had frozen on him, he was suffering from cramp and collapsed when he reached the road.'

Frank Card, 'Whensoever'.

The two aircraft from the United States Air Force base at RAF Lakenheath in Suffolk had been reported overdue from a low flying sortie during the afternoon of the 26 March – their contacts disappearing from radar screens whilst over the Cairngorms on a routine mission. It was very soon apparent that they must have crashed somewhere in the mountains. As the RAF SAR services are responsible for the location of missing military and civilian aircraft within the UK Search and Rescue Region (UKSRR), a major search was immediately launched by the ARCC. RAF mountain rescue teams from Kinloss and Leuchars were called out, together with the Cairngorm, Braemar and Aberdeen civilian teams and search and rescue helicopters from Lossiemouth and Boulmer. RAF Leeming and Tayside MRT were also called out, later that afternoon, to join a search in appalling weather conditions – freezing temperatures and driving snow, and the ever present threat of avalanches.

The initial search included a huge area of the Cairngorms extending as far west as Ben Alder. But, when the ARCC duty controller requested a 'radar replay' from the Distress and Diversion Cell at Prestwick ATCC, it yielded valuable information – crucial to the wreckage being found, close to the summit of Ben Macdui – the UK's second largest mountain. Helicopters, normally the trusty workhorses of search and rescue operations, were forced to play second fiddle to the all weather search and rescue asset – mountain rescue.

Sadly, during the second day of the search, personnel from the Leeming, Aberdeen and Braemar teams located the first body. With the permission of the Procurator Fiscal, the dead pilot was carried down the mountain to a point where he could be winched aboard a rescue helicopter. In desperate conditions, the search for the second airman continued. Further search teams were deployed by helicopter to a point as close to the

Navy 177 from HMS Gannet on exercise with Lomond MRT

crash site as the weather allowed, their journeys completed on foot. High level searches by helicopter were impossible, despite the courageous efforts of the aircrew, as the weather and minimal visibility severely hampered operations. The search intensified, but fresh snow and continuing poor weather made progress very slow. The incident was developing into a major search operation, the like of which had not been seen for years.

By the evening of Thursday 29 March there was still no sign of the second pilot and things were looking grim. So, with a reasonable weather forecast for the next

the wreckage. But one problem was immediately obvious. During the initial search, USAF personnel had employed their own means of transport to the site – their own 'Jolly Green Giant' helicopters.

A tail fin from the double F15-C crash on Ben Macdui

day, a major push was mounted. By morning, visibility had improved considerably. The second pilot was found around noon, completely buried under snow, still attached to his ejection seat, just fifty metres from the main search area. Two USAF armourers were brought up to disarm the seat before the body could be transferred to a waiting snowcat and taken down the mountain for onward relay by helicopter.

Both pilots now accounted for, the next phase – post crash management – began. Normally, mountain rescue would have withdrawn at this point, leaving the longer term crash guard, investigators and the 'crash and smash' team to identify and clear

Despite an improvement in weather conditions, the inhospitable terrain still posed a major risk to any non-mountaineers. To alleviate the problem, a rota system of all five RAF teams was set up, each team taking turns to provide safety cover in one week stints. It was agreed that all non-military personnel, including USAF Board of Investigation personnel, would be accompanied by RAF MRS members whilst on site and that 'gate guardians' be placed at the roadheads. A large container for use as an emergency shelter was uplifted by RAF Chinook and members of RAF Stafford MRT assisted police from Lossiemouth with the siting of anti-pollution booms in the Loch Avon and Lairig Ghru areas to protect

Royal Air Force Kinloss Mountain Rescue Team
Forres, Moray, IV36 3UH
Tel: 01309 672161 Ext 7671

INCIDENT REPORT A	**SERIAL NO: KIN/05/01**
Referring to Form R: 1115	DTG: 06 0830 FEB 01

Nature of incident: Missing walker   **Area**: Torridon
Mil or Civ: Civ   **Date**: 04 Feb 01
Total Personnel assisted this year: Mil: 0 Civ: 10

Times: Alerted: 01:05   Deployed: 01:05
    On Scene: 01:15   RTB/new task: 12.00
Personnel on task: 12   **Team strength**: 36
Total Personnel hours: 121   **Total Vehicle miles**: 150
Other SAR Forces Involved: Northern Police, Torridon MRT, SARDA

Comments on Communications: Poor VHF Comms.
Comments on Equipment: Nil
Comments on IEC: Nil

Weather: Gale force winds, blizzard conditions, very cold.

Narrative:
Chf Tech Price plus 11 were tasked by ARCC Kinloss to assist Torridon MRT in the search for a missing 50 year old male walker who had failed to return from a coastal walk in the area of Alligin Shuas 24/830590. Initial search of the tracks and buildings was carried out by SARDA and MRTs with nothing found. Shortly after commencing a first light search Coastguard helo (MU)observed a person waiving from the bottom of a crag. MRT were deployed to the location by MU. The cas was confirmed as the misper and IEC was carried out by Cpl Steatham KMRT, for lower leg and shoulder injuries. The cas was then lowered down the crag to a boat, uplifted by MU and taken to Broadford hospital. KMRT were stood down by ARCC Kinloss and then returned to weekend training at Torridon.

PRICE S J
Chf Tech
DTL
MRT

Incidents such as the double crash on Ben Macdui – indeed, all incidents – are fully documented both during the incident itself and afterwards. Should any questions arise later, those records provide an objective and accurate reference. The note shows an incident involving a missing walker, as recorded by RAF Kinloss MRT on their return to base. Kenneth Wright, a middle-aged sales representative was out with friends from a mountaineering club when he decided to take a coastal walk by himself whilst the others climbed one of the adjacent mountains in Torridon. At some point in the day he slipped on ice and fell onto a ledge sustaining a broken leg and shoulder injuries. Unable to move, neither could he alert anyone to his plight. It was only when his friends returned from their day's walk to find him missing, that the alarm was raised. RAF Kinloss MRT was in the area at the time on a training exercise. They joined the local Torridon team and three dog handlers in an initial search before dark, without success. At first light, a full scale search was mobilised including a Coastguard helicopter. Shortly afterwards, the walker was spotted waving his arms from the bottom of the crag where he had fallen. A Kinloss team member delivered immediate first aid but the combination of gale force winds, blizzard conditions and steep cliffs were causing severe turbulance – winching from such a precarious position was out of the question. Undeterred, team members lowered the injured man by stretcher onto a boat, which was able to move a safe distance away from the crags. The lift completed, helicopter and casualty made their way to hospital in Skye, and Kinloss team members returned to their weekend training.

against fuel contaminants. Meanwhile, members of the civilian Braemar team provided supervision, escorts and safety advice to the seeming hordes of daily visitors to the site. The entire incident – until every last piece of wreckage had been removed – lasted more than two months, from 26 March to 31 May.

None of this would have been possible without the organisation and co-ordination of the Aeronautical Rescue Co-ordinating Centre – the ARCC – based at RAF Kinloss in the north east of Scotland. There are other rescue co-ordination centres across the world, but this one is unique in the UK. It is one of three resources – along with the RAF Mountain Rescue Service and Search & Rescue Helicopters – established by the Ministry of Defence to provide cover for crashed aircraft – civilian as well as military – and cover for military operations, exercises and training. The Ministry of Defence, as you may by now have realised, is central to our search and rescue service and whilst these facilities were initially provided for military purposes, they are predominantly put to work for civil, aeronautical and land-based search and rescue operations. See, for example, a typical tally on the 'Total Personnel Assisted This Year' category on the Report A form.

In fact, all MOD assets and requests for assistance from the emergency services for a search and rescue capability on land, air or sea, are co-ordinated by the ARCC. The UK Search and Rescue Region (UKSRR) extends to the Faroes in the north, to the boundaries of continental Europe in the south and east and to the mid-Atlantic in the west. Quite a patch! It's a total area of over one million square miles of land and ocean. The centre deals with around 1500 incidents every year – primarily involving military and civil aviation, with much of its day-to-day effort going into the co-ordination of RAF and Royal Navy asset tasking during civilian search and urgent NHS hospital transfers that other agencies cannot fulfil.

When the north Cornish town of Boscastle hit our television screens during the summer of 2004, we watched transfixed at the sheer horror of the film footage rolling time and time again before us. A cataclysmic surge of muddy water swept remorselessly down through the picturesque harbour to the sea, apparently sturdy trees and precious cars bobbing like corks over rocks and

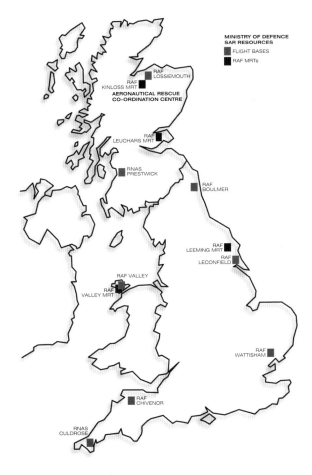

There were seven helicopters in action at the same time, dozens of blue light vehicles, casualty clearing stations working flat out, the air buzzing with non-stop comms traffic.
Police, ambulance and fire service personnel worked alongside coastguard, St John Ambulance and mountain rescue.

under bridges. Thankfully, not a single life was lost. We saw some remarkable rescues - families winched from the tops of their homes, a young man lifted from the roof of his parent's car, inflatable rescue boats ferrying frightened faces to safety. Andy Brelsford, of the Cornwall Rescue Group remembers, 'There were seven helicopters in action at the same time, dozens of blue light vehicles, casualty clearing stations working flat out, the air buzzing with non-stop comms traffic.' Police, ambulance and fire service personnel worked alongside coastguard, St John Ambulance and mountain rescue. It's during incidents such as these – and many less extreme situations – which affect entire communities, the lives of 'ordinary people', that these Ministry of Defence resources prove invaluable, especially in terms of personnel, hardware and co-ordination.

But how does this work in practice? Take something far less dramatic to the national media, but equally as traumatic to the individual involved – a climbing accident. If a mountain rescue team judges that the most effective means of treatment for an injured climber is to be airlifted from the accident site to hospital, how is a helicopter mobilised? Simple really. The team requests the use of a helicopter through the police who, in turn, contact the ARCC and ask for assistance. The co-ordination centre considers the request and carefully selects and tasks the appropriate asset, or assets, bearing in mind factors such as the weather, other incident commitments, crew duty time, serviceability of the helicopter and asset capability. If the weather is too bad for flying – and these aircraft will operate under atrocious conditions – or if the ARCC considers the incident not serious enough to use a helicopter, or that the resources on the ground are perfectly adequate, then the request for a helicopter would probably be declined. If the conditions are unsuitable for a helicopter, the ARCC may offer RAF MRT assets

Chopper stoppers

Whilst the Sea King can fly in most weather conditions, there are limitations. Low cloud, high winds, falling snow and icing all affect the aircraft's capabilities and may prohibit operations completely. In general, helicopters are unable to operate in cloud unless it is possible to hover in visual contact with the ground. High winds and the associated turbulence severely limit a helicopter's ability to pick up and may require casualties to be carried lower down the mountain to a more favourable location. Icing is a problem that affects all aircraft and severely curtails operations. Fuel is also a consideration. Whilst a Sea King is capable of carrying eighteen people, the number drops depending on how long it has to remain in the air before refuelling. At one time, night operations were impossible but the wearing of NVGs by the crew gives much improved night flying capability. All MRT personnel are required to switch off radios and mobile phones before entering the aircraft.

instead.

Teams have learned never to rely entirely on the availability of a helicopter. Sometimes the weather turns foul or mechanical problems mean the helicopter cannot be deployed. Very rarely, they are retasked whilst en route, to more serious incidents, but this is another facet of the ARCC's role. Military operations can, in theory, take precedence over civilian incidents but nobody can remember this ever happening in practice. Indeed, in the popular, high mountain areas such as Snowdonia in Wales, or Lochaber in Scotland, military helicopters are deployed in the majority of rescues. And it's not a one way street. When a major aviation incident

occurs – such as Lockerbie in the late 1980s – the ARCC will readily call upon the help of the civilian mountain rescue service. It's a good working relationship. There's a huge amount of respect and appreciation for the contribution of the civilian teams, and a deep understanding and sympathy towards mountain rescue operations.

With their purpose-designed centre and state of the art computer systems, the ARCC controllers have immediate access to a wide ranging database of emergency services and assets, which enables the logging of incidents in real time. Most of the controlling staff have either served on maritime patrol aircraft or search and rescue helicopters and all have the training, knowledge and connections to cope with a wide range of search related problems and situations. Tom Taylor is a typical example. The UK Mission Control Deputy Manager and ARCC Mountain Rescue representative, Tom has served on the controlling staff for some years. He was a member of the RAF mountain rescue service for twenty two years, serving as leader of both the St Athan and Kinloss teams, joining RCC Pitreavie Castle – predecessor to ARCC Kinloss – in 1992. Over the years, he's played his part, but stresses that 'everyone in the larger search and rescue 'team' contributes including the sitting (down) members.'

With one million square miles of land and ocean to look after – the watery bit clearly not the remit of mountain rescue personnel – the centre also serves as 'mission control' for detecting radio distress signals from mariners in trouble. When Tony Bullimor, round-the-world yachtsman, capsized in the North Atlantic, he activated the personal locator beacon on his boat. That signal was picked up, via satellite, by a co-ordination centre in Australia, which then rallied the necessary resources to save him. It was a New Zealand military vessel which ultimately found him. For those of you with an interest in the detail, the technological sophistication of the new generation personal locator beacons is such that, when activated, they can be identified anywhere on the earth's surface, often within a few hundred metres. At the moment, they're only licensed for maritime use in the UK and it is illegal to use them on land.

The chances are if you come a cropper whilst navigating the oceans of the world, it will be a Nimrod aircraft which comes along to find you. The Nimrod can fly to a distance of around 800 miles from base and then fly a search pattern in the incident area for about seven hours. They have extensive communications equipment which allows them to direct activities when at the scene of the incident. They can drop life rafts and survival equipment by parachute – with amazing accuracy – to survivors in the water, although they are more often tasked to direct shipping and helicopters to the scene of an incident. The RAF maintains one Nimrod at Kinloss, or a suitable diversion airfield, at sixty minutes readiness, twenty-four hours a day, for maritime search and rescue duties, co-ordinated by the ARCC.

Useful as they are, Nimrods are seldom used for land search and rescue operations. That's the domain of military helicopters. Regular visitors to the mountains will no doubt be familiar with the RAF Sea King helicopters. Who can resist a moment's speculation, as the yellow 'chopper' (earlier models were affectionately known as the 'paraffin budgies') passes overhead. Where is it headed? Who for? How serious? The MOD has helicopters located at eight bases around the UK coastline – Boulmer, Chivenor, Leconfield, Lossiemouth, Valley, Wattisham and two

Winching

1. The person being winched obeys the winchman's signals and instructions at all times.

2. They ensure that the earth strap on the winch cable makes contact with the ground before taking hold of the strop – this avoids any danger of static shock from the helicopter. (This can build up very quickly.) The winch operator always attempts to winch the strop to the person rather than the person moving to the strop.

3. They remove their rucksack before attempting to get into the strop and attach it to the hook below the strop.

4. They place the loop of the strop over and behind their head and under each arm, and pull the toggle firmly down in front of them.

5. When ready, they give a thumbs-up sign and stand still. As they are winched up they remain still with their arms to their sides.

6. As they are winched into the aircraft no attempt is made to correct any swing or to attempt entry. The winch operator does this. Once pulled into the cabin they are instructed where to sit, fasten their lap belt and the strop is then removed.

Royal Navy bases at Culdrose and Prestwick. The helicopters are all Westland Sea Kings, 52 foot long with a 70 foot rotor circle and weighing around ten tons. They've been in service for over 35 years and have many miles to travel yet! They can carry up to eighteen passengers, depending on the prevailing weather and the distance of the incident from the helicopter's operating base. They each have a crew of four – two pilots, a radar/winch operator, plus a winchman. They can fly for around six hours at a speed of 140 mph and have an operating radius of 280 miles, although this can be extended by

The winch operator guides the winchman and casualty into the RAF Sea King

refuelling from land bases, oil platforms and suitably equipped ships. All are on 24 hour standby. By day, they must be airborne within 15 minutes, 45 by night.

A comprehensive kit of immediate emergency care enables rear crew members to undertake a wide range of procedures to stabilise and sustain a casualty whilst en route to hospital. All crew members are trained in first aid, but the winchman – who is by definition the first on scene – is trained to Advanced Immediate and Emergency Care (IEC) level, involving the use of drips, drugs and other more advanced techniques. Sea Kings are also

equipped with the latest navigational aids to enable the crew to get to an incident quickly and accurately. It has to be said, however, that when forced to fly low because of thick cloud, the pilot may sometimes navigate by following roads and other ground features. The RAF SAR Sea King fleet is currently being fitted with an advanced Forward Looking Infra Red (FLIR) and low light TV camera installation, the purpose of which is to quickly find the casualty.

Once a Sea King is on scene it can hover, maintain height and position automatically. Once in position, the winch operator can manoeuvre the

aircraft using a remote control beside the main hatch. The electronic winch carries 245 foot of cable, strong enough to lift three adults simultaneously.

In practice, RAF and Royal Navy Sea Kings help mountain rescue teams in a variety of ways. They're very effective at carrying out searches, particularly on open or steep terrain and have an impressive success at night in clear conditions, especially when the casualty or casualties, have even a low-intensity light source – even the lit face of a mobile phone can suffice. They are not suitable for searching dense forestry or urban areas. They can cover comparatively large areas of ground in a relatively short period of time. The search pattern used by the helicopter is usually determined through consultation with the police or rescue team. Sometimes, aerial searches take only a few minutes to find a missing person or group, whereas a similar search by ground personnel could take many hours. At night, helicopters are best used to search specific features such as climbing routes, paths, streams and gullies, although Night Vision Goggles (NVG), radar and Forward Looking Infra Red (FLIR) have extended night searching capability considerably in recent years.

The facility to drop team members, search dogs and equipment on high ground can save time in the

THE CLOCK METHOD OF 'TALKING IN' A RESCUE HELICOPTER

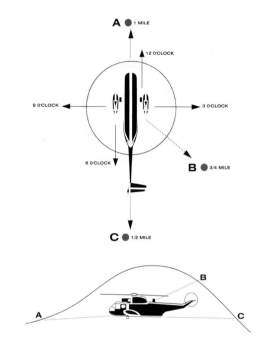

RADIO CALLS

MAN A: 'I'm in your 12 o'clock low one mile.'
HELICOPTER RESPONSE: Maintains course but descends till MAN A says '12 o'clock at the same height.'

MAN B: 'I'm in your 4 o'clock high three quarters of a mile.'
HELICOPTER RESPONSE: Turns to its 4 o'clock and climbs till MAN B says '12 o'clock same height.'

MAN C: 'I'm in your 6 o'clock same height.'
HELICOPTER RESPONSE: Turns 180˚ and maintains height. MAN C transmits when helicopter is at 12 o'clock

order of hours – quite possibly the difference between a successful outcome and tragedy. A helicopter crew, often with the assistance of the rescue team involved, can adapt their methods to suit the circumstances. Let's say, for example, the casualty site is swathed in cloud. The helicopter could fly team members as far up the mountain as possible, then wait for them to bring the casualty below the cloud-base. It's all about teamwork. And by the way, dogs are always tethered when on board, not left free to wander around, else they can cause havoc. On one occasion, a dog managed to free itself from its harness and scuttled straight under the feet of the pilot who was forced to make an emergency landing.

Besides their search capability and their ability to dump rescue team members in the middle of nowhere at a moment's notice, they are ideally suited for the swift evacuation of the injured from the mountainside, either to the nearest roadhead and a waiting ambulance, or directly to hospital.

Operating helicopters in mountains and confined areas is a hazardous task. Sometimes, because of the terrain or lack of a suitable landing site, the pilot may decide to winch members into or out of the machine. There are stringent rules and practices to be adhered to, with no room for sloppy behaviour or individual practices. Whether winching or landing, the down draught produced by a helicopter's rotor blades can easily knock a fifteen stone man off his feet. At such close quarters the noise can be pretty frightening too. So people, livestock and any loose equipment must be fully protected and secured – a loose polythene survival bag sucked into the engine intake or wrapped around a rotor blade could lead to a crash – and all non-essential personnel are moved well away from the winching/landing site. When it comes to transporting team members up the mountain, it's up to the pilot to determine how many passengers he or she can carry. To do this, he'll first establish the weather, turbulence and power margins on scene without the added weight and the implications of carrying others on board – and he or she always has the final say on these matters. Having safely switched off all radio equipment and mobile phones prior to embarking, once on board, personnel must ensure they have no loose head gear, axes are taken from rucksacks, or totally enclosed inside them, and crampons removed. Team members strap into an assigned seat and do not move until told to do so by a crew member.

When a helicopter leaves the scene of an incident, all those on the ground must secure their rucksacks – and any other loose bits and bobs – until the down draught fades. Operating in the mountains, of course, there are no purpose built, perfectly-ironed-flat, landing sites. More than likely the terrain will be rough, uneven and sloping significantly. The rotor blades can come very close to the ground on the upslope side. When disembarking onto a slope, team members are advised to stay beside the helicopter, allowing it to move away. On pick up, a crewman will signal, by 'patting' with his hand, that they adopt a kneeling position and remain still while the helicopter moves in. Praying is optional!

Sometimes, the pilot may choose to drop off the winchman to administer first aid. If he can competently cope with the situation, and mountain rescue team members have not yet reached the incident site, they may not be tasked to the scene.

However, when there are multiple casualties, the casualty is in a dangerous place or if mountaineering expertise is required, the helicopter generally returns from the incident location, following an initial survey,

PHOTO: DAVY GUNN

Winchman and MacInnes Mark 7 stretcher about to enter an RN Sea King

for team assistance. Then again, dependent on the situation, the helicopter crew may decide either to land near the casualty's position or to use the winch. Every situation is judged on its merits.

There are also established procedures for informing the helicopter crew where the rescue team is located on the mountainside. The crew will always

What do you say at times like this? How do you cope with 250 casualties? Never in our history have we dealt with something like this.

know where they are flying to and usually have a map reference. Once team members sight the helicopter, they can initially guide the crew to them using the radio. A smoke or flare is used to indicate the exact position – with the added advantage that it indicates to the pilot the approximate strength and direction of the wind, critical in determining the flight approach. If a smoke or flare are unavailable then the incident site can be marked with something bright, or a team member can stand apart from the others facing the helicopter with arms extended in a 'Y' shape. At night, a strobe light, flashing torch or camera flash is used, but caution is always exercised to prevent destroying the crew's night vision. Once it becomes evident that the helicopter crew is responding to the strobe or flare, and is near enough to positively locate the casualty's position, a couple of torches pointed at the ground are usually all that's necessary.

If the rescue team has radio contact, the helicopter can easily be talked in using what is known as the 'clock method'. Something like, 'I am in your 3 o'clock, 1000 foot lower, at two miles.' As the helicopter responds, refinements can be made until positive identification has been established.

The relationship between helicopter crews and mountain rescue team members is exceptionally positive. Most teams train regularly with either RAF or Royal Navy crews in order to understand each other's capabilities. Training typically takes the form of mock scenarios and safety or operational briefings with the focus on learning and practicing the strict operating procedures of embarking and alighting from a helicopter when it is on the ground or hovering close to it.

All well and good. But what happens when something really big happens? An incident so serious it involves every resource, every agency, every ounce of endeavour an organisation has to offer – with such devastating and far reaching consequences that the effects are still reverberating many years after the event, marking forever the minds of those who were there? The evening of 21 December 1988 was precisely such an occasion.

PHOTO: RAF KINLOSS MRT

Dave 'Heavy' Whalley

With only a few short days until Christmas, people everywhere were returning home to their loved ones, making their last minute preparations, looking forward to a break from work, a chance to relax, and party. But, for the families of a quiet Scottish market town, the two hundred and fifty nine passengers aboard a Pan American jumbo jet bound for New York, and emergency services across the UK, all that was about to change. At 7.02pm, a terrorist bomb exploded aboard the Boeing 747 killing everyone on board and eleven on the ground. Thirty eight minutes after take off from Heathrow, the plane had reached an altitude of 31,000 feet. At Shanwick Ocean Control, first one blip appeared on the radar screen, then three more, then five as the shattered pieces of the airliner fell from the skies. The impact of the crash was so strong, a blast of 1.6 on the Richter scale was registered at British Geological Survey stations in the south of Scotland. Minutes later, eye witnesses described a 'fireball' falling from the sky. It was virtually raining fire. The plane had broken up in mid-air so suddenly that the crew were unable to send any message, and so dramatically that wreckage and debris were scattered for miles – across the border as far south as Kielder Forest. The scene of the Lockerbie air disaster remains a 'Crime Scene' to this day.

In the cold light of the morning following the crash, the full horror of the devastation became apparent. The wings of the 747 had struck the A74, engulfing cars in flames. The fuselage had landed on a housing estate demolishing several homes, the four engines landed in the town, and there was a gash 155 feet wide and 196 feet long slewed between two rows of houses. Twisted fragments of metal littered streets and gardens. Bodies lay strewn around the towns and fields, often mutilated beyond recognition. The most abiding image for Frank Card, in his history of the RAF MRS was 'the sight of the cockpit and nose of the 747, half buried in a field at Thundergarth Mains three miles from the town, the bodies of the crew still inside.'

At times like this – undoubtedly Britain's worst air disaster to date – a contingency plan swings into action which brings into play every possible appropriate resource. All the agencies – the emergency services, local authorities and voluntary organisations – involved in dealing with the incident have to be co-ordinated. Once alerted, the ARCC deploys search and rescue helicopters and RAF mountain rescue teams to the area. When the aircraft has been located, the responsibility for co-ordinating the activities of all the responding agencies passes to the police. Effectively, the police chair a co-ordinating group at which all agencies are represented, and a police incident officer co-ordinates activities at the incident site. A Forward Control Centre is established close to the site and a rendezvous point designated to cope with the influx of emergency service vehicles.

Mountain rescue teams are deployed as fast as possible on arrival, to search for and recover survivors, provide specialist advice to civil emergency services, assist with the cordoning off of the crash site and the provision of communications. A Temporary Restricted Air (TRA) space is quickly invoked, followed by an Emergency Restriction to Flying Regulations (ERFR) – the area and altitude dependent on conditions. The fire services specialise in the immediate area of the crash site in dealing with fire and toxic hazards. A press centre is established for relatives and journalists wanting information.

On that fateful evening in 1988, Dave 'Heavy' Whalley, team leader of Leuchars MRT, was just beginning to enjoy a spot of well earned leave. With more than a hint of irony, he recalls his parting shot to colleagues. 'Don't call me unless a jumbo jet crashes in the mountains.' It's the sort of thing you might say, never imagining for one moment it will happen. And, of course, it never does. Until that once. It was the first day of his break, just as he was making plans with his girlfriend, when the call came through. At first he assumed it was a wind-up. His deputy having a laugh. But then 'Raz' suggested he turn the telly on and see for himself.

'I switched on. It was like a dream – a nightmare. I quickly sorted my gear, left my girlfriend and shot down to base. The troops were dashing about – the usual organised chaos before the brief. What do you say at times like this? How do you cope with 250 casualties? Never in our history have we had to deal with something like this.

'Already, troops from RAF Leeming were airborne for Lockerbie with RAF Stafford in hot pursuit. Raz left with the team whilst I followed behind. Before leaving I phoned the police as the motorway was closed. Very kindly, they escorted me all the way but we travelled so fast that my dog Teallach, who was in the back of the car, was even more terrified than normal! It was a weird experience driving down the M74 with no cars in sight. As we approached Lockerbie, the police had blocked all entrances and the press were everywhere. There was wreckage all over the road and the sky was illuminated with reflections from burning fires. It was also full of helicopters – the scene could easily have been Vietnam. An engine had impacted into the road, aircraft panels had landed on roofs, there were open suitcases and Christmas presents spread about – quite an incredible scene. The smell of fuel was overpowering – a smell that will remain with me for the rest of my life.

'The police took me to where the troops were located, held back whilst Leeming MRT carried out an initial search. On their journey up, they'd been listening to the radio and hoping to save lives or help casualties. But there was little to do. The scene was utter mayhem and confusion with a real danger from the uncontrollable fires. But very quickly, and with quiet efficiency, the head of the RAF MRTs, the Inspector of Land Rescue, Sqn Ldr Bill Gault, set up control.

'I was told to keep the teams happy, find a base and control the helicopters to avoid the real chance of a mid-air collision. Communications with the outside world were non-existent. The satellite phones had broken down and landlines were severely damaged by the crash. Somehow, we managed to set up a landing site for the choppers and gained some type of control into search areas – extremely important for flight safety. Eventually, the police gave us a briefing in the school, which was to become the co-ordination centre for the disaster. There were over five hundred people present including ambulance, fire and police personnel, coastguards, voluntary services and RAF and civilian teams. There was, as one would expect, chaos. The civilian teams from the Borders looked to the RAF teams for guidance. As luck would have it, we'd just

carried out exercises in the Borders a few months previously when the scenario was an aircraft crash. Through this exercise we had made key contacts, which were to prove invaluable in the days ahead.

'It was decided at the briefing to wait until first light, as it was too dangerous to search in the dark with the fires still raging. Frustrating for the troops who were keen to go out and help, but they accepted they had to sit and wait. Few slept.

'Information was hard to gain and I decided to recce on my own. Lockerbie is a small town, situated just off the motorway near the Borders. It has the smallest police, fire and ambulance authority in Scotland, which was completely overwhelmed. A local policeman and myself went around the crash site in the dark. It was a scene from hell – bodies, wreckage, Christmas presents and clothes all over the place. The smell of fuel and death filled the air. Fires still burned fiercely. These scenes will remain in my mind forever. Nothing can prepare you for this. Even after a lifetime of rescues, it was hard to accept what I saw and felt. We located the main wreckage, which gave us vital information to guide our search areas the following morning.

'The plan was prioritised into a casualty count and a map of all the wreckage and main aircraft parts. The RAF teams had done this many times before, but never on this scale. By now, based on reports and what we had seen, we reckoned the chances of live casualties being found were extremely limited. The brief to the troops was one of the most difficult ever given. We made sure they worked in pairs with an old head alongside a newer troop member and explained what horrors they might expect to find. In the days to come, the RAF, civilian rescue teams and SARDA handlers were all to do a magnificent job in the face of the untold death and destruction. I will never forget their efforts. After the brief we gave each team specific areas to search. We explained the importance of looking for

the aircraft's black box, which was found very quickly by a Stafford team member. This impressed the police and especially the 'men in suits' who had arrived in the middle of the night.

'By now it was common knowledge this wasn't a normal crash and that terrorism was the probable cause of all the death and destruction. The teams worked together in shifts listing wreckage and casualties on the 'crash map'. The debriefings with team members were harrowing but all worked very professionally, gathering information, reporting to base, and going out to another area for more of the same. The casualties were left where they fell but mountain rescue personnel covered the bodies with fleeces and clothing and a policeman guarded each casualty, once located. As the list grew, the enormity of what had taken place began to sink in. Everything was now being treated as a scene of crime. There were countless members of the press present, desperate for information. To make matters worse, some mindless individuals had entered the area, removing possessions from some casualties.

'At times of great tragedy, the basic things in life come to the fore, and heroes emerge. The WRVS established a base in the school kitchen and produced meals 24 hours a day for several weeks. These ladies brought a touch of sanity to the scene and they worked tirelessly throughout. Helicopters carrying experienced mountain rescue team members flew across the area to plot the wreckage from low-level photographs. Casualties were found in the main town and in the fields across a vast area. By the end of a long first day the troops were tired and very stressed, but had located three quarters of the casualties. We tried to relax by going into the village but, the town had been thrown into mayhem. Many local people had been killed, several streets had been demolished and wreckage was

Navy 177 from HMS Gannet on exercise with Lomond MRT

everywhere. However, some of the pubs were open. The locals, who knew we had been working very hard in a difficult task, made us very welcome. We all felt guilty drinking and trying to relax but it was what we all needed because it served as a safety valve. Very few slept that night. Many had nightmares and were aware that it was going to continue the next day.

'Within a short period of time things took on a degree of order. The police, other emergency services and teams had risen to the challenge and knew exactly what to do. Mountain rescue troops flew out with the helicopters locating casualties and wreckage. Everything was plotted – casualties, belongings, parts of the aircraft were found and marked. Additional resources were mobilised, making life better for us all. Members of the world's media were ever present, all wanting information and to record how we felt. By the end of the third day, we had accounted for all the casualties. Now, there was little left for us to do and so we pulled out but, before so doing, we submitted all of the 'crash maps' to the police. They highlighted the enormity of the tragedy. Each life a tragedy to their families and friends, lives lost because of evil. The local mountain rescue teams worked with the search dogs for weeks after we left, searching for human remains and other items.

'On my return to Leuchars, I was tasked with reporting on the event and, most importantly, identifying the lessons learned. Many members of the team came to see me, disturbed at what they had seen and done. In those days, there was no training in post-traumatic stress – all counselling was carried out 'off the cuff'. Little did I realise how this would affect me later on in a fairly serious way. We have now moved on and manage stress in a much more sophisticated manner.

'For a while, mountain rescue was the flavour of the month. Teams received letters from the Prime Minister, Members of Parliament and many others. A few weeks later the Kegworth aircrash took place. Leeming and Stafford team members did it all again. This time they saved lives and what a difference that made to all the troops. It took a long time to go back to Lockerbie but I did. The garden of Remembrance and the Memorial are impressive. The village is back to normal and life goes on, but I found it easy to visualise what had happened on that dark night and will never forget it. I thought I would never see such a scene again but a few years later I was one of the first on scene at the Shackleton crash on Harris and then the Chinook on the Mull of Kintyre.

'Mountain rescue has been built from years of experience, dedication and service. God willing, nothing like Lockerbie will happen again. But in this mad world in which we live, you never know. All of the RAF teams are now part of the UK's Disaster Planning structure and all team members have the qualities necessary to rise to any scenario. Mountain rescue and SARDA all did an exceptional job during Lockerbie. We are all very proud of the part we played.'

Bill Batson, who left the RAF MRS in April 2004 after twenty six years, having latterly served as chief instructor, was Leeming team leader at the time – the first team on scene. The team's parent station had been effectively rebuilt in preparation for the arrival of the F3 Tornado. It was while the team was celebrating the grand opening of the new section that news of the crash came in. Bill's account of the incident appeared in the *Mountain Rescue Magazine*.

'Memories, flashbacks, call them what you will – a host of images from that first night remain. A fire hose lying unattended and writhing like some great serpent, casually spouting precious water into the street, forming great, useless puddles where we knew the water supply had been damaged. Sherwood Crescent, or what was left of it. Burning. A 747 engine, almost intact, driven deep into the

the structured way an RN helicopter conducts a search

Early one November, the alarm was raised when a man in his 30s was reported missing from his home in Tillicoultry, Central Scotland. He was known to be suffering from depression and the police were concerned that he might harm himself. A search was commenced in accordance with 'Missing Person' data (see Chapter 6). The police requested a member of the local MRT fly with the helicopter crew and direct them to local beauty spots as well as tracks and roads leading to the hills. A search of these locations plus known locations of previous suicide attempts was conducted for approximately three hours without success. Failing light and low fuel ended the day's search, but the MRT was put on standby that evening in the event that further information became available. The missing person was found dead in his car the following day by police.

The following report describes the flight pattern of the helicopter whilst carrying out the search. It illustrates the meticulous manner in which details of the route were recorded so a full account could be relayed to the search managers. To follow the route in more detail, refer to Ordnance Survey 'Landranger' map number 57.

From	To	Search Area
Forthbank landing site Stirling (15.00 hrs)	Gartmorn Dam	Flew directly to the dam, following a tree-lined track at GR 900933 to the dam head. Circumnavigated the dam and overflew the track leading to Gartmornhill Farm. Overflew the road leading from Longriggs and the road in the surrounding wooded area.
Gartmorn Dam	Old Railway Tillicoultry	Followed the railway to Dollar, paying particular attention to laybys parking areas, etc.
Dollar	Rumbling Bridge	Followed the Devon on the S side. Inspected the waterfall at 005988 and what could be seen at Rumbling Bridge.
Rumbling Bridge	Dollar	Flew on the N side of the Devon to Dollar.
Dollar	Castle Campbell	Checked all of the car parks and what could be seen of the quarry. Checked the track leading into Hillfoot Hill.
Castle Campbell	Castlehill Reservoir	NE over Maiden's Well to Glenquey reservoir. Followed track to main road (A823) and Castlehill reservoir. Flew round Castlehill reservoir.
Castlehill Reservoir	Glensherup Reservoir	Followed road north then cut off for Glensherup reservoir. Checked this then headed back to the main road.
Glensherup Reservoir	Upper Glendevon Reservoir	Flew up main road then cut up for the Frandy fish farm. Followed road up to Backhills Farm.
Upper Glendevon Reservoir	Tillicoultry	Flew up Broich Burn and down the Gannel burn to Tilly. Checked the quarry and the road leading up to it.
Tillicoultry	Menstrie	Followed back road to Alva. Checked Farriers and Woodland Park. Followed back road to Menstrie.
Menstrie	Sherrifmuir Road Logie	Followed track to Lossburn reservoir. Headed on to Sherrifmuir Road. SE down road checking Cocksburns Wood and Archer's car parks. Headed on down to Logie.
Logie	Tillicoultry	Headed E just S of the main road (A91) checking various lanes etc.
Tillicoultry	Dollar	Overflew the Harviesoun Estate and back road to Dollar.
Dollar	Muckhart	Overflew back road from Dollar to Muckhart covering the various farms on the way.
Muckhart	Stirling	Headed S of the King O' Muirs Road (B9140) then W, following the general line of the road to Manor Powis. Then to Forthbank landing at about 16.30 hrs.

tarmac road by the impact, only feet from a group of houses, all occupied. The fleet of yellow council transit vans, waiting patiently for the bodies to be brought in by the helicopters, moving off one at a time like some surreal taxi rank, to carry their silent passengers to the town hall. You need a lot of space for 250 bodies. Difficult times indeed.'

Even now, with the no-holds-barred, technicolour imagery – both real and contrived – which assaults our senses on an almost daily basis, it is hard to imagine the awful sights, sounds and smells which confronted Dave Whalley and his colleagues during those dark December days. Frank Card told of images which never made the front pages – although one wonders whether they might do these days. 'Bodies – of adults, children and babies –- were to be seen in fields, caught against fences like fish in a net, on rooftops, some still strapped in their seats.' But this happens in mountain rescue. And it's worth mentioning that it wasn't only the local teams who gave their time. Search dog handlers and rescue team members from across Scotland, England and Wales left their homes and families, and work commitments, to do what they could. Lancashire handler Peter Durst described arriving with his dog Jan at midnight and spending 'all night searching in the hills to the east of the town, finding eleven of the victims. We stayed for eight days over the Christmas period, working in the midst of tragedy.' True, it was an extraordinary situation - sometimes, you have to be prepared to see and do things which are quite shocking and alien to your everyday experience.

Team members respond to tragedy in different ways – some cope well and others less so. Most will try their best to treat incidents involving death and serious injury as 'jobs to be done'. Indeed, these are the very occasions when resolve, skill and efficiency must prevail. Emotions, sympathy and feelings must be cast to one side for the duration else they could easily impact on the smooth and safe operation of the rescue. It is never easy confronting death –

particularly for the first time. Peter Hancock was on his very first call out with the RAF Valley MRT in the late 1950s when he came face to face with tragedy.

'The first call out one never forgets. Mine was at the back of Ro Wen above the Conwy Valley. A young midshipman's Vampire had crashed into the hill of hard volcanic rock. I still clearly recall his name. The explosion, presumably on impact, and the engine behind his seat having driven through him, had resulted in extensive fragmentation and scattering of his and the plane's remains over a wide area. I helped to search for and gather the body fragments into a small cotton bag bearing his name. This was quite an experience for an eighteen year old. Yet it was natural to take it in one's stride. Immediately afterwards, in the local pub with post-event beer and crisps, I remember the eerie sensation of feeling my own fingers feeding crisps into my mouth having just picked up and felt similar pieces of anatomy of the unfortunate young pilot. However, I recall no signs of post-event trauma on my part or on the rest of the team.

'Today, after similarly horrendous events, professional rescuers such as the police and firefighters can have problems living with the experience and counselling is provided. It is interesting to ponder the change and the reason for it. Was it the MRT spirit and sense of military duty and our childhood wartime experiences with air raids and bomb-sites that enabled us to take it all in our stride, or was it because we talked frankly and openly about the events, viewing each rescue, however tense and dramatic, as no big deal?'

On a lighter note – banter, camaraderie, and humour are powerful tools. If the casualty can be involved then all the better. This applies to RAF teams as much as their civilian colleagues. There is no better first aid treatment than joking with a casualty whose broken leg is giving them a bit of pain! The curious mix of professionalism and banter carries everyone along on a high and always helps steer individuals through their fatigue, pain or bad weather. Such a 'style' was clearly evident in the early days of the RAF MRT service as its longest serving member, and a distinguished team leader, Ray (Sunshine) Sefton recalls.

'Additionally, the party carried a one inch Verey pistol, cartridges and some thunder flashes for signalling with. The illuminators were good for getting off the hill at night, and it was not unknown for the thunder flashes to be used for fishing. Health and safety was not a problem. We loaded the Bedford with all the kit plus twenty jerry cans of petrol, the troops climbed in, smoked and sang or played cards all the way to the base. Civilian clothes were not allowed – we travelled in Service kit with berets!!

'Social life at this time was brilliant. The troops could easily attract the girls like a magnet. There was usually a good ceilidh or dance on in the villages. We took our boots off and danced until the wee small hours. Usually we had somebody who could play the accordion or guitar and had great sing songs in the pubs. Sometimes the guitar player didn't buy a pint all night.'

In the matter of uniforms and magnets, some might agree, things never change.

A female casualty is evacuated from Ben Nevis by RAF winchman from Rescue 137 watched by members of the Lochaber MRT

chapter eight

LEARNING THE ROPES

On an exacting rescue each moment is remembered with amazing clarity, for one lives at a higher pitch than usual when risks must be taken which wouldn't normally be contemplated. Only too often it is a fight for life: there is nothing more satisfying than the successful evacuation of a critically injured person on a highly technical rescue, where a single mistake could result in death for the casualty. It is, on a grand scale, a game of chance in which Nature holds most of the cards.
Hamish MacInnes

Mountain rescue, under the extreme conditions and enormous pressure that some incidents demand, may indeed be a 'game of chance' but, as Edward Whymper observed, 'the true satisfaction is to be found not in courting unknown dangers for which you are ill prepared, but in matching your own skill and experience and the danger and difficulties of which you are aware.' Nature may hold a good many of the cards, but the training practices and distillation of experience – sometimes measured in hundreds of years – which are central to every rescue team are surely the aces up their collective sleeves?

The general perception of mountain rescue work is that it is highly dangerous and that team members place their lives on the line every time they sally forth to rescue some incompetent, ill-clad numpty who should know better than to be in the mountains in the first place! We think, by now, you'll have taken our point that this is very, very rarely the case – walkers and climbers, in general, are not numpties, their gear is more often than not of the highest order, and

rescuers do not court danger. They tend to value their own skins and have better things to do with their time, quite frankly. Yes, of course, there are exceptions – and these stories are seized on only too gladly by those who enjoy a more sensationalist viewpoint. And, yes, there are risks involved. In fact, there have been a few fatal accidents, over the years, involving rescue team members.

In 1983, Mike Rudall, team leader of the Bridgend MRT, was killed when protecting a casualty from falling rocks. In 1987, Harry Lawrie, leader of the Killin team was killed when he was thrown from an RAF helicopter which crashed as it attempted to touch down on a steep mountain slope and, in 1992, Phil Jones, team leader of Assynt MRT was killed on a training exercise when he was carried by a small slab avalanche over an outcrop onto boulders.

Mike Rudall had been out on a navigation exercise with a group of novice team members. It was the first day of May. The Morlais MRT (now Central Beacons MRT) had just recovered a young

PHOTO: JEZ HUNTER

PHOTO: IAN DAWSON

person with a knee injury from an adjacent mountain, Fan Fawr, when news came over their radio that people coming off the hill had reported whistle blasts in the vicinity of Pen y Fan. At the same time, Mike – from his position on the shoulder of Pen y Fan – called on the radio and agreed to investigate. He eventually came across a young scout, one of a party of four, who had fallen sustaining a leg injury. By this time, the Morlais team had completed the first rescue and evacuation and were on their way to assist Mike with the scout. As they began the steep climb to the summit, their radios crackled into life. There was a shout, 'Below!!' Then silence, even when further radio calls were made. Fearing that something very serious had happened, the Morlais team made their way as quickly as possible up to the summit, where they met one of the trainee members, left there by Mike as a radio link. He was deeply shocked, but managed to update them with what information he had.

The injured scout had fallen on steep ground below the summit. He was being attended by Mike, and a passing walker Daryl Camplin, when a large block of rock detached itself and began to tumble towards the boy. Instinctively, both Mike and Daryl laid over the lad to protect him. Both were struck by the rock and knocked about 140 foot down the near vertical face and very steep ground. They came to rest at the bottom of the crag, although the scout remained where he had originally fallen. One member on the ground with Mike, who had witnessed the accident, managed to make his way down to Mike and Daryl. He did not know where he was on the rockface – the whole mountain was now swathed in mist and it had started to snow.

Peter Howells, deputy team leader of Morlais at the time, called for help from the Brecon and Bridgend teams and the RAF helicopter from

The Lomond team practicing stretcher handling on steep ground at Aberfoyle quarry

Brawdy. Then using ropes for the 500 foot descent, he and Dave Llewellyn climbed down a very hostile and fragile cliff to the bottom of the crag where they eventually located both casualties. To their absolute horror, they found that Mike had been killed outright by the falling rock. Daryl had received multiple, but not life-threatening, injuries. The first party from the Brecon team arrived with equipment and together they lowered Daryl to the base of the cliff. As the weather worsened, and now in the dark of the night, the helicopter came and lifted him from the mountain.

A little later, Bridgend team members arrived to relieve the Brecon party on scene. They conducted an all night vigil with Mike, carrying him out to the roadhead at daybreak. In the meantime, the original scout casualty was located by Morlais team members, near the top of the cliff face, where he was treated and evacuated off the mountain.

Incidents like these are quite exceptional. Archie Roy's accident – mentioned earlier – when he slipped through a snow bridge whilst out on a search with the Lomond team, is perhaps more typical.

'I was relaxing after dinner around 7.00pm on 2 January 2001, when the call came to attend a search on Ben Lomond for a party of four who were overdue. Fresh snow had fallen on the Ben that day and it had been bitterly cold during the entire festive season. Bob Sharp and I met up with the rest of the team at Rowardennan and while the main party was being organised to conduct a search on the south east slopes of the mountain, we took off up the South East Ridge, the main tourist route, to sweep to the summit and provide a radio link.

'Snow conditions were poor with fresh unconsolidated snow making progress awkward. At around 2000 feet, I dropped into one of the many concealed holes in the snow and as I hit the bottom there was a whip-like crack just above my knee. There was an instant spasm of pain and I knew immediately something had given way. Bob heard my yell and ran back to help. I was in considerable pain, which made it extremely difficult for him to pull me out of the hole onto more stable ground. It was pretty obvious that I was going nowhere fast and we agreed that I should remain where I was, and that he should continue with our original task. He had very mixed feelings about leaving me but I insisted he did, as the radio link was crucial to the operation of the overall search. By this time, the team had been deployed below us on the hillside and had commenced a sweep search of the most likely areas. Following additional reports from relatives and friends, the number of missing persons had risen to eight. A Royal Navy Sea King from Prestwick was scrambled to assist.

'As I sat alone on the hillside, I recalled some sound advice given to me when I joined the team. "Make sure you are self-sufficient because you never know what might happen." I had everything I needed for a long night on the mountain although I did contemplate how long it would take to crawl the 1200 feet descent to the Land Rover track! Meanwhile, the search continued and, for about four hours, I watched the torches of the team sweep the mountain in search of the missing persons.

'Around midnight, the team successfully located six of the missing eight. They were quickly evacuated by the helicopter which later returned to uplift me from the mountain. The remaining two persons were reported to have entered the forest and, although the search continued, they were not located until first light. The winchman helped me onto a stretcher and I was winched on board the helicopter. I was taken immediately by ambulance to hospital in Stirling – alongside one of the lost casualties from the search, who was suffering from severe hypothermia. As to my injury, a surgeon diagnosed a severed main tendon at the base of a quad muscle, which required immediate surgery. This was followed by three

risky business - spikie the jack russell goes missing!

Darkness had been closing in when Spikie's owner Iain Anderson and his three dogs picked their way down the mountain A'Chrois, near Arrochar in Scotland. As Iain, a member of Arrochar MRT, reached the half way point down the mountain, he came to a large clump of heather in the fading light and decided to jump over it. But as he glanced over his shoulder to check where his dogs were, he realised he had just leapt a narrow crevice which ran deep into the mountainside. Before he could react Spikie, a twelve year old bitch, had plunged into the abyss. Iain couldn't see her, but he could hear her pitiful yelps far below as he called her.

Iain ran down the mountain with his other two dogs and called his friend Mark Leyland, Arrochar team leader. At first light next day, Iain, rescue team members and a group of friends set off to climb up the mountain to the fissure down which Spikie had vanished. However, despite scrambling 120 feet down the narrow fissure they could find no trace of the dog. Exhausted, they returned to the top and agreed Spikie must have perished at the bottom of the craggy crevice several hundred feet below.

The following day – almost 48 hours after Spikie had vanished – a disconsolate Iain and his girlfriend Fiona Jones, returned to the scene yet again and once more tried calling Spikie's name. Astonishingly, they heard a slight whimper, then a yelp and finally a full-blown bark. While Fiona kept watch at the edge of the abyss, Iain returned to Arrochar and alerted once more the Arrochar team. This time,

PHOTO: LES GALLACHER

Spikie with owner and team member Iain Anderson following his dramatic rescue

fully equipped and buoyed with the knowledge Spikie was still alive, the party set up ropes and belays for the hazardous descent into the crevasse. Once again Iain climbed into the deep and narrow fissure squeezing through subterranean rocks. At one point he escaped serious injury when a falling rock missed him by inches. He managed to scramble across a slippery ledge and his torch picked out Spikie trapped on a ledge twenty feet long on the other side of what appeared to be another deep crevice. Iain's rope wasn't long enough to reach Spikie and a second difficult descent with a longer rope had to be made to rescue the frightened animal.

By this time it was dark and raining heavily. As Iain returned to the spot 150 foot below the surface he managed to get to the ledge and lay his hands on the shivering and bedraggled Spikie. He could see that she was terrified and deep in shock and refused to come forward even just a few inches so that he could grab hold of her. By inching forwards very slowing he managed to grab hold of her and stuck her inside the empty rucksack he had tied to his safety harness. Spikie was then hauled, with Iain, to the surface by the team.

Iain said after the rescue, that even though the odds were stacked up against the dog surviving the fall, he never gave up hope she would somehow still be alive. The following day, following a check by the local vet she was pronounced fit and well with only a minor cut on her head to show for her ordeal.

months in plaster then a similar period of physiotherapy. I did, however, achieve my personal goal of climbing to the top of a 3000 foot mountain in mid-May later that year.

'My memories of that night are many and varied. It was a surreal experience and I found myself taking a detached look at events as they unfolded. I was reminded how important it is to take nothing for granted during mountaineering activity, to be prepared to handle anything that might come along and to live with the consequences. I also witnessed the professionalism and expertise of my friends and colleagues and I reflected on the sobering experience of being both rescuer and casualty.'

The first principle of the emergency services – look after your own safety first – is well established in mountain rescue work. So, when a team is called by the police to an incident, members know what skills and resources are essential to effect a successful outcome. Teams train and equip themselves in full knowledge of what is required and the risks involved. They train in all kinds of weather conditions, day and night, focusing on the skills and procedures relevant to the sort of accidents they're likely to meet. They get to know their 'patch' extremely well – especially the regular 'black spots'.

Risk assessment typically follows the line of identifying the hazards, who is at risk and how the risks are managed. Whilst there are many similarities between teams, the differences will broadly reflect a team's geographical area. Teams operating in lowland areas may focus on the risks associated with search operations, whereas those in the more mountainous areas will develop risk assessments which include the implications of extreme weather, avalanche and steep cliff rescue.

In other words, teams work within the boundaries of their skills and expertise. Individuals rarely work alone. Team members support one another, work in small groups and look to the safety of each other. When they find themselves dangling on the end of a rope or balanced on steep exposed ground, safety systems ensure that high risk

with nature which left them frightened for their own lives – a very rare phenomenon. Everyone involved listed numerous bruises the next day. Unfortunately, some newspaper reports chose to sensationalise the story with an eye-catching tale of two foolish and apparently ungrateful rock climbers snubbing their heroic rescuers. Readers were invited to contact the newdesk with the identities of 'Britain's most selfish climbers.'

Teams must practice stretcher handling on the sort of terrain commonly found on their home patch in the best and worst of conditions they are likely to meet, day or night

The UK had suffered a generous dose of winter weather and there was more to come. Many mountain rescue teams had already been involved in rescuing lost souls in the diabolical conditions. In the Lake District alone, seven teams were out during the afternoon, working with RAF Stafford mountain rescue team members, covering six separate incidents. The two men in question had climbed Skiddaw in worsening weather, but

procedures are fail safe. That said, there are occasions when the elements do their best to conspire against even the best laid plans. It is precisely at those moments when the rigorous training instilled into team members – combined with the basic human instinct to survive – comes into its own.

In 2001, while the rest of the country was looking forward to celebrating the start of a shiny new year, Keswick team members were involved in a battle

found conditions so severe that they were forced to ground 100 metres from the summit, at 930 metres. They raised the alarm by mobile phone but were then out of range for the next couple of hours. Team members eventually spoke to them just ten minutes before finding them, and asked them to shout.

Conditions were so bad, with extreme wind and blown ice crystals that, crawling up to the cairn which sheltered them, it was impossible to either see or hear them until they were literally alongside. Actually getting to them was not easy – the only way to move was in scrums of three members. And once they got there, all they could do was get the hell out of it. Downwind. And fast. One of the casualties had already lost both his gloves when the bivvi bag he had been trying to open blew up like a sail and tore the gloves right off. During the rescue, several items of equipment were lost, including a stretcher and two headguards – not exactly lightweight! It was three days later before the stretcher was found.

The two men were told unless they got out, they would die. They were dragged off the mountain, everyone involved getting off the way they were blown. There was little alternative. But bruised or otherwise, everyone survived. Why the paper treated the story as they did is anybody's guess. Pandering to the stereotype, perhaps? Reckless, self-centred mountaineers who put others at risk in their search for kicks? And heroic mountain rescuers risking their lives for others, neither of which captures the truth. We've said it before, but those who find themselves in trouble tend not to be reckless, ill-equipped or thoughtless, just unlucky. There are very few mountain rescue team members who would see themselves as heroes. They're generally an unassuming bunch who prefer to see the efforts of the team applauded, rather than those of any one individual, however remarkable.

The day after the news report, the team made it quite clear that it had been a 'difficult rescue – generally well reported.' As for the 'ungrateful climbers' – they had, in fact, thanked the team expressing their own view that their rescuers were all heroes. And far from making quick their escape they had provided their names and addresses as routine.

HAZARD 1	Steep snow, ice and rock faces
RISKS/LEVEL	Possibility of falls leading to injury/death. Low risk
AT RISK	Team members/casualties
CONTROL MEASURES	Only team members with appropriate skills to carry out steep face rescues
	Routes chosen are appropriate to team member's abilities and prevailing conditions
	Appropriate personal protective equipment to be used
	The possibility of injury is understood and accepted by all involved

HAZARD 2	Weather
RISKS/LEVEL	Exposure to extreme weather conditions, hypothermia, exhaustion, frostnip or frostbite, particularly on prolonged exposed cliff rescues. Low risk
	Snow blindness, sunburn. Very low risk
	Avalanche or cornice collapse. Extremely low risk
AT RISK	Team members/ casualties
CONTROL MEASURES	Specialist and local mountain weather forecasts consulted where available
	Personal protective equipment appropriate to weather conditions carried/used by team members
	Casualty equipment carried - appropriate to weather conditions
	Team members trained in avalanche awareness and avoidance techniques

Extract taken from a team's risk assessment for technical rescues in winter

standard operating procedures working with helicopters

● With the aircraft on the ground

Helmets should always be worn.

A helicopter should never be approached during start-up or shut down.

Only approach or leave the helicopter when cleared to do so by a member of the flight crew giving a 'thumbs-up' signal.

Approach and leave only in the direction indicated by the aircrew. (For the Sea King helicopter this is between 1 o'clock and 3 o'clock.) Never approach or leave near the tail, or out of sight of the aircrew.

Ensure there is no loose gear. Radios should be turned off. Keep your rucksack in your hands and make sure no damage is caused to the aircraft by ice axes or crampons.

Once in the helicopter, strap into your assigned seat and do not move until told to do so by a member of the crew.

● When winching is involved

Obey the winchman's signals and instructions at all times.

When signalled to do so, remove your seat strap and move towards the door of the helicopter. First, however, the winchman will help you into the strop, making you secure and will direct you to the door opening. Your rucksack (or someone else's) will be hung on the grabhook.

The winch operator will now winch in the cable and by doing so, draw you out of the aircraft and into a position hanging just outside the door. The winch operator will then lower you to the ground. During lowering, the arms should be kept by the sides, avoid the temptation to grasp the cable as doing this could result in you falling out of the strop. Initially you may feel a slight jerk and an increase in the rate of descent. Don't worry, this is quite normal.

Once on the ground, make sure you have a secure footing before removing the strop but DO NOT anchor yourself to anything while still attached to the aircraft. Remove the strop FIRST then remove your rusksack from the grabhook. At this point you may, if you wish, give a 'thumbs-up' indication to the winch operator, who will be watching from the doorway of the helicopter. At this signal, or as soon as he sees that you are safely removed from the strop, he will winch in the cable ready for the next lower. You are now free to belay if necessary, to await the arrival of the remainder of the party.

● Winching up into the helicopter

This is basically a reversal of the above.

Allow the earthing strap on the winch cable to make contact with the ground before taking hold of the strop – this avoids any danger of static shock from the helicopter. The winch operator will attempt to winch the strop to you rather than you moving to get the strop.

Attach your rucksack to the grabhook BEFORE you slip the strop over your head.

Place the strop over your head and under each arm, pull the toggle firmly down. When ready give a 'thumbs-up' sign and then stand still – do not

A 'Stokes' litter being hoisted into a RN Sea King from a point on 'Curved Ridge' in Glencoe. The rope technique is called 'highlining'.

move around in an attempt to get what you believe is a better winching position once you are in the strop. As you are winched in, do not attempt to correct any swing nor attempt your own entry into the cabin. Allow the operator to do this. You will be pulled into the cabin with your back to the aircraft. Then do as indicated by the winch operator.

They realised what an epic it had been for everyone involved and that, but for their mobile phone, they would not have survived.

Because mountain rescue is voluntary, teams don't have a statutory responsibility to comply with government legislation such as the Health and Safety at Work Act. But they do have a duty of care to safeguard themselves and others. Central to this duty is a requirement to demonstrate to the police that they operate safe practices. Standard Operating Procedures (SOPs) do exactly that.

So what do teams actually do when they train? Well, they practice and develop the kinds of skills you'd expect – first aid, casualty handling, radio communications, security on steep ground, avalanche awareness, pyrotechnics, searching, working with helicopters, incident management and so on. Teams that work in the high mountains where climbing is popular, such as Glencoe in Scotland, Keswick in the Lake District and Ogwen Valley in Wales, work on the technical skills required to recover climbers from steep rock faces or snow and ice filled gullies. Those that operate in open moorland and forested areas, such as teams in the mid-Pennines or Northumberland National Park, might devote less time to technical wizardry and more to search techniques and management. But, whatever the differences, some skills are fundamental to the effective operation of all mountain rescue teams, whatever piece of mud and rock they call home – namely, how to treat and handle a casualty, communicate by radio and work with helicopters.

First aid training is especially important. Team members may train to various levels – basic, advanced, emergency technician and so on – but everyone must have the basic skills to save life. Far better the person first on scene comes equipped with the confidence to set about dealing with a casualty's injuries than be forced to hang impotently

Rigging for Rescue using the Piken Pivot method

around, unable to do anything. More often than not, training is carried out in-house or using various qualifying organisations such as the St John or the British Association of Ski Patrollers. Some teams have links with hospital A&E departments, which permit members to shadow doctors during busy times. Others use 'professional casualties' to beef up their expertise. Bob Sharp recalls his own experience of medicine in the front line.

'Alaisdair, a local GP and our medical officer at the time had a very good relationship with one of the hospitals in Glasgow. He regularly worked in the A&E department and arranged for interested team members (who were brave enough) to spend a Friday or Saturday night in the department. We would arrive around 9.00pm, don white jackets and wait for the first casualty to arrive. Usually, little happened until the early hours although, on one occasion, we had only been there ten minutes when we heard the sound of someone crying in pain. A young woman wearing a wedding gown and clutching her hand in anguish entered the cubicle. "Come and look at this," said Alaisdair. Knowingly, he whispered that we were about to witness a miracle! The girl had been married earlier that day and was sporting a wedding ring that was clearly too small. It was constricting blood flow to her finger which, in turn, had swollen out of all proportion. Actually, her predicament was quite serious. There was a danger the ring would damage blood and nerve supplies with disastrous consequences. Alaisdair produced a small, circular cutting wheel which, with the help of a little lubricant, he used to cut through the ring. Within a few seconds the ring split open and popped off her finger. Pain relief was immediate, although when she saw her damaged ring we were treated to another flood of tears!

'Through the course of the evening and early

morning, we experienced many and varied injuries and ailments. On one occasion, a young lad accompanied by a police officer walked into the hospital with a meat cleaver loosely embedded in his head. Steadying the offending item with his hands, he was adamant that it had dropped onto his head as he walked under a bridge on his way home! The lad was so inebriated that he required very little painkiller when stitched up. On another occasion, a middle-aged man was carried into the hospital with serious abdominal pains. He was ashen and looked really bad. It transpired he had a history of kidney stones and was clearly suffering. Following confirmation of the problem, Alaisdair proceeded to administer a pain killing injection – or rather, he suggested that I administer the injection! Having previously practiced on oranges, I prepared to inject my biggest 'orange' to date. Once again, Alaisdair said we would be surprised by the speed of reaction. True to his word, within about five minutes, the man's colour reappeared and he visibly relaxed. He started to talk and thank us for removing such a dreadful pain. I've never forgotten that moment. Relieving pain is one of the most significant things you can do as a first aider. And one of the best ways to do this is with a bit of TLC and reassurance.

'The A&E experience is not for everyone. I recall one visit when two of us were exposed to a variety of blood curdling scenarios (well, what do you expect in Glasgow on a Saturday night?) The eventual downfall (literally) of my colleague began when we overheard a discussion between two young consultants about who would attend a road traffic accident. Neither wanted to go as it seemed likely the driver would have to have his leg amputated at the scene. We never found out what happened but the chat sent my colleague into a very pensive mood. Matters got worse when we attended a youth with a dislocated shoulder joint. We both stood by as Alaisdair manoeuvred the boy's shoulder in preparation for a

Rigging for Rescue using the Kootenay Highline System

final tug. We were both asked to help steady the boy. My eyes were firmly planted on the boy's shoulder, but I couldn't help notice that Jim was beginning to sway unnaturally backwards and forwards. Just as Alaisdair tugged, my colleague dropped to the floor like a lead weight! I managed to break his fall and position him into a recovery position. I suppose he was unconscious for a few seconds but none too worse for his ordeal. After dusting him off and administering copious quantities of hot tea, he said he'd had enough and wished to go home – so much for macho mountain man!

'So, this is not everyone's cup of tea and not every team is able to arrange hospital experience for their members. The advantage is it allows team members to condense more medical experiences into one night than they might see in several years in the mountains. A 'second best' is first aid training with so-called 'professional casualties'. Dotted around the country, there are groups of people who are very competent at mimicking the sounds and sights of people with serious injuries and they offer their expertise to rescue teams and other groups. I'm not too sure what motivates these people, but they're very competent at what they do. Perhaps they're out of work actors? To give a flavour of what they do let me recall a training session we had one dark, wintry night in January.

'Our training officer told us to assemble at a local woodland car park and be prepared for a 'helicopter crash'. With all manner of first aid equipment to hand, members assembled at the due time. Within moments, the unmistakable sounds of people in pain and distress were heard from within the woods. The helicopter had obviously crashed! We quickly made our way into the wood to find a vast number of people lying on the ground, in bushes and across rocks suffering from the most horrific injuries. My first encounter was somewhat unusual. Rather than meeting a person, I came across a leg complete with protruding thigh bone and torn flesh! Nobody was in sight. For a moment I had difficulty deciding what to do. How do you resuscitate a broken leg? So, I tucked the leg under my arm and followed the blood trail that led along a path. The owner was not far away and in clear need of urgent first aid treatment. Three of us dealt with the person's injuries, but I never did get to find out what we should have done with his leg!

'Experiences like this are superb training. Not only are they shocking and dramatic, but they're

Knit one, purl one...

very real. Most important, because you don't know the casualties and because their screams and injuries are authentic, you tend to treat the incident as if it were real.'

Teams typically set up annual training programmes, meeting on a regular basis across the year, either on outdoor exercises – getting to know their own terrain and the nature and range of incidents they are likely to meet – or indoors, in the form of lectures and demonstrations. Training is usually carried out 'in house', using the skills and knowledge of the more experienced team members, but outside specialists might be used where expertise is lacking or where external validation is required. Some teams encourage members to undertake mountain leadership and instructor courses.

Bob Kerr is a member of the Assynt MRT (the most northerly in the UK). In the autumn of 2003, he was one of nine mountain rescue team members to put themselves through a 'fun-packed summer mountain leader training course,' delivered over three weekends by three qualified instructors.

'Doing the course this way, it meant we had to spend three Friday nights and two Saturday nights out socialising. We'll never think of Grantown on Spey as a quiet village again! But why did we do the course, what was covered and what were some of the highlights?

'The nine members came from two Scottish

Technical training for water rescue

teams, neither with the luxury of members holding instructor qualifications. However, both teams wanted to help develop their members' mountaineering skills, through recognised qualifications, thus reducing the risks faced when out on training exercises or call outs.

'The syllabus of the summer mountain leader training course covers key skills like navigation, river

A full depth slab avalanche on the Great Slab of Coire an Lochain, Cairngorms.

crossings, basic ropework, emergency evacuations, weather, group management and environmental knowledge. The instructors covered the syllabus very well and delivered it in a relaxed cheerful manner. Initially, we thought the course may become disjointed, carried out over three weekends instead of six days in a row. But this wasn't the case. Everyone was fresh and enthusiastic throughout. Splitting the course provided useful periods of consolidation that helped the delegates' learning process and suited work commitments.

'Some of the most memorable parts included the complete immersion of someone doing a river crossing; singing soprano during abseils; topless karaoke in Grantown on Spey; malt whisky tasting at the overnight camp; and the majority of one navigation group being 180 degrees out! Not bad for a group of mountain rescuers!'

Training boards also focus on the special skills of winter mountaineering. The mountains in winter attract walkers and climbers in vast numbers – with the attendant consequences. When the snow and ice conditions are just right and the sky is painted wall-to-wall azure, nothing can touch it for sheer breathtaking beauty and sporting pleasure - but people beware! Reduced daylight hours, extra physical effort and additional risks – not to mention the capricious mountain weather – make the very slim line between safety and challenge that much finer. Trip over your shoelaces on a summer path and you might bruise your knee. Do the same in winter and you could fall 1000 feet – or trigger an avalanche.

Thankfully, there's a great deal known about the weather factors that lead to high avalanche risk. But avalanche prediction is not a perfect science and an unfortunate few find themselves taking an unexpected rollercoaster every year. One such group, a party of six on a basic winter skills training week, were climbing an easy route on Lochnager called 'Black Spout Gully' led by their two instructors. They were divided into two lots of three, each comprising an instructor climbing solo and unroped, and a climbing pair, roped together. One group was positioned just below the exit to the gully and under a small cornice of snow. The roped pair had set up a belay in the middle of the gully and were about to tackle the cornice. The other group were about 200 feet below. The roped pair were anchored to the snow for security whilst their instructor was ahead looking for suitable anchors. At this moment, an avalanche released from the right wall of the gully. It missed the higher party but hit the lower group, sweeping all three down to the bottom of the gully and out of sight. Miraculously, all three survived the fall. One of the roped climbers and the instructor were uninjured, but their companion suffered ankle and shoulder injuries.

Not all those who are avalanched are so fortunate. Two male climbers in their mid-thirties were overdue from climbing a winter route in Glen Cova in the Southern Cairngorms. Following an extensive search involving three rescue teams they were both found dead at the bottom of the gully. One was completely buried and the other partly buried in the avalanche debris and both had sustained injuries which would have proved instantly fatal. The manner in which they were roped together suggested they were retreating from the gully. What we'll never know is were they overtaken by an avalanche from above? Or, as often occurs, did they trigger the avalanche themselves?

There's a common thread to both these stories – the wisdom of which might be questioned – and that's the use of security ropes on snow and ice. If one climber falls, they invariably take the other one with them. Consequently, accidents tend to involve both climbers. But, it's not just climbers who are caught out, as a couple of walkers discovered to their cost in early January 1997. Swept down a

what you need to know about avalanches

Avalanches are less common in the UK than elsewhere in Europe but they do occur, sometimes with tragic results. They've been reported in the English and Welsh mountains but, more typically, avalanches are a Scottish problem. Anyone who ventures into the mountains in winter should know something about the basic theory behind their evaluation. The ability to make an informed judgement about a snow slope and what to do if involved in an avalanche (either as a victim or observer) are critically important skills.

A knowledge of how snow accumulates and how avalanches occur is important in avoiding them. Snow cover is usually made up of layers. It's the way in which these layers are bonded together that determines how stable or unstable the snow layer is. Weather history and the nature of the terrain are also factors. Avalanches occur when the bond between layers weakens and gravity takes over.

PHOTO: DAVY GUNN

Find by a Golden Retriever. The casualty was buried two metres down. The picture, taken in the Alps, is a good demonstration of avalanche debris

Avalanches tend to be described according to the type of breakaway – single point or entire area (loose or slab), entire slope or only part (full or partial depth), channeled or not (confined or unconfined). They can also be airborne or flowing. Powder avalanches – not common in the UK – usually take place during or just after a snowfall and involve the surface layer of snow sliding over a harder underlayer. A wet snow avalanche sets like concrete when it comes to a halt, making it impossible to move if caught up in one. Wind slab avalanches are more common and result from a build up of windborne snow accumulating in sheltered areas.

So how do you avoid avalanche? There are three things to consider – weather, the snow pack and the terrain.

● Weather. Heavy snowfall signals a high risk, particularly in the 24 hours following the fall. A sudden rise in temperature may help undermine upper layers and high winds will increase the risk of wind slab. Weather history is critical. If, for example, snow has fallen for several days accompanied by high winds from the north, then it's a fair bet that south facing slopes will be at high risk from wind slab avalanches.

● Snow pack. Signs of recent avalanches indicate that similar facing slopes may also be avalanche prone. If the snow cracks easily or collapses when placed under pressure then the snow is unstable.

● Terrain. Slopes that are convex in nature are more likely to slide than concave ones. Lee slopes and wind-sheltered gullies are at high risk, as are slopes angled between 30 and 45 degrees.

Mountaineers can also take advantage of the sportscotland avalanche information service, which *gives an avalanche risk on a five point scale. This service covers key mountain areas in Scotland but it only provides a risk estimate (albeit based on highly sound testing). Anyone going into the winter mountains – anywhere in the UK – should always be conscious of the risk and use as much information as possible to make an informed judgement. If there is any doubt about a snowslope, then stay away or select an alternative route such as a ridge where the risks are minimal.*

What do you do if caught in an avalanche? There's a lot of theory and many practical tips on this subject – roll to one side, use your ice axe to slow down your movement, release your rucksack, try to swim on your back to keep close to the surface. It's also suggested that if you are caught then, as the avalanche slows down, try very hard to make as much room for your face and try to thrust a limb out of the snow. Whilst these ideas make sense, often the speed of the avalanches, disorientation or accompanying injuries probably make any attempt to escape fruitless.

If you see someone caught in an avalanche then it is critical you note their start position (if possible) and certainly the last point seen. Do not take your eyes off that point. Then quickly make a check for further danger and call for help. It is vital to carry out an initial search within minutes by probing the snow with a walking pole or ice axe. Experience has shown that the first fifteen minutes are critical. The likelihood of finding someone alive falls from 90% to 30% within half an hour.

Cairngorm mountain by a slab avalanche, knocked unconscious and buried to a depth of eight feet, they survived – thanks to a remarkable combination of luck, effort and sheer dogged determination. Their story is featured in the classic text on avalanches *A Chance in a Million* by Bob Barton and Blyth Wright.

'Coire an Lochain in the Cairngorm massif is a classic avalanche site. The full depth springtime avalanche on the Great Slab is a well known feature of the Scottish mountain calendar. Its date is always a subject of conjecture but it has occurred as early as 11 April and, on at least one occasion, as late as the third week of June. The lochans which give the coire its name nestle in a bowl at the foot of the Great Slab but avalanches from all round the back of the coire run out on to the surface of the lochans, which usually consists of ice up to half a metre thick. Occasionally, the huge impact of a large avalanche smashes the ice and drives it forwards out of the lochans into a pile of blocks metres deep.

'Saturday, 11 January 1997, was not particularly inviting from the point of view of hill walking. However, on that day three mountaineers, accompanied by a pet dog, approached Coire an Lochain, bound for Ben Macdui. Two of the walkers were about to be involved in one of the most remarkable avalanche survivals ever known. Visibility was poor and winds were about 30 mph from the south west. There had been some fresh snow and avalanche risk was known to be high. At the bottom of the slope which leads out of the coire and onto the plateau, the group stopped to review the situation. One member of the party decided that he didn't wish to continue and turned back. The remaining two carried on, along with the dog.

'Generally, an avalanche-safe route exists close to the path ascending the west side of the coire. However, it requires to be followed closely and may not be easy to follow in poor visibility. Both to the right and particularly, to the left, just beyond the Twin

Members of Lomond MRT undertake helicopter training with Navy 177 from HMS Gannet

Burns, steeper slopes exist which are frequent avalanche paths. It appears that the party wandered in the poor visibility too far left, on to that part of the slope where the maximum accumulation of new windslab lay. The result was not long delayed and without warning, both were carried off in a large slab avalanche.

'The exact sequence of events is unclear in the minds of both victims, but what is certain is that they were carried from near the plateau, down through a vertical interval of about 500 feet, onto the lochan and buried. It seems that both were unconscious for a time and that initially they were completely buried at a depth of about eight feet. At that stage, their survival for more than a few minutes would have been most unlikely.

'Then came the event which transformed their no-hope situation into one which, almost incredibly, gave them a chance of survival. It seems that, as the full force of the avalanche came to bear upon the surface of the lochan, the ice fractured and allowed a substantial mass of the debris to pour into the lochan itself. As this happened, cracks and crevasses opened up in the debris. One of the victims regained consciousness. He was aware of being buried, trapped. However, he was also aware of being able to breathe. Astonishingly, he could hear the dog barking. It had evidently survived the avalanche. He shouted and was immensely relieved to receive a reply from his companion but from what position or direction he was unable to determine.

'He gradually became aware of his position, which was bizarre in the extreme. He was buried, still at a depth of eight feet, with his body held immobile in the snow. However, his face was exposed in the wall of one of the crevasses which had opened up and he had a clear air passage through to the surface. He could hear his companion, but still not identify his position. The dog stood guard at the top of the crevasse, barking

furiously. The will to survive took charge. The only part of his body which he could move was his head and that only in a restricted, nodding fashion. Using this ability, over a period of time which must have amounted to hours, he succeeded in burrowing down to his right hand which as fate would have it, was held in the debris just above the left breast pocket of his jacket. Having freed his hand, he was then able to open the pocket, which contained his compass. Using this implement as a shovel, he then proceeded to dig himself out of the snow.

'Darkness was falling and relief at his own extrication was tempered by concern for his companion. He was alive, but where was he? Then the first survivor made the amazing discovery that the two of them had actually been buried beside each other, with the second man's arm touching the first man's leg. The second victim was much further from the wall of the crevasse but eventually, with the aid of his ice axe which he had held onto, he was also liberated.

'It would have been understandable if, exhausted by their efforts, the pair had stayed put and awaited rescue. After all, their friend who had turned back would have been concerned at their failure to arrive back before dark and might already have alerted the rescue services. This is in fact what had happened and the Cairngorm mountain rescue team was gathering to search for them. However, the two survivors showed further evidence of their self-reliance by setting off back in the dark, to reach the car park at the ski area just as the rescue team was setting out. An ironic final footnote to this remarkable story is that, even without their own heroic efforts, the two men might well have survived. When a couple of days later, they came to relate their tale at Glenmore Lodge they revealed that, at no time during their burial had they felt cold. They would probably have survived until the rescue team's arrival and, in addition, the faithful dog would

skills required for mountain rescue

Mountain Rescue (England & Wales) established a set of National Training Guidelines in the 1990s. The list itemises the key areas of work and the skills required by a full hill member of a rescue team.

The Full Hill Member should be able to:–
• **Personal Kit.** Pass a check of personal equipment and clothing required for the conditions within the team's area. State the requirements for the inspection of personal protective equipment as it relates to mountain rescue equipment.
• **First Aid.** Hold a current first aid qualification.
• **Hypothermia.** State the causes, recognition and treatment of exhaustion hypothermia.
• **Navigation.** Demonstrate the ability to produce and navigate to a six figure grid reference, night or day, in any weather conditions.
• **Equipment.** Demonstrate and relate the use and storage of team equipment. Relate the general requirements for inspection and maintenance of team equipment.
• **Stretcher.** Assemble the team's current stretchers and prepare for the loading of a casualty, night or day, with and without a casualty bag.
• **Casualty Handling.** As part of a team assist with the handling, carrying and transporting of a loaded stretcher across varied terrain.

• **Rope Work.** State the types of rope in common use and the required inspection and care. Tie these knots (as listed by British Mountaineering Council Technical Committee) – bowline, bowline on a bight, figure of eight on a bight, overhand knot on a bight, fisherman's bend, double fisherman's bend, clove hitch, tape knot.
• **Belays and Abseiling.** Set up a personal belay and belay another person. Abseil down a vertical face.
• **Rescue from Heights.** Assist in the setting up of a belay system, capable of taking the load of a stretcher, casualty and handlers, for a vertical lift. Assist in the preparation of a stretcher for horizontal and vertical lowers and assist in the lower of a stretcher.
• **Search Techniques.** As a member of a search party, carry out the search of an area using current acceptable field techniques.
• **Helicopters.** Have a working knowledge of the requirements for working safely around military and civilian helicopters.
• **Control.** Have a working knowledge of the major functions performed at a rescue and search control, including the normal chain of command. Be aware of briefing and debriefing requirements at a personal level.
• **Radio.** Operate vehicle and hill radio sets in command use and pass messages.

still have been barking to indicate their position.'

Had the team been required to search for the two walkers in the avalanche debris, they would have carried out a sweep search using avalanche probes. These are strong, thin steel rods up to ten feet in length that are pushed into the snow to feel for the buried person. A sweep search of avalanche debris is highly disciplined. Members stand shoulder to shoulder and probe the ground immediately in front of them. On command, they move forwards a couple of feet and probe again, and so on, until a probe detects something.

Besides teams sharing their in-house expertise, the two national committees also arrange courses and seminars on a wide variety of topics, often with visiting experts – sometimes from mountain regions outside the UK. In 2001, the Mountain Rescue Council invited Canadian Kirk Mauthner to introduce his Rigging for Rescue techniques to a small group of team members from across England and Wales. RAF mountain rescue team members had already attended the Canadian course and implemented many of his techniques. Based in Invermere, British Columbia, between the Rockies and the Purcell Mountains, Kurt has been involved in mountain rescue since the early seventies. This first, and subsequent courses, encouraged teams to evaluate the dynamics of whatever rigging systems they were currently using, to look outside their own capabilities at what other teams and other countries – were doing. There were new techniques to learn, ideas to exchange and develop, as well as the satisfaction of reaffirming existing team skills. The expectation with courses such as Rigging for Rescue is that those selected to attend will cascade their new found knowledge down to their colleagues through regional and team based training sessions.

The concept of learning from our mountain rescue colleagues across the water is not new. In 1986, inspired by a presentation on search management at a National Association of Search and Rescue (NASAR) Conference, and a subsequent course in Florida, Peter Howells determined to introduce some of the methods to search operations in the UK. Two years later, the first one week Search Management course was launched. Attended by police officers and mountain rescue personnel, and taught by Rick LaValla and Skip Stoffell of the Emergency Response Institute (ERI) in the States, it was a roaring success, and continues to develop. In the late 1990s, Dr Don Cooper joined the instructor team, originally to teach Tracking and Clue Finding. He began research into the original work on search theory, collaborating along the way with Jack Frost, a specialist in the subject contracted to the US Coastguard. Between them they published a number of articles in the USA which described the application of search theory to land search – which, in turn, led to a complete revision of the MRC Search Planning and Management course.

The Tracking, Clue Finding and Field Skills courses, initiated in the early 1990s, were influenced by the work of the US Border patrol and ex-military personnel. The theory is that any missing person will leave many clues as they pass through an area. The course teaches searchers how to read those clues.

Teams operate within the bounds of accepted mountaineering practices to ensure – as far as is reasonably possible – that the safety of individual team members, casualties and any one else directly involved is never compromised.

The police also have a common law duty of care when civilian personnel act under their control or direction. To discharge this duty of care, the Chief Constable must be satisfied that members of mountain rescue teams have the equipment necessary and can demonstrate appropriate skill levels. On a national level, both the mountain rescue committees have devised sets of guidelines to help teams meet their duty of care. For example,

Mountain Rescue (England & Wales) has identified a set of basic skills which it considers fundamental to all team members, which includes first aid, knowledge of personal kit, navigation skills, rope work and working with helicopters. It has also established a set of skills important for party leaders such as team briefing, managing the scene of an accident and communications. The individual teams are free to develop and use these as they feel appropriate to their own circumstances. In Scotland, a broader set of guidelines covers the same basic topics along with avalanche evaluation. They focus on the need for training to be structured, monitored and recorded, with team members deployed according to their skills and abilities.

The training undertaken by teams is always monitored. Some teams use personal logbooks which might include a checklist of skills, in which team members must demonstrate they are competent. On a lighter note, it's not unusual – in these days of public awareness, education and mountain rescue 'brand' building – for teams to take the brave step of inviting outside comment on their training and standards, in the form of journalistic review. Felicity Martin was one such member of the press who spent a day training with the Tayside team.

'I remembered the warning about the deafening noise and blasting downdraught, but in the rush, I forgot that the sill of the door was at an awkward height. A shove from behind helped me to make an undignified entry on my belly into the Sea King helicopter. Within seconds, we were airborne and through the open door I watched the Glen disappear in the gloaming as the crew from the RAF helicopter whisked us up on to a 500 metre high ridge in the hills. A thumbs up from the winchman and we unclipped our seatbelts and quickly exited. Crouching together in the heather like frightened animals, we waited for the assault on our senses to fade with the departing chopper. My first mountain rescue training exercise had begun.

'Night was falling rapidly and I pulled up my hood against the wintry blast that emphasised our exposure. Looking around, I saw that the broad hillside ahead seemed to be covered with demented glowworms as a scattering of lights flickered back and forth across it. Other members of the team had arrived ahead of us and were searching for accident victims. The next few minutes passed in a blur as we hurried to make the most of the one hour flying time from the RAF. We located and administered first aid to two 'casualties' who were then stretchered back to the landing area and airlifted off one by one.

'By now, the rain was lashing and it was difficult to hear each other against the gusting wind, but the team leader managed to brief us on phase two of the exercise. We were to look for three more casualties using a fine search. Initially, with our backs to the wind, we maintained the line despite having to clamber over peat hags. Powerful torches caught mountain hares scattering like crazy snowballs from under our feet and a lone red grouse that resolutely refused to budge. The weather deteriorated rapidly. Turning into the teeth of the gale, I staggered like a drunk into the buffeting wind. With eyes screwed almost shut against the stinging hail we were no longer looking – just surviving – and before long the team regrouped and abandoned the search. Had it been a genuine emergency we would have changed our approach and kept going – all night if necessary, although as the team leader said, "The number one priority is to bring the whole team off safely."

'The attractions of being in a team are similar to those of being in a mountaineering club – regular trips to the hills combined with a good social scene – but with the added benefit of helping others and receiving regular training in first aid, ropework and other valuable skills. The volunteers I accompanied included a teacher, a lecturer, an engineer and a manager with Scottish Natural Heritage. Individuals can only commit to the team if they have a public spirited employer prepared to release them at a moment's notice to attend a rescue. As well as spending time on rescues and exercises, everyone takes part in the regular round of fundraising activities to cover the cost of equipment.

'Given the strong social and community spirit shown by teams I wondered why, when women make up nearly 50% of mountaineering club members, there are so few of them in mountain rescue. Across Scotland, women make up barely 5% of teams. Some people say it may be that a macho image puts off a lot of female would-be members. Despite the atrocious weather conditions, there was certainly nothing in our night exercise that other women in my mountaineering club could not have coped with. Everything was carefully controlled and we even managed a few laughs along the way. Perhaps if mountain rescuers were lauded more for their judgement and skills than for their brawn, more women would be inclined to join the teams. They are likely to receive an encouraging reception – and even the occasional shove in the backside when necessary.'

Now there's a thought! Why so few women in mountain rescue? Five per cent is about right overall, although it's extremely variable. Some teams have no women while others have around 20%. Perhaps there is a perception of gung-ho, macho men. Or earnest, grey haired men with beards and pipes, in plaid shirts and corduroy trousers. You might spot the occasional stereotype amongst the sea of fleece and technical fabrics but, in the main, that's just what those images are – stereotypes – unduly fixed mental impressions. Women have been involved with mountain rescue for many years. Molly Porter was a founder member of the Cairngorm team in 1964 and its leader for ten years from 1972 to 1981 – probably the first female rescue team leader in the UK. Her contribution to the Cairngorm team was

exceptional. She was, for many years, both team leader and secretary, and also ran the training programme for team members. Her colleagues at the time were in awe of the exceptional amount of time she invested in team affairs. Besides mountain rescue, she was a qualified mountain guide and took part in many mountaineering expeditions across the world, at one point gaining the interesting accolade of 'Britain's Highest Housewife' from *Woman's Own* magazine.

Ted Burton, leader of Buxton MRT for sixteen years through the seventies and eighties, recalls his own team having five female members during his leadership – all able mountaineers. Even in those earlier days of equal opportunities they were treated no differently than their male colleagues. 'They were simply considered as team members,' said Ted. 'In fact, I often used an all-female section on incidents and felt nothing unusual in that, knowing they could, and would, do whatever was asked of them. Indeed, when dealing with young female casualties I always considered them invaluable. My wife Eve was one of these and is still a very active member thirty odd years on.'

So what was it that made the young Eve want to join a rescue team in the first place? Is that motivation the same amongst today's newer female team recruits? Eve recalls just 'drifting into' mountain rescue after meeting a member of the Buxton team through Ted's work connections. 'In those days', she explains, 'there weren't the formal application and training procedures we have today. People came along, joined in at training and call outs and, if you were good enough – and you fitted in and had something to offer – you were in. Ted and I were both into the outdoors – walking and climbing – so it was a natural extension of that interest. If you were good enough to be on the hill – and you could navigate – you were accepted.'

Recognition of just how far into mountain rescue

Eve had drifted came in late 2004 when she was recommended for a Mountain Rescue Council Distinguished Service Award for her work not just with her own team, but for the Peak District's regional organisation and the national body – only the third woman to receive the award in England and Wales, and the first in England. Approaching her seventieth birthday, she is as committed as ever, still active on the hill and intends to remain so for as long as she is able.

Women may well have been part of the civilian teams for over thirty years but it was 1992 before the RAF conceded the point, accepting SAC Donna Flanagan at RAF Leeming as the first female novice. Women had already been absorbed into the command structure, were flying as combat aircrew and mounting armed guards at RAF station gates, so it seemed somewhat churlish to deny them the opportunity to join the mountain rescue service. As would be expected, female team members were asked to reach exactly the same standards as their male counterparts, echoing Eve Burton's sentiments. If you had the skills – and the commitment – you were in.

Eve's feeling is that motivation, especially amongst newer female recruits might not be the same nowadays. But then perhaps things were simpler thirty, forty years ago. The path might well already have been trodden many years ahead of them, the equal ability of women in the rescue environment already established, but younger women – who've grown up in an atmosphere of constantly having to prove themselves equal in the workplace – might naturally assume they also have to do that on the hill.

Gail Todd was inspired to join Rossendale & Pendle after witnessing the Aberglaslyn team deal with her friend's accident in North Wales. On a sunny day in June, whilst some of their party went up Snowdon, and the less energetic hit the shops, Gail and three others had decided to take a gentle walk by the river. Freshly fed and watered and wearing all the right gear, her friend's leg simply went from under her on the gravel, snapping her tibia and fibula. It was clear from the angle of her foot what she had done, so the other three set about immobilising it before two of them went for help. Only 150 yards from a back road, they had been unable to attract any attention. An ambulance was called and they, in turn, called out the team. Paramedics were unable to move the casualty so the rescue team loaded her up and carried her to the waiting ambulance. Chatting to the team members as they made their way down the path, someone mentioned there were rescue teams local to Gail's home in Lancashire. By pure coincidence, only a month later an item appeared in the local paper, inviting interested people to an open day at the Rossendale team headquarters. It could be argued Gail's drift into mountain rescue was no different to Eve's. In fact, we suspect most of those deeply involved in mountain rescue never quite imagined they would become quite so involved; as Eve observed, if you have something to offer, the work has a way of drawing you deeper and deeper into its web, until you begin to wonder how life was without it! If proof were ever required, you only have to take a look at the number of long service awards totting quietly up in the background – twenty, thirty, forty years and counting. Gail remained a support member of the team for twelve months, helping with fundraising and joining in socially, attending the odd lecture. Eventually it was suggested she sign up as a trainee, and two years on she is fully operational. And her motivation? 'I enjoy being part of a team, learning new skills, getting to do things I've never done before. And I want to take myself as far as I can with it.'

In an organisation and culture where most people involved get their 'high' from being out there at the sharp end, it often bemuses operational team

Extract from a typical MRT Training Logbook

5.2   Safety on steep ground (summer conditions)

	Signed by	Date
5.2.1 Identifying when it is appropriate to use safety measures		
5.2.2 Awareness of objective dangers		
5.2.3 Basic knot tying		
5.2.4 Improvised harnesses		
5.2.5 Use of natural anchors (spikes, threads)		
5.2.6 Linking anchors		
5.2.7 Tying on to anchors		
5.2.8 Different belaying techniques and devices used		
5.2.9 How to hold a fall		
5.2.10 How to exit from the belay system		
5.2.11 How to perform lowers		
5.2.12 Descending using basic equipment		
5.2.13 How to use a classic abseil		
5.2.14 Ascending using basic equipment		
5.2.15 How to set up a safe abseil and how to solve common problems which may arise		

members when someone appears to derive as big a buzz from taking a support role. Bob Sharp has spoken of his experiences as member and team leader of a busy Scottish team, but what about co-author Judy Whiteside?

'The fact that mountain rescue even existed in this country had never entered my consciousness until I found myself sitting opposite an old work colleague – subsequently my partner for five years – waxing lyrical about his newfound interest as a team member. Up until then, mountain rescue was something I'd witnessed on several occasions during ski trips to the Alps – a set of skis crossed and planted upright in the snow, the 'blood wagon' (a stretcher on sleds with two long handles at either end, one for each of the pisteurs) hurtling down the fall line with their petrified casualty aboard, or the red rescue helicopter landing dramatically on the piste before whisking an injured skier off to the nearest hospital. I was fascinated.

'Some weeks later, he took me off to Snowdon for the day. It was January – cold, but blue skied and sunny as we left Manchester. Later, as we scrambled up towards the exposed Crib Goch, the weather became very different. The howl of the wind drowning out my voice, specs misting with fine rain, strands of hair obscuring my vision and the hood of my jacket flapping angrily against by face, my bottle went. Under my feet, a slippery dark greyness fell away into the valley. Above my head, a seemingly vertical face, and me, clinging to the rock like a limpet. Petrified. Unable to move a hand or foot else I plummeted to certain death!! (A touch melodramatic perhaps, but such is the power of fear.) It mattered not that barely five minutes earlier a solitary walker had strolled past, miraculously upright, inordinately tall to my Neanderthal crouch. The two men had engaged casually in conversation, fag on lip, hands in pockets, while I peered pathetically upwards from all fours, unable to trust myself to a mere two points of contact. It turned out the other chap was a National Park warden and local mountain rescue team member. The day before, a man had been blown to his death in 40 mph winds and the warden was up there taking photographs. Argh!! There they stood, windswept and masculine, exchanging whatever signals mountain rescue people do when they meet on the hill - establishing provenance; wise words about the weather; assumed nonchalance.

'As the warden wandered off with his camera, and the wind battered me flat again, dissolving into tears and gibberish, half remembered prayers suddenly playing in my head, Andy was speaking very loudly across the wall of wind and flapping hood.

'"Just step across to your right." Easy for him to say! Next thing I knew, he was behind me. Behind me?! "I've got you."

'"What do you mean? You've got me?"

'Even more calmly this time. Measured. "Jude. I've got you."

'My panic-stricken brain struggled in vain to imagine, comprehend. "But what the hell are you standing on? Who's got you?"

'It was the scene in Superman. The one where Lois Lane dangles from the helicopter, high above Metropolis, about to meet her doom, and Superman catches her in his supermanly arms before carrying both her and the helicopter to safety. Many, many skyscraper floors-worth below.

'"It's okay. Just move across to the right. I'm behind you."

I still couldn't picture it, didn't have a clue what he was standing on. But there was something deeply reassuring in his voice, something I hadn't heard before – in charge, trustworthy. A couple of deep breaths, blink to clear the tears from my eyes and finally doing what he said, we moved together, stepping to the right, finding a footing and the courage to move my hands. Two steps more and I dared to glance down again, adrenaline coursing through me like a dose of salts. Suddenly feeling stronger, protected and safe. The bad dream gone.

'Impressed by the confidence and assurety of this new man in my life – and the stories I was beginning to hear of mountain rescue in general – I became involved with the Rossendale team, first as one of the girlfriends at team socials, but gradually finding myself roped in to help with sponsored walks, the odd tinshake or open day. Because my professional life involved design and copywriting, I took on producing the team newsletter, an anarchic mix of protocol, officer's reports, anecdote and distinctly dubious humour. Invited to represent the team, along with Andy, at the regional meetings, we found ourselves propelled onto a national sub-committee, looking after publications and information for rescue teams across England and Wales. Hardly a year in and I was asked to edit the national newsletter, an infrequent concoction of photocopied reports, stapled together and distributed in somewhat random manner. Five years on it's a thriving quarterly magazine with a loyal readership and ever-widening distribution. Meanwhile, back in Rossendale, it was suggested I might stand as team secretary, which I did and was duly appointed. The more involved I become, the more I learn, the more fascinated I am by mountain rescue and the people who do it. That anyone is prepared to get out of a warm bed in the early hours of the morning to stand around a police station for several hours waiting to be deployed in a search for a missing person, or to leave their work and family to stride off into an inhospitable hell to rescue someone in trouble on the hill, I still find remarkable.

'And, yes, I too am constantly asked why I'm not operational. How can I be so involved without going the whole hog? I guess I get a different sort of buzz. With me it's about being able to use my professional skills to make a difference. I doubt I could find the time to do what I do in that capacity, commit to callouts and still manage to earn a living!'

In whatever capacity, support or operational, it's still not clear why so few women join, but it can't all be down to masculine imagery. Women have been retaining their femininity on the mountain for over a century – take a look at the long skirts, delicately cinched waists and wide brimmed hats gravure-plated into the climbing manuals of old. There might not be too many hooped underskirts around but, thanks to the wonders of technology, we do now have lycra! Perhaps the answer lies in the number of women, compared to men, taking part in any sort of outdoor activity in the mountains. In a paper summarising ten years of its annual survey into sports participation in Scotland, sportscotland revealed some interesting, although not altogether surprising, patterns. Overall, male participation in sport is significantly greater than for women and men participate in a much wider range of sports than women. Data on mountain accidents and incidents suggests that men are three times more likely to be involved in an accident compared to women. But this could simply mean more men are involved in climbing and walking – or that they take part more often – or perhaps they just tend to go for the more hazardous pursuits, so come to grief more often. And, given that men are far more likely to be involved in accidents where the ground is rocky, snow or ice covered – or to fall, become avalanched of cragfast than women – it makes sense that they'll also be more attracted to helping extricate others

Rossendale & Pendle team members practice steep ground work with the Bell stretcher

PHOTO: CHRIS BOYLES

from those same higher risk situations.

In recent years, teams from all corners of the UK have come together for the bi-annual Mountain Rescue Conference. Lectures, small group workshops, practical sessions and outdoor scenarios focus on current issues and developments in medical and technical equipment and techniques. These events aren't just a two day freebie away from the pagers, telephones and domestic chores or a chance to drink oneself into oblivion in the company of like-minded souls. True, a fair measure of alcohol is consumed and taps do tend to run dry – despite repeated advance warnings to the bar tenders concerned – but there are a few really good reasons why rescuers get together. Debate and discussion in mountain rescue has always been of fundamental importance in clarifying and modifying ideas on issues of central concern. In recent times, Mountain Rescue (England & Wales) has adopted the principle of central funding and the MRC of Scotland has designed a brand new stretcher and casbag. These developments would never have taken place without the will to change, a desire to listen to people from outside mountain rescue and the confidence to take a few risks. Conferences are occasions when traditional, current and new topics are discussed through the interaction of people from varied backgrounds. Indeed, one of the most critical benefits they offer is the opportunity to take individual members away from the familiarity of their 'patch' and place them in the company of others with different views, expertise and philosophies. It's a salutary experience to find that someone else doing a similar job has a much better way of doing it, even when you have practiced and refined your own approach over many years. But these things only count when team members are prepared to listen, consider their own ideas in the light of what they've heard and then rework their own practice with a view to change. Events like this are especially valuable for new team members, as Richard Glover from the Assynt team discovered when he attended the annual Scottish MR seminar held at Balmoral Castle.

'The weekend at Balmoral was great. The weather met us with a small covering of snow and was cold, but good and clear all weekend. The event was organised and led by the MRC of S Training Officer in his own inimitable style. As well as the skilled speakers and instructors many teams had experienced members in them and I picked up lots of useful information and skills throughout the weekend from all sources. We arrived on Friday evening at Ballater Barracks, which was the overflow accommodation from Balmoral. I managed a wee tour of local bars, purely to be sociable obviously! On Saturday, breakfast at Balmoral set the standard for the weekend's food and service which was superb and got better and better. Lots of information was received on many aspects of rescues, equipment and new developments. Being a fairly recent member this all helped put together a good overview of how things are done within the organisation and what changes are ahead. Teams were split up for afternoon activities and I was pleased to end up with a simple technical ropeway while others were involved with swift water rescue, radios and GPS or stretchers and casualty bags. The emphasis was on rope rescues with a minimum of equipment, simple techniques and good safety - some really useful new stuff learned and some good reinforcement and reminders of basics. Saturday night was late and loud and required consumption of regular liquid refreshment. (The view that mountain rescuers drink copious amounts of alcohol at every opportunity is not a myth we are able to dispel!)

'Sunday saw a few worse-for-wear faces and the prospect of another immense breakfast. Some of us had definitely put on weight by this time. More speakers and information in the morning and a session from the RAF on Sea King helicoptors including an explanation of the Sea King's capabilities, requirements and equipment, a good look around the aircraft and practical demonstrations of winching and safety etc. What brain cells any of us had left were tested after lunch with the team quiz. With most of us stuffed full of food all day and sociable liquid all night it was not surprising our running skills in the team challenge were not at their best. Running and carrying a casualty on a stretcher over different terrains, straw bale obstacles and a Tyrolean ropeway was the objective. We did complete this without being disqualified, which is more than can be said for those teams caught dragging their terrified casualties as if on sleds, over all terrain including a flight of stone steps! We didn't win any awards at the end of the weekend but then most of our team were new to rescue work. We all gained a lot from the weekend in terms of knowledge, skills and enjoyment. The location was excellent and the food and service amazing - all in all an excellent weekend.'

If setting challenges and encouraging team members to think on their feet with volunteer 'casualties' from amongst their peers is the name of the game, then Harold Burrows, an experienced paramedic and SARDA dog handler has, on occasion, been known to take the concept a couple of steps further, as he explains.

'How do you give mountain rescue first aiders an experience that will bring home the importance of what they do and let them live through the experience of trauma, so they feel it through the casualty perspective, while enjoying the experience and, as a bonus, bring teams closer together to work for the good of the casualty? That was the simple task I set myself while in South Wales. The result was an experiment which went so well that stories of people being put on the edge, and becoming better first aiders for it, have become the stuff of legend several years on.

'The courses were run during the winter months, every session geared to give students the experience of working in the outdoor setting. Instructors had to be well versed in pre-hospital care with an ability to make the students want to learn more. There was a framework of topics covered by the casualty care course, but instructors had to be aware of the needs of the student and ready to change the topics as necessary. The idea was to see things from the casualty's point of view – they don't fully understand what we are about or what we are going to do to them – and to encourage students to take time to speak to the casualty and explain their actions.

'For starters there was a pre-course test paper to get the students to read the books and get them in the mindset of first aid. Then the first session, straight after breakfast – airway management with 'vomit' (a special Harold mix) put in to each student's pharynx for their colleague to remove before they ran out of air. Inevitably, there were always some who would give their colleague 'projectile vomit' to deal with as well, which all added to the experience for the student – from both sides of the vomit!

'We often deal with hypothermia, and most of our casualties will also be suffering from shock (in its many forms) which leads to the shutting down of peripheral circulation. They look odd and feel cold – rather like the piece of pork you get out of the fridge before you put it in the oven. So how do you get students to experience that? Ask for a volunteer, put them in a stream with just their underwear on (preserving their modesty) and wait until they become cold enough. Then get the rest of the group of five to reheat them and look after them. What begins as a bit of a joke very soon changes as the volunteer and the group realise how vital it is to look after their team mate.

'But how do you experience a casualty going in to shock? Ask the course for a volunteer who does

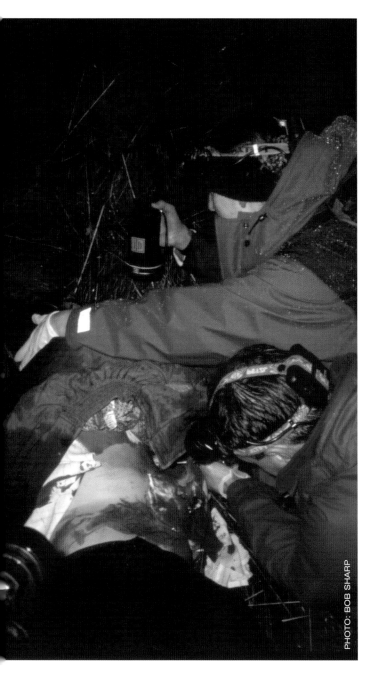

Night exercise – practising first aid with a 'simulated' casualty

not like needles or the dentist, keep a close eye on the reactions and persuade the person to volunteer to be hooked up to an ECG machine. Students first note the normal ECG trace on the machine before one of them is delegated to make a noise each time he feels the pulse. It soon becomes apparent that the beep of the machine comes just before the sound of the student feeling the pulse. Incidentally, it's also wise to have some oxygen handy at this point, but out of view of the volunteer. You should be getting the picture of a caring group with a paramedic mopping the volunteer's brow. Another paramedic now appears with a long venflon needle. The caring paramedic looks worried and asks that he use a thinner needle as this volunteer doesn't like needles. The ECG and the 'pulse person' are still making the bleep sound and everyone can now see and hear that the pulse is increasing. If it goes really well the volunteer might faint in front of the whole class and you have a great learning session for all! Students see what a shocked person looks and feels like, the volunteer feels what the casualty will feel and gives the explanation in their own words, not in medical terms.

'Team members are often required to give injections to the casualty and must be mindful that on cold, wet and windy days we don't operate to the same degree. So how can we experience that one? Simple, get the group to practice on each other. Do it at night with just a head torch for light, then put your hands in a bucket of icy water until they are cold. And make sure all the aseptic techniques are observed, and the safe disposal of the needles and syringes are followed.

'To give students an appreciation of the apprehension and fear of a casualty during asthma attack, we asked them to hold a plastic drinking straw with their lips, then breathe through the straw while squeezing their nostrils together. Then walk around a bit. It soon becomes apparent you can't get the air out before your lungs are screaming for you to take in the next breath. The fear is real and most only last a couple of minutes before giving up and gasping for a full breath of air.

'It goes without saying that the practicals are outdoors and, as long as we maintain a steady supply of hot drinks, we all have a great day. Then there's the written exam. As we operate in the open air, the exam should be out in the open too. Be it raining, snowing and blowing, they must be able to keep warm and dry for the hour the written exam takes.

'While casualty care training must be practical, the instructors must be supportive to the students, both in a physical and emotional way. Perhaps surprisingly, all the students volunteer for something on the course, and the result is the first aiders understand when a casualty feels fear and apprehension, as they've been there too. We must never forget that a casualty is a whole person. The broken leg or asthma attack belongs to them – it's not just something for us to practice with.'

A sentiment which could equally be applied to any area of training!

PHOTO: PETE HILL MIC

Many team members further their personal skills through Mountain Leader training. Some work in the outdoor industry as instructors, mountain guides or leaders.

chapter nine

IT'S A DOG'S LIFE

The more I see of men, the more I admire dogs.
Mme de Sévigné

The 'Rough Bounds of Knoydart' in Wester Ross are aptly named. 'The wettest, roughest, remotest and wildest peninsula in these islands,' according to the guidebooks. 'Any expedition here is an adventure.' But, with adventure comes risk and, often, tragedy. One of the last wilderness areas in the UK, the mountains here are renowned for their rugged nature and amount of exposed rock. Three mountains in particular, Luinne Bheinn, Ladhar Bheinn and Meall Buidhe, are popular with walkers, not only for their Munro status, but also for their remoteness and stature. In the spring of 2001, a lone, forty year old walker had gone to the area to climb these mountains, but had been missing for several days.

Already, two days of searching had taken place involving the Lochaber mountain rescue team, RAF teams from Kinloss and Leuchars, helicopters from RAF Kinloss and the Stornoway Coastguard, along with search and rescue dog teams from both SARDA Scotland and Southern Scotland. Neil Ross and his dog, Blaven, had not been involved in the earlier extensive searches but, on the third day, he and another dog handler and mountain rescue teams were deployed from Fort William and Mallaig. An RAF helicopter took Neil and Blaven – together with another search dog team and a party from RAF Kinloss – to the bealach (bealach is the Gaelic word for col or saddle – the low point between two hills) at the eastern end of Luinne Bheinn, in the heart of Knoydart. Weather was fair and a favourable breeze was blowing – very good conditions for dog searching.

Bob Scott and Clyde

PHOTO: SANDY SEABROOK

PHOTO: BOB SHARP

Knoydart

Both dog handler teams were tasked to search the north east face of Luinne Bheinn. Neil's colleague and his dog, Meg, took a high route not far below the ridge, whilst Neil and Blaven commenced a gradually rising traverse across the face of the bealach. The plan was to meet at the far side of the coire to reassess their search plan.

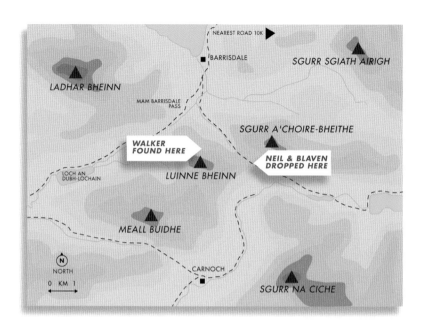

After about forty minutes of searching, Blaven struck down into the coire from whence the wind emanated. After descending about eighty metres, he negotiated a short terrace and crossed some ground to a group of boulders, where he began to bark. As Neil moved down to the terrace, he spotted the red clad legs of the casualty. There was no verbal response – the walker was dead.

Other searchers were informed by radio of the location and condition of the casualty. Twenty minutes later the RAF helicopter was on scene. The crew lowered the winchman and a stretcher before leaving to refuel in Broadford on the Isle of Skye. Between them, the winchman and Neil packaged the casualty in readiness for evacuation. Three Kinloss team members arrived and helped carry the loaded stretcher to a safe winching site and, before too long, the helicopter was fading into the late afternoon sky, its sombre load safely on board. It was with mixed emotions that Neil and his fellow team members made their way quietly back down the hill. Sure, it had been a successful find but such a tragic outcome is never easy.

There are many, many stories involving dogs of all shapes and sizes getting into doggie scrapes and causing team members to miss out on a hot dinner or their afternoon nap. The Lake District is particularly prone to dogs either losing their nerve over Striding Edge and having to be talked back from the brink, or thinking 'To heck with it,' and launching themselves into a fifty foot base jump off Helvellyn. And living to wag their tail. Others are not so lucky. You'll recall our earlier tale from Lancashire, where a family dog and his owner slipped and fell more than sixty feet at a popular beauty spot, just yards from where they had parked the car. The gentleman in question survived... thanks to his dog breaking his fall. A tragic outcome to a normal afternoon stroll.

If we're really being honest – whatever we might have said so far – in the world of mountain rescue, it is very often the dog who is the hero. It's the dog who is doing all the hard work and wearing a nifty little search and rescue number. It's the dog who is calling the shots on the hill, though their human handlers (and their other two legged team mates) might beg to differ a little.

Search and rescue dogs and their handlers are categorically a breed apart. They tend to eat, sleep and play together. Never has there been a more appropriate phrase than 'Love me, love my dog.' Dog handlers go to black tie social functions and take their dog with them. If they fall out with the missus, they sleep in the back of the van with the dog. Sometimes, they even have to be coaxed back into the house.

But there's good reason for this. They have to be dog lovers to do the work. The trust between a dog handler and his or her dog is paramount. They need to invest huge amounts of time in training and assessment. As there is only a small number of handlers scattered across the UK they are likely to be called to incidents, perhaps hundreds of miles outside their own operational area, in order to assist other teams. Consequently, they have to bear a significant financial burden in terms of travel, accommodation, dog food, vet fees, clothing and equipment. The understanding spouse (or partner) goes without saying.

Search dog handlers are all keen mountaineers (when they get the time to enjoy it!), competent in all aspects of mountain rescue work, including navigation, first aid, radio communication and self sufficiency. They frequently work alone, often in extremely hazardous environments, in atrocious weather conditions, with little sleep. The handler is often the first person on the scene of a fatal accident or suicide. All of which only adds to the satisfaction, the sheer buzz of training a dog to the peak of its ability and making a 'find'. But let's just take a look at how it all started.

SARDA (Search and Rescue Dog Association), the umbrella organisation for air scenting search and rescue dogs in the UK, was conceived by Hamish

PHOTO: CHRIS BOYLES

Even the search and rescue dogs must learn helicopter protocol!

MacInnes, in the early sixties. Leader of the Glencoe team and one of Scotland's foremost mountaineers and mountain rescue experts, Hamish was invited by the International Red Cross to attend a training course for avalanche dogs in Switzerland. The Swiss Alpine Club was already using the dogs' natural scenting ability to find people buried under avalanche debris. On his return, keen to explore the techniques within British mountain rescue, he began to train his own two dogs, with impressive results.

In December 1964, MacInnes invited six handlers with their dogs to a pilot course in Glencoe. The results were so encouraging that, in May 1965, the Search and Rescue Dog Association was formed. Six months later, handlers from Scotland, England and Wales attended the first training course in Glencoe.

In 1971, SARDA divided into three separate organisations representing Scotland, England and Wales. Twelve years later, the Scottish Association divided yet again into Highland and Southern Scotland Associations and, in the same year, the All Ireland Association was formed. However, the gradual process of rationalisation didn't stop there. In 1992, a group of handlers who had previously been part of SARDA (England) broke away to form SARDA (Lakes). In 1996 the two organisations in Scotland became SARDA Scotland and SARDA Southern Scotland. This remains the current set up.

Nowadays, the Search and Rescue Dog Association as a whole is responsible for not only the training and deployment of dog teams, but the assessment of dogs and handlers – the prime objective to maintain consistently high standards. The need for continuous assessment is perhaps the most important and demanding part of the work. Dog teams travel many hundreds of miles to attend training weekends. These typically involve handlers from different mountain rescue teams, as well as other organisations such as the RAF or Royal Navy helicopter flights and HM Coastguard. As there are only around 100 dog teams in the entire UK – against a total mountain rescue membership in the region of 3000 – they tend to be a close knit bunch, despite the huge distances separating them.

Why are dogs good for searching? Well, if you have ever seen a group of walkers toiling up a demanding scramble or inching their way across a particularly exposed ridge, whilst their canine companion skips ahead without a care in the world – only pausing to double back and see what's keeping the humans – then you'll know they are able to work in a variety of terrains and reach their goal far more quickly than their two legged friends. But it is their sense of smell which really singles them out.

The part of a dog's brain which deals with scent is four times the size of a human's. So their capacity to scent is between 1000 and 10,000 times better than ours. In ideal conditions, they can pick up a scent from about half a kilometre. It has been said that a dog is able to detect one drop of petrol in a whole swimming pool of water! In fact, recent trials have shown that they are also capable of locating bodies underwater.

There is often confusion between so called 'sniffer' dogs and search dogs. A sniffer dog is trained to detect the scent from a particular individual through the use of a 'starter article' – perhaps a piece of clothing or personal effect. Search dogs find missing people by following human air scent carried on the air. It's an ability which puts them way out in front of their human counterparts on a search – in more ways than one – and means that large areas of ground can be searched quickly and efficiently.

There is a slight drawback to this wonderful ability to detect the smell of human being in that it does depend very much on the conditions prevailing at the time. The nature of the terrain, wind direction and air temperature all factor into the equation. For example, if the wind direction is in the same direction as a moving dog, it will most likely fail to pick up any smell. And if the terrain is very broken, the air currents generated will also be broken. But in terms of overall effectiveness, a search and rescue dog is equivalent to about twenty fellow team mates in good conditions and many more in poor conditions.

This story, of how a young search dog called Bonnie made her first find, demonstrates just how vital her natural sense of smell could be in poor conditions. Derbyshire police received a mobile phone call at around seven in the evening. Two walkers and their dog had been overtaken by darkness on Kinder Scout in the Peak District National Park. They had no torch and had alerted the police in an effort to prevent a major search being mounted. In the best of conditions, Kinder Scout is acknowledged as wild and exposed. Not the sort of place you would want to be lost in darkness with a storm brewing.

Up until 1932, there was no legal access to the area. Kinder was a jealously preserved grouse moor, patrolled by keepers who had little compunction about taking a stick to trespassing hikers. Then, on Sunday 24 April of that year, Benny Rothman, a twenty year old unemployed motor mechanic from Manchester, led a group of 400 ramblers in protest across the moor. There were a few scuffles with gamekeepers above William Clough (that's a place, not a junior gamekeeper!), no doubt wielding their sticks, and Rothman was one of five people arrested and charged with various public order offences, including 'riotous assembly'. Sentences ranged from two to six months' imprisonment. But the Kinder Mass Trespass brought to a head the whole issue of access to the countryside. It paved the way to the creation of our National Parks.

It was undoubtedly the heady mix of rock buttresses and escarpments, boggy peat-hagged ground and deep cut, fast moving water channels –

the potential for a challenging and exhilarating exercise – which drew these protesters in their hundreds, and no less so today. But Richard Gilbert, in his *200 Challenge Walks in Britain and Ireland* gives out a word of warning to those setting out in winter '...darkness falls quickly and the deep groughs and oozing bogs make progress imperceptible. The Kinder plateau, at over 630 metres, is not the place to be benighted. Accurate compass work is imperative and a wide margin of safety must be allowed.'

So it was in this context that the Edale Mountain Rescue Team decided to mobilise a small party to escort the walkers to safety. Five members, including the team leader, one of the team's doctors, and dog handler John and his German Shepherd, Bonnie, set out from Grindsbrook Booth. The walkers had described their location as the edge path of the main Kinder Scout plateau at a point where a small stream falls over the crags into Grindsbrook. It was about four kilometres from the start point and a climb of 300 metres.

The group searched towards the location in three pairs, Bonnie and John following about 500 metres behind the doctor and his companion along the edge path, which runs right round the plateau at an altitude of 600 metres. By the time they reached the plateau, the forecasted storm had arrived, with a vengeance.

The familiar path quickly transformed into a trench of liquid mud. As the human search party struggled against gale force winds and a low cloud base which had reduced visibility to just thirty metres, Bonnie appeared unconcerned by the conditions, using the wind to her advantage. She appeared and disappeared in the mist as she quartered the moor to the north of the path. By 9 o'clock, all six members of the search team met near the reported position of the two walkers, having found nothing.

scouts in the mist

'A group of six Scouts were taking part in a three day expedition as part of their Queen's Scout Award. By the second day of the expedition, a strong westerly wind was generating low cloud and rain. Conditions were not ideal. During the afternoon, one of the party began to complain about not feeling too good and was

was tasked to get out on to the hill, with one other member of the team to carry the casualty bag and act as navigator. As we left Search Control and ascended we were soon in the mist, well before we reached the ridgeline. We walked in a general northerly direction with the wind on my left cheek. To my right was the crag line coming off the ridge, which was important to keep away from.

'I set Kim, my search dog, off to locate the three scouts and their tent. Kim ran off to my left and right, but due to the poor visibility, once she was more then twenty feet away, she would disappear into the mist, reappearing and disappearing every couple of minutes. With my navigator about ten paces to my left, we walked northwards, calling out the names of the group.

'At one point, Kim disappeared into the mist and did not return for a good ten minutes. When she reappeared, she came running towards me, barking once before turning away in a north westerly direction, back into the mist. As usual, I turned to the direction Kim had disappeared, to go after her. My navigator and I went off, still not too sure what we would find. After another twenty minutes, Kim reappeared, barked once at me and ran off. It was then that my navigator said how strange that Kim was running off, as her normal indication was to bark at my feet until I said the words 'Show me'. It was only after that Kim would run back to the casualty.

growing colder by the minute. With the added poor visibility, the group had made very slow progress. In the late afternoon, the decision was made to stop along the ridge they were walking, put up the tent and place the young lad inside for shelter. The five remaining scouts decided to send three down for help, while two stayed with the boy in the tent. The group of three made a note of their grid reference and location description, along with the names and description of their friends, then set off to continue along the ridge and make their way down to phone for help.

'Around eight o'clock the call came to the police and the local mountain rescue team was called out. I

'We took this to indicate some urgency and broke into a jog in the same direction as Kim. She continued the pattern – running back to me and giving her one bark as an indication of the find, but not waiting for my response. By now, we were both running when, out of *the mist, I could make out the shape of a tent. We stopped running and began to walk in an attempt to catch our breath and gather our thoughts, wondering what we might find. The hairs on the back of my neck were beginning to bristle and both of us were quiet as we approached the door to the tent.*

I slowly unzipped the doorway to the tent. There staring back at me were three young faces! Dry and rosy cheeked, with a slight smile on their faces. All were in good spirits and the lad who had initially felt ill had now recovered from his ordeal. I checked out the three of them and all were fine. They'd done the right thing by stopping, putting up the tent, putting their hypothermic friend in a sleeping bag and giving him some food. Needless to say, my navigator and I were jubilant – if a little wet ourselves.

'Now, normally, Kim would want her reward for finding the casualty, but there was no sign of her by me in the tent. I looked outside to see her sheltering between the tent and the flysheet, her head inside the cookpot the boys had used to cook up some Irish stew. So that was why I wasn't getting her normal indication – she'd been helping herself to regular samples of stew! So, as an extra reward, we let her lick the pot clean. I swear it finished up as clean as the day they'd begun the expedition!

'We walked the boys off the hill, where they were reunited with their friends, no worse for the excitement of a rescue. We had all learnt a lot that day about what to do in an emergency. And I had learned a little more about my dog's eating habits!'

Harold Burrows
SARDA Wales & North East Wales SRT

By this time, radio conversation with the Edale base revealed that the missing persons' mobile battery was now flat. The rest of the Edale team was called for, including Geoff Allen with his dog, Haggis. This was now developing into a serious incident.

Conditions were too severe for Bonnie and John to continue working alone, so another member joined the pair as they began a new search pattern westward across the moor towards Crowden Tower. They made good progress by keeping off the boggy path and out of the peat hags. 500 metres on, they heard shouts and a distress whistle. Bonnie pricked up her ears and disappeared, the lightstick around her neck bouncing away into the darkness. The shouts and whistles increased so John moved quickly after her. Within minutes, Bonnie came running back to indicate her find. The group were soon together and shaking hands. A flare was fired and a radio message sent to base to indicate that all was well. One of the walkers had apparently twisted his knee earlier in the day. To carry him off by stretcher would have extended the rescue by another four or five hours. Instead, he bravely limped off with the aid of two walking poles. The party finally arrived at base an hour later where a welcome was waiting for the missing walkers and Bonnie – fresh from her first find.

Bonnie, of course, is a German Shepherd, but the most popular choice for search and rescue is undoubtedly the Border Collie. Ask any dog handler, dog 'body' or rescue team member what it is that endears these talented creatures so and you will be several hours late for whatever you were planning to do next. Quite apart from their air-scenting abilities, the naturally companionable search and rescue collie will happily snaffle all your butties, pee on your boots and give you a generous face wash in the time between indicating your whereabouts to its handler, toiling up the hill in its wake, and his or her breathless arrival. And before we move on, think

first call out lockerbie

'Following eighteen months of intensive search dog training, I had qualified as a novice search dog handler in November 1988 and waited eagerly for my first call out. It came on 21 December 1988 around

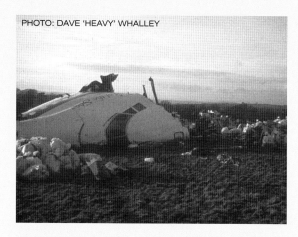

PHOTO: DAVE 'HEAVY' WHALLEY

20.00 hours. I'd already seen the newsflash interrupting 'This Is Your Life' and anticipated that we may be called. I was told to make my way south to Lockerbie. The name would come to haunt me, and probably will for the rest of my life.

'After being redirected by the police at Moffat, I travelled along an eerily quiet A74. In the distance, I could see a red and golden glow – Lockerbie. I made my way to the police station through scenes you might encounter in a disaster movie set – flames shooting to the sky, the strong scent of kerosene in the air, badly damaged houses and a massive smoking crater with debris all around it. I joined two other dog handlers and we were tasked to search some fields quite far out of Lockerbie. On the way, my headlights lit up my first

sight of that nose cone. I can still feel the shock wave I experienced all those years ago and, to this day, when I catch sight of it on the TV I still have a reaction.

'The search started. Within minutes, our search dogs had indicated on luggage, bundles of cargo, piles of debris all scattered around the field. The dogs were confused at the amount of scent, particularly my dog on her first real search – what to indicate on first? We praised the dogs but continued looking for life. I find it unbelievable now that I was naïve enough to think there might still be a living soul waiting to be rescued. It truly didn't occur to me that humans falling over 30,000 feet would have no chance of survival, or that the impact would leave some bodies in a horrific state. Or that some scenes would be so surreal I still question whether I truly witnessed them. Truth to tell, no preparation could have helped me cope with what I experienced over the next twenty hours. The sights encountered are firmly imprinted on my subconscious and rise to the surface in the form of nightmares at times of stress.

'I am asked why I continue to devote much of my time to mountain rescue as a volunteer search dog handler after that horrific experience fifteen years ago. It's a difficult question to answer, and I'm not sure I understand why I do it myself. One answer would be that I enjoy the challenge and pleasure of training and working with a dog (my current search dog, Buidhe, is my third). I also thrive on being out in the Scottish countryside experiencing different seasons, the ever changing scenery and being self sufficient in fairly remote areas.'

Jan Millar
SARDA Scotland & Lomond MRT

about this, it's been calculated that the Border Collie is the second most intelligent dog in the world of dogs. This begs the obvious question – which is the most intelligent? Well, it's the French Poodle! But we'd hazard a guess – although we could be wrong – that no self-respecting mountain rescuer would be seen on the hill with a fluffy, manicured pooch called Mademoiselle Mitzi.

These may well be genetic characteristics dating back to the days when the next meal was much harder to come by and certainly didn't come wrapped in a tupperware box alongside a packet of salt'n'vinegar and an energy bar. All dogs, regardless of breed have a common ancestor – the wolf. The transition from wolf as a creature of the forest to man's best friend took around 10,000 years. Our ancestors would observe the way the wolves hunted – in particular, their ability to separate a chosen animal from a herd and bring it to ground – and, as the relationship grew, learned to harness this characteristic to assist in their hunting activities.

The forerunners of modern search dogs are generally considered to be the dogs of the monastery at the summit of the Great St Bernard Pass. In the seventeenth century, the dogs (now known as St Bernard's) were introduced at the monastery to work as guard dogs. They would often accompany the monks on rescue missions, breaking trails in the deep snow. Their unerring sense of direction rendered them invaluable as guides in bad conditions. These dogs are reputed to have been responsible for saving the lives of many lost travellers and even avalanche victims. Records reveal that a particularly prolific St Bernard called Barry saved forty lives during his lifetime. During the First World War, dogs were trained for use with the Red Cross to locate injured personnel on the battlefield during lulls in the fighting. They were trained to 'find' by using airborne human scent.

There is a reported incident in the winter of 1937, during an avalanche search, when a rescue team member's dog showed continued interest in one particular place, which had already been probed, and eventually began to bark. After reprobing at this location, the victim was found alive. The incident prompted a Swiss dog training expert to train four German Shepherds to search for avalanche victims. These were then presented to the Swiss army. In London, during the Blitz, dogs were used with great success to find victims buried in buildings, again using airborne scent. After the war, the Swiss Alpine Club reviewed its normal method for finding the victims of avalanches and decided to train dogs in avalanche work for their own rescue network. So successful was this that avalanche dog training centres are now widespread throughout the Alps. In

Mark Richards, of the North East Wales team, with search dog Wesley

Quite apart from their air-scenting abilities, the naturally companionable search and rescue collie will happily snaffle all your butties, pee on your boots and give you a generous face wash in the time between indicating your whereabouts to its handler, toiling up the hill in its wake, and his or her breathless arrival.

Skye with owner Marion

more recent times, search and rescue dogs were used to locate bodies following the Lockerbie air crash on 21 December 1988, and have been used to assist in many natural disasters.

It has been said that any dog can be trained provided the chemistry between dog and owner is right. Though the majority of search dogs are Collies and German Shepherds, there is a significant proportion of Labradors and cross breeds. The herding instinct that we saw in our ancestors' wolvine companions is very strong in the Border Collie and it is this which is developed by handlers as a basis for training a dog to search in a systematic manner. It is well known that Collies have an irrepressible tendency to round up almost anything that moves, including people and vehicles, sometimes to their cost! But they also have a number of other characteristics that make them ideal for the job.

They have a natural desire to work long and hard and are generally gifted with intelligence, endurance and agility. They are also extremely devoted to their owners. But it is their physical attributes which really give them the edge. Their water-resistant coats give excellent protection from the elements. The very dense, long, coarse outer coat sheds rain and snow easily. The softer, thick under coat insulates against the cold and the abundant mane and collar protect the vital organs. They have relatively small ears that are not easily frostbitten, their muzzle is exactly the right length to warm the cold air before it reaches the lungs and their legs are just long enough to keep the chest and abdomen above snow, heather and bracken. Made to measure!

If enthusiasm for work, learning ability, stamina and vitality are the key criteria for a good search dog, the same criteria might apply to the owner! The fact that there are very few handlers reflects the highly specialised nature of their work. Entry requirements for becoming a handler vary slightly between member associations but, in general, trainee handlers must be proposed and supported by a mountain rescue team and have been a full

Now you see me... now you don't

PHOTOS: ROHAN HOLT

hours – even weeks – of their free time, to making up a flask and butties and wrapping up in their warmest clothing, for the dubious pleasure of lying in a snow hole or under some unforgiving bracken reading the paper and awaiting discovery by an over-excited bundle of hair intent on showing its affection – and supplementing its diet! Because that is what these selfless beings do in order to assist their team colleagues in the training of their dogs.

Many dog bodies are non team members, looking for a satisfying, if slightly different – some would say bizarre – way of spending their free time. There is one couple we know of who, on retirement – and having no previous experience of search dogs, or even mountain rescue –

team member for more than twelve months. Overall training could take two years – one year as a trainee and one as full member. The mountain rescue team to which a handler belongs trains the handler in mountain rescue techniques, whilst SARDA covers the actual dog training. Although, in practice, most handlers begin their association with SARDA before they even acquire a dog or begin training with it, often acting as dog 'bodies' to existing handlers.

Dog bodies, it has to be said, must be almost as mad as the dog teams themselves about the whole process of canine search and rescue. Why else would otherwise perfectly sane individuals devote

decided to buy a caravan and offer their services to SARDA. Throughout the year, weekend after weekend, come rain, shine, hail or snow you will find them crisscrossing the country, hiding in holes for fun. And loving every minute of it!

Other dog bodies are full team members who enjoy working with the dogs and their handlers. Although, it has been observed that the novice body should perhaps omit to mention his or her mountain rescue experience (heaven forbid!) when first standing in line at a training weekend, waiting to be deployed. Given their assumed skill base, they may well find themselves in a far more precarious and remote position than their non-team counterparts – they do like to test the dogs, you see. And accidents do happen in the most unexpected of places.

So when the moment arrives that a seasoned dog body, tired of hanging out in the bracken – or, indeed, any other team member – decides to become a search dog handler, what next? Training for search work usually starts with games of hide and seek, when the dog is a few weeks of age. Early on, they are expected to obey the usual commands such as 'Come', 'Sit' and 'Stay'.

Given the Collie's natural tendency to 'round up', an important early stage is the livestock test which involves presenting the dog with a small group of sheep. The dog is unleashed and made to 'Stay,' while the handler walks to the other side of the flock, then called to 'Heel' through the sheep. Dog and handler then walk towards the flock and the dog must show no tendency to chase after the sheep. All this takes place under the gimlet eye of a shepherd with the power of veto! Many a dog has failed at this stage of its training. In fact, the stock test is probably the most anxious part of the initial assessment for any aspirant handler. Changes in the wind can always be blamed for failure to detect a hidden 'body', but there are no excuses acceptable should a dog chase after a sheep!

A bit like play school through to sixth form, the learning starts out as fun, gradually growing more complex over time. Once started, it never stops, and most handlers spend several hours each day exercising and training their dog. The hide and seek games of early training are developed, dog and handler working together to find bodies hidden at increasing distances from the search starting point. More difficult ground is used to test the ranging ability of the dog – not to mention the handler's fitness!

The handler's ability to take account of wind direction and speed, and how these vary with terrain, is a critical process. It's been shown that a dog working in a search pattern across the wind can cover ground most efficiently. A sudden change in the dog's pace and direction – or posture – usually indicates that a human scent has been detected. Handlers watch for such signals and encourage their dog to go 'Find'. Indeed, the entire process is one of encouragement. Human scent brings praise, whereas the indication of hares, deer or birds fails to impress.

Training the dog to go back when a casualty is found, or to return to the handler and lead them to the body, are further skills demanding patience for perfection. Communication between dog and handler is vital and the learning process is far from one sided. Handlers, too, must show consistency in command and tone of voice. They must be able to motivate and reward their dog, to constantly revise their own acquired skills. They must both learn to work as a team. Most importantly, a handler must be kind to his 'bodies'! The odd beer never went amiss.

The training required of a dog and handler is very demanding and exceptionally time consuming, through a programme that extends to five grades. At Grade 1 level, the handler is given the location of the body (within an area of about half a square kilometre) and the dog is given 20 minutes to find the body, return to the handler indicating, and then lead them to the body. At Grade 2, the location is unknown and the search area extended to about three quarters of a square kilometre. The dog should be capable of ranging over a greater distance and be able to find more than one body in the area. At Grade 3 (novice search dog) the search area is extended to about one square kilometre and the search time to two hours. By now, both dog and handler should be competent in dense forest and able to find medium sized articles at night in all weathers. The dog should be capable of 'sends away' to specific points and the handler able to direct along specific boundary lines. In a 'real life' search situation it may be the dog team

Dog bodies, it has to be said, must be almost as mad as the dog teams themselves about the whole process of canine search and rescue.

alone working a search area, so it is absolutely vital that the handler can plan search areas using maps, justify the working of an area and assess the overall search strategy. Some might say, a one man (or woman) search team! At this level, dog and handler may be added to their team's call out list as a resource (although, as we have said, the two-legged part of the duo will already have been an operational member for some time, possibly several years).

At Grade 4, the dog/handler should be able to demonstrate a high level of competence in areas such as dense forest, boulder fields and crags, and also be able to perform an effective shore line search around a loch. And, just to up the ante, they should be quite capable of working in areas that have been fouled by other people and dogs. Grade 5 is full search dog standard. At this level, the dog/handler team should be capable of working in front of a rescue team and alongside other dog teams, with no distraction or interference problems. They should be able to clear any area and maintain a high level of performance for at least two days.

A key feature of assessment is the presence of 'outside' assessors from other mountain rescue teams, even countries, to ensure the strict maintenance of standards. Dogs and their handlers are assessed on a regular basis throughout the working life of a dog. Such is the enthusiasm of the average search dog handler for his or her work, that they frequently go on to train second and third dogs when their first has died or reached the end of its working life.

Once on the call out list, a dog team may be called to assist, not only in their own team's area, but anywhere in the UK, whenever someone is reported missing in the mountains, hills or forests. They're often the first resource to be requested by police and the rescue team manager if a large area has to be

Rangi finds Stephen, the dog body, in an avalanche tip

covered, such as mountainside or forest, or if a night time search is required. The beauty of this capsule rescue team is their immediate effectiveness. Thanks to good relationships between SARDA and the RAF and Royal Navy search and rescue squadrons, a dog team can be quickly deployed by helicopter to remote areas and begin the search whilst other search resources are still being marshalled. Troopers that they are, the dogs soon become accustomed to being winched in and out of helicopters!

Their use is far from confined to a mountain environment, however. Increasingly, particularly in semi-urban or farmland areas of the country, SARDA members are asked to search for missing children, or older people who have strayed from home. Harold Burrows, of SARDA Wales, tells the story of one old lady who had gone missing at 3pm from a North Wales coastal town. She was suffering from dementia but quite able to walk without difficulty. Having lived in the area for many years, she might easily have wandered some distance from her home.

This is often the case. Some years ago, the Rossendale & Pendle team was asked to search for an allegedly frail and vulnerable old lady, last seen wearing slippers and a cardie and in the company of her dog. She was eventually located, having walked a full twenty miles. She was fine, if a little weary and, incidentally, still in her slippers. Her dog was knackered. Not content with her little adventure, the lady repeated the exercise six months later, setting out from the same nursing home, at the same time of day on precisely the same journey. Suspecting there may be a pattern developing, the team advised police to search the Keighley Road area. This they did and picked her up – still with her dog.

But back to Wales. A search control was established and dog handlers deployed to specific areas. By now it was 9pm, the temperature falling and the situation urgent. The local mountain rescue

avalanche find at white coomb

'In the early hours of a Monday morning in the spring of 1995, I was asked to join a search for a missing hill walker in the hills near to Moffat in the Scottish Borders. Heavy snow had fallen in strong

Search dog Tarah

winds, a couple of days before. This was followed by a rise in temperature and low level snow melt. The walker was reported missing on the Sunday evening after failing to return home and his car was found at a popular car park. The weather that evening was windy with blizzards and the initial search teams could find no trace. As darkness descended, the search was abandoned but scheduled to resume with the assistance of dog teams the following day.

'The morning was clear and cold. Five search dogs were deployed into the search area, tasked to search the area around White Coomb and Loch Skeen. In particular, we were to concentrate on areas of potential avalanche activity. Although the weather overhead was

good at the start, conditions underfoot for both dogs and handlers were difficult. The snow was soft and lying deep in the peat hags. On more than one occasion the dogs and ourselves floundered as we unwittingly walked off harder ground into waist deep snow. Several hours into the search, three of us identified a significant channelled avalanche. The dogs showed a degree of interest in this area but nothing positive. As we continued to move around the hill, a helicopter from RAF Boulmer was deploying ground teams onto strategic points.

'In the corrie to the north east of White Coomb, we came across the debris of a huge avalanche. (We later estimated the width at the crown wall to be around 500 metres). I was with two other dog handlers. We split up and started to move across the debris. The snow was in blocks but not too difficult to walk through. Within minutes of starting I could see that my dog Tarah was showing some interest. This was more positive than on the avalanche that we had crossed earlier. She made for a point some twenty to thirty metres ahead of me and started to dig at the snow. Very quickly, she came back to me, indicated strongly, and dashed back to the spot where she had been digging. As I approached, I could see a mitt lying at the bottom of the hole that she had scraped. The mitt was not empty!! I called the other handlers down and alerted the base. Within minutes we were digging to clear the snow and it became clear that the casualty's arm was raised and outstretched and that his body was several feet deep in *the snow. Tragically, there was no sign of life. The casualty was airlifted by the helicopter and taken to the base location where a doctor was present to confirm death. Back on the hill, the weather was beginning to deteriorate again and we started to walk back down to the base.*

'I had very mixed feelings about the incident. I felt extremely sad on account of the tragic loss of life but, at the same time, a sense of exhilaration because the dog I had spent the past two and half years training had made the find on her second call out. The avalanche was so large that it would have taken days to search with human teams equipped with probes. The fact that Tarah was able to locate the casualty lying several feet below the surface within minutes is testimony to the tremendous benefits that a search dog can provide in any search. All of her training was worth that one find alone. All dog handlers feel a very special relationship and sense of teamwork with their dog which is heightened when the training comes to fruition on a real incident. Needless to say, Tarah was given an extra helping of supper that evening and a special spot by the fire!'

Steve Penny,
Team Leader, Tweed Valley MRT.

The full story of this rescue is in
'A Chance in a Million'

team had also been called in. The dog teams were given small areas to search and slowly moved further and further out from the lady's last known location. Just after midnight, Harold was given an area close to her friend's home to search, about two miles from the lady's own house.

'As my navigator and I looked through the windows of the house, Sam, my search dog, went around the garden and garage. He came running back and barked his indication to me to say that he had found something. I followed him to the garage, whereupon he started to sniff frantically around the garage door. I tried to open the door but it was firmly locked from the inside. I walked around to the side of the garage and looked in through the side window, where I was met by an old lady looking back at me! It did make me jump as I had been calling out her name for some time. Eventually, I opened the side door and made my way in to see her. She was unsure about my presence but was quite happy to have Sam alongside her.

'A quick radio call to search control brought the police and ambulance to their location. Sam, courteous to the last, walked the lady to the door of the ambulance. Only when she was safely inside did he bound back to his proud owner!'

Usually, handlers from several rescue teams are called to assist in a serious search. They are almost always tasked prior to the arrival of other personnel, to avoid the risk of contaminating the search area. The dog handler works with the designated search co-ordinator – usually a police officer or mountain rescue team leader – to take into account details of the missing person and their likely whereabouts, the nature of the terrain and wind direction.

Once on the hill, the dog works in partnership with its handler and runs free under their direction, the key factor being the ability to range and cover vast areas of land in a relatively short time. The task for the handler is no less daunting – not only do they

how the search dog team works an area

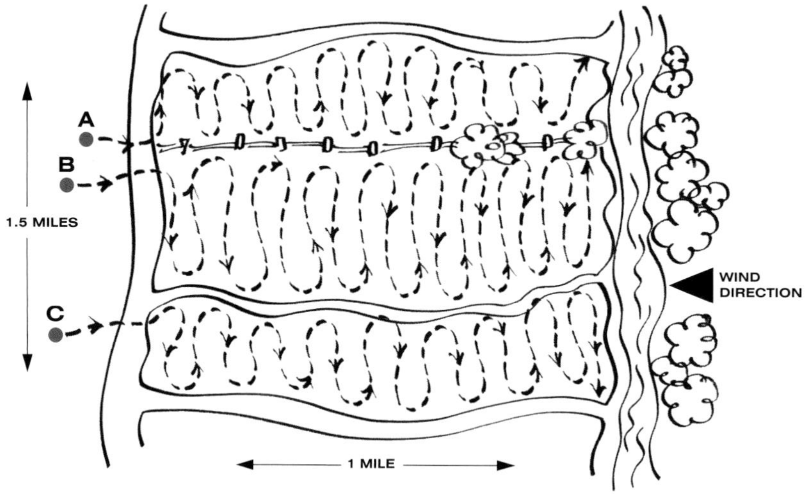

A

B

1.5 MILES

C

WIND DIRECTION

← 1 MILE →

Search dog teams work into the wind in a structured manner, with obvious features such as hedges, fences, streams or pathways used to divide the area into sectors. The diagram shows a simple search with no obstacles – such as boulders or clumps of bushes – along the designated search paths.

have to direct and observe the behaviour of their dog, they must also navigate successfully, follow an agreed search plan and look after both their own and their dog's safety. And all, no doubt, in the sort of conditions you wouldn't normally let a dog out in. Quite a challenge. Perhaps, at this point we should mention the navigator. Not every time, but quite frequently, a handler will take along another, equally competent mountain rescue trained, person to take responsibility for the navigation, leaving the handler and dog to do the searching. Needless to say, it is important that all parties in the arrangement stick to their tasks – navigator navigates, dog team searches. For certain, it often helps to have another

human being on hand. Imagination can be a dangerous thing, as Robert Davidson from Ochils MRT knows from experience.

'One night, just after midnight in March, we were asked to search an area on the west shore of the loch. After a few hours, my dog came back and indicated to me, went into the woods and lay down. It was pitch black, windy and raining heavily and I could see nothing. But then I noticed a baseball cap next to where she was sitting and a set of keys not far away.

'You have no idea what to expect next – either a body hanging from a tree or someone in a less than normal state of mind, perhaps not wanting to be found. At that point I started shouting to the other dog handler in the area. We found nothing that night. But, the point is that, at that time of night, when you're woken from a deep sleep and then forced out into the wind and rain, your mind can play funny tricks.'

Once an area has been identified it might be searched thoroughly by several resources – dogs and handlers, mountain rescue teams, helicopters – with increasing intensity, from a rapid sweep to a finger tip search. This might continue for several days before a search is terminated. It may even be resumed several months later if there is a strong feeling the body is still located in the area, or fresh evidence comes to light.

As we've already noted, trained search and rescue dogs are highly effective in case of avalanches. In good conditions, they can search an area in about one tenth of the time it takes a team of twenty of their human counterparts, equipped with probes. The average time for a thorough search of a 100 metre wide square, by a well trained dog, is abut 30 minutes for a general search and one to two hours for a fine search. But times can be much faster depending on the type of snow.

Certain conditions can make life difficult for the dog. Compact snow, which is non-porous and icy, limits the passage of the buried person's scent, other people in the area create a variety of distracting scents, and poor weather conditions can mask the scents entirely. Trained dogs are invariably worked into the wind and, once a smell is detected, they are always encouraged to dig down to the source. If a dog is immediately available, other rescuers will be kept away from the avalanche debris to avoid confusing scents. If many people have already been searching the debris, then 'resting' the slope for ten minutes allows for false scents to dissipate. This said, a search by people on the spot would never be delayed in expectation of the appearance of a dog. Finding someone alive is, of course, the prime motivation! Dog handlers and other personnel searching avalanche debris are always required to wear electronic devices to aid their detection should further avalanche occur.

Most of the rescues we've looked at have involved adults, perfectly capable of making informed decisions about their environment and welfare. Sure, they often meet with extenuating circumstances which push them to the brink of endurance, sometimes with tragic results. But, what about when it's a child? When a child goes missing, the emergency services move heaven and earth to

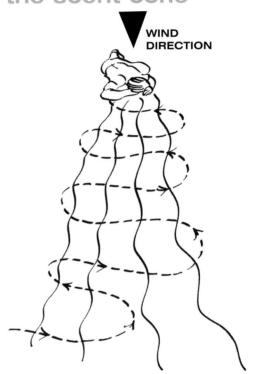

how a dog works the scent cone

WIND DIRECTION

Scent is carried downwind in a cone shape, narrow at its source – the person – and widening with distance. The diagram shows the likely path taken by a dog once it has picked up the casualty's scent. When the dog strays outside the scent cone, it senses a change and turns back towards the scent, creating the zig zag pattern indicated.

What a dog actually picks up might be a combination of rafts of dead skin – skin cells which the body sheds at a rate of around 40,000 every minute – water droplets from the casualty's breath or tiny hormonal droplets – such as adrenaline, if the casualty is frightened.

PHOTO: ROHAN HOLT

Search dogs come in all shapes, sizes and breeds - not just Collie. Tyke the Golden Labrador pictured during a SARDA Wales training week in Scotland 2004. Tyke and her handler, Ian Bunting, are members of the Edale team

help. Children are vulnerable, less able to look after themselves – though Lost Person Behaviour indicates they do possess an instinctive sense of survival when lost, often found curled up and asleep in a 'safe' place. Of course, when the cause of that disappearance is abduction, events can unfold in a deeply tragic manner – as in the case of Rosie McCann – but, even in the face of mounting evidence to the contrary, there is always hope that a missing child will be found alive. So, when the call comes, there is no question or hesitation. Whatever the time of day or weather, the response from teams is 100%. It's stories such as this one – of three year old Cameron Munro – which make it all worthwhile.

Cameron's mother had taken him and his younger sister Annie-Rose for a walk at the Falls of Shin near their home in Ardgay, in the north of Scotland. A very popular tourist attraction, the area is surrounded by thick woods, a steep gorge and fast flowing river. Whilst Cameron's mother strapped his sister into the car, she briefly took her attention away from her son. When she turned around, he had gone. She called his name hoping this was just a game and he would pop his head from behind a tree. But within a few minutes, she realised he was missing. For almost two hours, and with the help of others, she searched the area near the visitor centre but, as darkness fell, she called the police. Initially, the police helicopter, using a thermal imaging camera, flew over the wooded area where it was believed Cameron might have strayed. But this proved unsuccessful. Many local people arrived on scene with offers of help but no one was permitted into the area until the helicopter had completed its search. Around 6.30pm, a full scale search was launched, involving several mountain rescue teams, the police and dog handlers. RAF Kinloss MRT was on a training exercise in Central Scotland but made a five hour journey to assist.

Dog handler Dave Riley and his dog Rosie

how scent travels away from the casualty

The search becomes slightly more complicated, depending on the time of day or night. During daylight hours, and when the ambient temperature is warmer and the air still, normal body heat will make scent rise and disperse loosely in a cone shape.

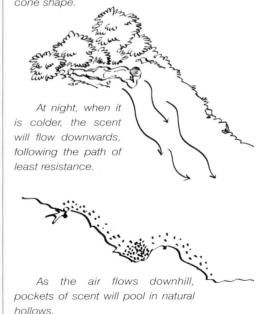

At night, when it is colder, the scent will flow downwards, following the path of least resistance.

As the air flows downhill, pockets of scent will pool in natural hollows.

wind movement and scent pockets

The job becomes even more complex when the scent flow changes course and nature, according to wind and any obstacles in the way. Handlers learn to work with their dogs, putting them into areas to use their scent to the best of their ability. When wind meets an obstacle such as a wall or tree, it creates a circular movement of air behind the obstacle which forms a scent pocket.

The circular movement of air behind the obstacle, combined with the flow of wind over and beyond the obstacle, in turn creates an area of dead air where the scent might be lost.

In the second diagram the scent has flowed over the first tree, creating a pocket behind it, then over the second and third trees, forming an area of dead air in between, and a further scent pocket after the third tree.

searched throughout the night. Then, just after daylight, Rosie found Cameron, sleeping under an upturned tree root covered in bracken. He had survived some sixteen hours alone – and just half a mile from his mother's car. Fortunately, he was wearing several layers of clothing, which helped to keep him warm and prevent hypothermia. When Cameron was asked about his ordeal he said that he had made a nest for himself under a tree where he was warm and cosy.

When he was reunited with his parents Cameron told them he'd been hunting for dinosaurs. His father explained that whenever his son saw fallen trees, he imagined they'd been knocked over by dinosaurs. So wrapped up was he in the prospect of finding one, he just wandered into the woods without a second thought.

Needless to say, Dave Riley was delighted with Rosie's find. He said, 'I would never have found the little boy without my dog – when she started barking I knew everything was going to be okay. Cameron was in a very rough and difficult place but he had used almost adult intelligence in crawling into a spot to get the most shelter. I was amazed how cheery he was. He didn't even say he was cold or hungry. When I went to put my jacket over him he told me, "I don't need that, I've got a jacket." It is very rewarding to find someone alive, particularly a child.'

A couple of months after his rescue, Cameron finally came face to face with his favourite beasts at Glasgow's Hunterian Museum where an exhibition based on the BBC's *Walking with Dinosaurs* featured real remains and life size replicas. A happy ending to the tale. But, just to prove that even search and rescue dogs have their moments, the following February saw eleven year old collie Rosie vanishing in a white-out blizzard whilst out searching for missing hillwalkers in the Cairngorms. She survived three whole days at sub zero temperatures before being found. Handler Dave reckoned it was the smell of sausage rolls which finally drew her in from the cold.

He said, 'I had been out for three days with friends looking for the dog. We were about to give up when we decided to have a break. I had sausage rolls and had just finished the last of them when Rosie came running over looking as fresh as if she had just been out for thirty minutes'.

Remarkably, Rosie had not just survived the bitter cold but had found her way off a 4000 foot plateau negotiating icy tracks and gullies!

Start 'em young. In the early stages, training is all about play

PHOTO: BOB SHARP

chapter ten

AND THE LAST WORD...

Deep down I will always be proud that he's so dedicated.
I know he would move heaven and earth for his family.
It's just that when that bloody bleeper goes off – so does he....

Nothing brings home the fragility of our own existence more than witnessing the end of another, cut prematurely short by a tragic twist of fate and circumstance. To watch someone's life slip away, despite making every effort to save it is a sobering experience. Only hours – seconds – before their fatal fall, they were a vital human being with everything to live for. There but for the grace of God...

At least when accident befalls a grown-up, the chances are they have taken measured risks, made decisions based on experience and knowledge and had all the right equipment. They were responsible for their own safety. When a young person or child is involved, the sense of utter devastation is palpable. In 1971, an incident in the Cairngorm mountains saw six young people die in what was to be remembered as the worst tragedy in UK mountaineering history. It would not only change the lives of their own families and those immediately involved, but rattle the windows of Westminster and change the way outdoor education was delivered for ever.

Saturday morning, 20 November had dawned clear and bright – seemingly a great day for hillwalking. Twenty one year old leader Cathie Davidson, a third year physical education student, and twenty three year old Ben Beattie were heading for the summit of Ben MacDui, with fourteen youngsters from the mountaineering club of Ainslie Park School in Edinburgh. A competent and experienced instructor, Ben was Ainslie Park's outdoor activities leader. His drive and enthusiasm was infectious, an inspiration to his pupils. Their monthly meets had already included visits to Skye, Glencoe and the Lake District, climbing or walking by day and using bothies for overnight stops. The trip to Ben MacDui was devised by Beattie as a test of their navigation skills, pushing them a little harder than on a normal hill walk. But, by late Saturday afternoon, conditions were deteriorating rapidly. The low cloud base restricted visibility to fifty metres, a

Memorial on Beinn Tarsuinn in Wester Ross

PHOTO: BOB SHARP

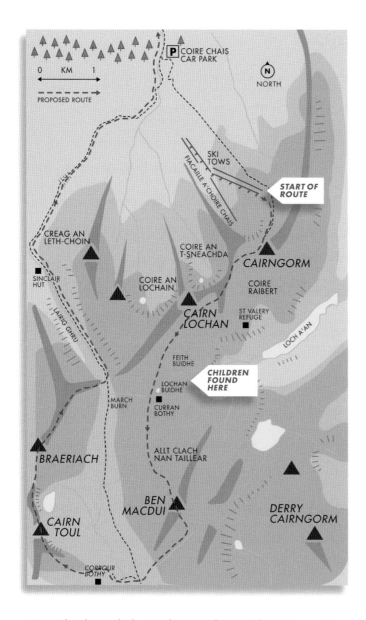

by the wind. The worst blizzard to hit the Cairngorms for years had arrived.

Over in the Spey Valley near Newtonmore, members of the RAF Kinloss team had reluctantly abandoned their weekend exercise – evidence, were it needed, of the dreadful conditions. Yet, shortly after returning to their base on the Sunday evening, they would find themselves on the road back whence they came, to join the search.

For the children, the adventure had begun innocently enough. After school on the Friday, the two leaders and their party – all between the ages of fourteen and eighteen – had driven to an outdoor centre at Lagganlia, in the shadow of the Cairngorms. The following morning each child was equipped with ice axe, crampons, sleeping bag, survival bag and adequate clothing. General equipment was shared among the party including food, cooking gear, flares, whistles and torches and the fourteen pupils split into two groups – one of eight fitter and more experienced children and one of six slightly less able.

The overall plan was for both parties to cross the Cairngorm plateau on the first day and meet at Corrour bothy for Saturday night. Beattie planned to lead the stronger party himself on a more demanding route, hoping to incorporate the traverse of Cairn Toul and Braeriach on the walk out on the Sunday. Cathie Davidson would lead the second group – boys and girls, all aged fifteen and sixteen, and an eighteen year old student teacher – through the Lairig Ghru for a rendezvous with Beattie at Loch Morlich. Her initial plan was to make for the

strengthening wind, veering to the south-east, driving crystal shards straight into their faces. It was hard to tell if the snow was falling or being picked up summit of Ben Macdui via the cairn on Fiacaill a' Choire Chais, the rim of Coire an t-Sneachda and Lochan Buidhe, before descending into the Lairig Ghru by the Allt Clach nan Taillear. As an alternative to the meeting place at Corrour bothy for the Saturday night it was decided that, in the event of bad weather, the two groups should head for the Curran bothy near Lochan Buidhe. Shelagh Sunderland, an eighteen year old student teacher, who was at the Lagganlia Centre hoping to become a temporary voluntary instructor, was allocated to Cathie Davidson's group. Completed route forms were left with the staff at the centre. The party, in high spirits, and now seventeen in number, was driven to the Coire Chais car park, below Cairngorm, arriving at about 11.15am.

Already the fine morning was deteriorating, but not enough to deter any well equipped, experienced group. To make up for their late start, Cathy's group made use of the chairlift, stopping at the top to eat their packed lunches. Meanwhile, Ben set off with his party for the summit of Cairngorm at 4084 ft, about 45 minutes ahead. As they traversed the col at the head of Coire Raibert, a venture scout unit from Stirlingshire, which had stopped for lunch by the cairn at the top of Fiacaill a' Choire Chais, saw them pass by. The scout leader, having heard the forecast and observing the threatening weather, abandoned his plan to skirt the rim of the Northern Coires as far as Cairn Lochan, deciding instead to descend Cairngorm by way of Coire an t-Sneachda.

PHOTO: BOB SHARP

The Cairngorm plateau on a good day

Having traversed most of the upper reaches of Coire Domhain, Ben's group met unfavourable snow conditions on the uphill western side. Unconsolidated powder snow, often knee deep, made walking particularly arduous. Progress slowed considerably. Reduced visibility rendered the landscape featureless and forced the group to use the method of navigating by one member walking ahead to allow bearings to be taken from him. It was soon apparent that the planned route to Ben Macdui and Corrour was over-ambitious and would have to be cut short. Their immediate goal had to be Curran Bothy – a very small shelter in an exposed situation, at over 3600 foot on the plateau near Lochan Buidhe, roughly midway between Cairngorm and Ben Macdui.

Because it was small, the shelter was often snowed over and, in the vastness of the plateau and adverse weather, could be extremely difficult to locate. After an hour or so of very hard going, this party reached the refuge at 3.15pm. They had to dig out the door to gain entry. With three miles of difficult walking and treacherous descent into the Lairig Ghru between them and their intended stopping place at Corrour and the weather very bad, Beattie decided to stay put. So nine people crowded into the twelve feet by eight feet of floor space to settle down for the night. As Cathie Davidson had not arrived with her party, Ben assumed she had cut short her walk and made for the St Valery shelter, on a promontory between Coire Raibert and Coire Domhain, not far off her route. Although that wasn't a planned bad weather alternative, he knew she had been there before and it seemed to him a logical detour to make.

Sadly, he was wrong. The truth was that the smaller party had met with extreme hardship. Having traversed the head of Coire Raibert and the rim of Coire an t-Sneachda without any major problems, they found walking becoming increasingly difficult as they crossed Coire Domhain. Soft snow, which would not bear a person's weight, was knee deep, sometimes deeper. The wind had strengthened and it was snowing heavily. Some of the girls were becoming distressed and were crying. Each slow, painful step forward took them further into the remoteness of the plateau and further from an escape to the lower ground to the north.

Somewhere on this leg the party arguably passed its point of no return, when to retreat would prove as hazardous as going on. As the afternoon dragged on, realising she must head for Curran bothy to get her children out of the blizzard, Cathie decided to follow the Feith Buidhe (the burn which drains Lochan Buidhe to the east) to the Lochan, then make for the bothy, only a short distance away. But the Feith Buidhe, being in a natural snow accumulation area, was virtually covered over. Only a short section of the burn was found before it disappeared under the snow. With the children tiring rapidly, the onset of darkness and the bothy still some way off, they decided to bivouac before becoming totally exhausted.

Even their efforts to dig a shelter were frustrated as the soft snow simply collapsed and they could not dig into it. But, with great difficulty, they achieved a semi-circular wall of snow about three foot high. The children huddled behind it in their sleeping bags and polythene bags. By then the weather was vicious, with a raging wind, continuous blizzard and visibility only two metres. Time and again through that bleak night, this exhausted young woman left her sleeping bag to help the children sweep the snow off themselves. At first they succeeded but eventually the snow covered the children faster than it could be cleared, threatening to bury them.

On the Sunday morning, Cathie tried to go for help. Taking the strongest boy with her, she set off towards Cairngorm, but the weather was so bad they could not stand and the snow so deep they found progress impossible. After only 25 metres they were forced to return to the party. They tried to dig out the others, but one boy was completely buried. Two of the girls, in struggling out of the snow, had lost their sleeping bags and were unprotected. An equipment bag was emptied and the girls placed in it – the discarded equipment quickly lost to the elements. As Sunday passed, Cathie continually sacrificed the meagre shelter of her sleeping bag to uncover the children but they were becoming increasingly buried and, weakened through her constant efforts, she was unable to cope with the snow.

In the meantime, Ben Beattie, unaware that the second party was less than a kilometre away, had left the Curran bothy and made a hazardous descent into the Lairig Ghru down the March Burn. His group walked out towards Loch Morlich where, about 6.30pm, they met the principal of Lagganlia. At once they realised that Cathie was in trouble and the alarm was raised. An immediate, desperate search was organised from Glenmore Lodge with three parties of two instructors going out in atrocious conditions. Two went into Strath Nethy and the others onto the Plateau before going down Coire Raibert and Coire Domhain, heading towards Loch A'An. The pair in Coire Domhain passed within half a mile of Cathie Davidson. So bad was the night that one of the parties failed to find the St Valery shelter in the blizzard. It wasn't long before the searchers themselves were fighting for their own survival.

At first light on Monday morning, mountain rescue teams from RAF Kinloss, police in Speyside and Deeside and the local Cairngorm team assembled at Glenmore Lodge and were allocated search areas. Over fifty team members searched on the ground. In the air an RAF helicopter struggled through the dense cloud. Cairngorm team members found themselves struggling through waist deep snow in an attempt to sweep into the Northern Coires of Cairngorm – Coire an Lochan and Coire an t-Sneachda.

By dawn most of the party were either completely or partially buried, and several were probably dead and Cathie was on the point of collapse. Soon after daylight, she made a last desperate attempt to go for help. She tried to persuade the same boy to accompany her again but he was by then too weak, so she set off alone. Suffering badly from exposure and frostbite, she started out on hands and knees in the direction of Cairngorm.

A few hundred metres on, a temporary break in the cloud above her, she was spotted by a Glenmore Lodge instructor acting as observer aboard the helicopter. As they picked her up, she managed few words – 'Burn. Lochan. Buried' – but it was enough to indicate where the children were. But thickening cloud, and the urgent need to get her to hospital, forced the helicopter to pull out and the information was passed to Glenmore Lodge. With increased urgency the rescue attempt was concentrated on the Feith Buidhe. A second helicopter, a Royal Navy Sea King, was drafted in.

Late in the afternoon, the stricken party was found buried under four feet of snow by Ben Beattie and the principal of Lagganlia. Of the seven Cathie had left, only Raymond Leslie remained alive, eyelids flickering. Completely buried but with an air space round his head, his only chance of survival now was evacuation by helicopter, even in the appalling conditions. And thus began a remarkable piece of skill and teamwork, as Frank Card relates.

'Bruce (RAF Kinloss team leader) explained the situation to Lieutenant Hockey, the RN helicopter. He agreed to do what he could, but he would need a guide who was very familiar with the terrain. Bruce said he would go himself and put one of his team in charge of the radio link. He positioned himself by Hockey's shoulder and guided him up Glen More and over the saddle north of the Cairngorm and then up Strath Nethy into the Loch Avon basin so that they could keep below the cloud as long as possible. However, when they reached the head of the loch they had to cross the headwall and go up to the cloud level. Bruce kept up a running commentary to the pilot, describing almost foot by foot the terrain in front of him, which he had walked so often with his team. Hockey, totally trusting a man he had never before met, was flying blind in the white out conditions and needed constant reassurance by Bruce that it was safe to ascend into the cloud. Then there was a slight break, and they could see a snow field. Here the pilot landed.

'Bruce checked his map. They were now very close to their target. Asking the pilot to stay there, he

Cairngorm plateau

jumped down from the helicopter and moved forward to find the stretcher party, who should have been not far ahead. He pulled out his Verey pistol and fired flares over the ridge to attract the attention of the stretcher party. His silhouette broke the white out for the pilot and Bruce could hear the engine note change, telling him that the chopper was moving forward in short hops.'

Once Bruce had made contact with the stretcher party, and the lad was safely aboard the helicopter, all that remained was to guide the pilot out again. Picking up a doctor on the way, 'he followed the railway line which runs down the valley and used that as a point of reference to guide the pilot to the hospital in Inverness'. Raymond Leslie and Cathie Davidson were both lucky. Back on the hill, the deteriorating weather forced those on the ground to retreat. It was the following day before clearing weather allowed helicopters to fly to the Feith Buidhe and recover the bodies.

Normally, mountain accidents affect only those directly involved but this incident – 'The Cairngorm Disaster' – aroused great public interest. Every detail was reported by the media. Questions were asked and statements made in the House of Commons. The local MP called for a 'harbourmaster of the hills' with authority to permit or prevent people going to the hills according to the weather conditions – not for the first time in mountain history – an idea which never materialised. February of the following year saw a Fatal Accident Inquiry at Banff in which every aspect of the incident was scrutinised. The issue which raised most debate was the presence of high level bothies in the Cairngorms. Did they attract less able people into remote areas as they offered safety and shelter in adverse weather?

After six days of evidence the jury rejected pleas by counsel to apportion blame, and returned formal verdicts on the deaths of the six children. It was concluded that a succession of human errors led to the loss of young lives. The tragedy prompted local authorities to introduce new guidelines for outdoor education as well as the development of a UK-wide mountain leader training scheme.

Cathie Davidson married and moved to the US. Ben Beattie was later appointed as an instructor at Glenmore Lodge. He quickly became an international authority on avalanche assessment but – somewhat ironically – died in the Himalaya in 1978 when overtaken by a massive avalanche. The Curran bothy shelter and several others were eventually removed from the Cairngorms. Flight Sergeant George Bruce was awarded the Queen's Commendation for Brave Conduct for the part he played in the rescue.

Death on the mountains and hills of the United Kingdom is relatively rare. The majority of team members might never be in the position of witnessing first hand the results of a fatal accident. But every time that pager bleeps, it brings with it the fleeting speculation, wrapped with the buzz of fear, that this could be the moment. Sometimes, there's no knowing how long a shout will take, what the outcome might be, even the risks involved. Yet off they go, anyway. It's a challenge, an adrenaline high, an opportunity to test their own mettle and the team's resources. The camaraderie and the banter is as vital to their safety and sanity, as to the casualties they rescue.

But what about the others? The ones on the other side of the bed when the call comes in the midst of sleep. How do they feel? Throughout this book we've related the words and experiences of many people, but there's one group we've so far omitted to mention. And, in a way, they're the most important of all, because without their support and understanding, things would be a great deal different. Partners, mothers, wives, husbands and children frequently have strong opinions about mountain rescue and what they say encapsulates the feelings, moods and challenges of everyone involved. They don't have – nor would the majority want – that first hand experience of excitement and activity. But they see its effect on their loved one. How do they feel when the phone rings? What does a husband or wife think while waiting for their other half to return from the mountain? Have they made mountain rescue part of their lives and how does it affect family life? When you listen to them speak, there are often notes of discord – some will sound hurt or hard done by, others express feelings of pride and concern. But most are strongly supportive. It's a confusing mix of emotions perhaps best summed up by these long-suffering people in their own words. We couldn't put it better ourselves.

'The most amazing thing about a mountain rescue call out is the complete transformation of priorities it causes. Everything is dropped. Meals are left uneaten. Friends are left without a host. Long planned outings are postponed. On one memorable occasion, I was left with a full mix of plaster and requested to "put it on the wall as best you can", by my husband as he disappeared out of the door. Quite a few call outs seem to be at the end of the day. If my husband is on childcare duties (tea, bath or reading a story) then he can barely conceal his delight at being called away! At times like that I bite my lip and remind myself that it's all in a good cause. I know few things would come between him and answering a call out, so I accept them. And being in the team probably doesn't take up any more time than if he was to play golf every Sunday.'

'When his bleeper goes off, it always seems to be at an inopportune moment. The worst time was when we'd arranged a birthday party for him. I had literally just lit the candles on his cake and the children were all singing to him when the pager started beeping. He quickly blew his candles out, gathered his gear together and dashed off. As it

Teamwork in action as Lomond team members carry the stretcher down hill

turned out, despite the team's best efforts, he spent his birthday evening with a casualty who died in his arms. He was very quiet when he got home. This made me realise that it's not just physically hard for members, but the emotional side must be considered too. Probably the worst thing is you don't know what dangers he is dashing off to. You've no idea of the time scale. I can't relax until I've heard from him and know he's all right. Team members have died on rescue work. It's not until I hear his key in the door that I can heave a sigh of relief and really know that I've got him back in one piece.'

'It can put a strain on family life and domestic harmony at times, when the children need attention or need to be taken to parties or school. And I do resent the time the team takes up. He already works a full day, sometimes in the evenings. Yet, when the bleeper goes, I'm there to make up the sandwiches, fill the flask, make appropriate soothing noises and, once he's gone, wait uneasily for his return. Sometimes I could scream, wondering if he'll be okay to go to work after being out all night. What if there's a road accident because he's overtired? Sometimes I grumble about all the things he never gets round to doing. I worry about the men on the hill. Will they injure themselves or become exhausted? And I sometimes wonder why does he do this to me? I haven't made the rescue team part of my life, more like my husband has made it part of mine! Having said that, I do enjoy the camaraderie between team members and do like to take part in the social and PR events.'

'Life's too short to worry every time she's called out. I do have a lot of faith in the team and know how well they work together on the mountain. I believe she's in the best possible company and I know they all look out for each other. I think it helps when you know the other team members well. Even though I'm not a mountaineer, the rescue team has become a part of my life in a really positive way. They're a good bunch and a lot of us meet up socially. While the team is made up of a real cross section of people and professionals, they all have one common interest – the mountains. I know how much being part of search and rescue means to her and the dogs. It gives her a great purpose as well as a lot of enjoyment. And many of her best friends are in the team.'

'To be honest, there are times when rescue is a dirty word in our house. Perhaps I'm getting intolerant in old age, but our life just seems to revolve around the team. It's the number one priority. But when they're out, my first thought is for the casualty and the pain they may be suffering. Generally, I don't resent the time given to the team. Some children of team members have grown into adulthood with the team an ever present part of their family life. The daughter of one team member was asked to write a story when in primary school, describing in graphic detail the smell of damp rope, soggy clothes and filthy boots! Many of her childhood memories are filled with Dad's mountain rescue experiences. She even drew a wonderful picture of him sliding down a steep mountain sitting on a stretcher shouting out "Yippee!" The poor casualty strapped behind was shouting with equally vigour "Help! Help!" Thirty years on she tells me that whenever she smells wet clothing or shoes, be it in a garage or the boot of a car, she has visions of helicopters, dogs and bleepers going off – and Dad rushing out of the house at full speed stuffing a chocolate bar in his rucksack!'

'Deep down I will always be proud that he's so dedicated. I know he would move heaven and earth for his family. It's just when that bloody bleeper goes off – so does he...'

acknowledgements

Of course, mountain rescue is all about people helping one another and working together towards a common goal. Writing this book has been very similar. We have shared common skills, contributed our own special areas of expertise and worked closely as a team. But we have also benefited greatly from the expertise and experiences of the wider mountaineering fraternity. All those we have sought help and guidance from have been exceptionally obliging and willing to assist us in what has been a long and complicated task. We are greatly indebted to the following people for providing gems of insight and permission to use their stories and photographs. We have credited most people throughout the text, but for completeness we list everyone here by name and designation. If we have missed anyone out please forgive us!

Aiguille Alpine Equipment, Alan Crichton (Aberdeen MRT), Allen Fyffe (Mountain Guide and Photographer), Alex Gillespie (Photographer), Andrew Fellows (Witness to accident & Lomond MRT), Andy Brelsford (Cornwall Rescue Group), Andy Nisbet, Andy Simpson (Rossendale & Pendle MRT), Angie Jackson, Angus Jack (Dundonnell MRT), Dr Anthony S G Jones MBE (MRC), Archie Roy OBE (Lomond MRT), Barry Robinson (Rossendale & Pendle MRT), Bill Amos (Dundonnell MRT), Bill Batson MBE (Former RAF Mountain Rescue Service), Bill Rose (Killin MRT), Bill Seville (Oldham MRT), Blyth Wright (sportscotland Avalanche Information Service), Bob Kerr (Assynt MRT), Bob Sparkes, Bob Stokes (Rossendale & Pendle MRT), Brian Lochrin (Photographer), Brian Wills (Llanberis MRT), Charlie Orr (Scottish Mountaineering Trust), Chris Boyles (Rossendale & Pendle MRT), Dan Hudson, David Allan (MRC Chairman), Dave Freeborn (Patterdale MRT), Dave 'Heavy' Whalley MBE (ARCC), David Paine, David Syme (MRC of S Medical Officer), Davy Gunn (Glencoe MRT), Duncan Tripp (RAF 202 Squadron), Eve Burton (Buxton MRT), Felicity Martin (Freelance Writer and Photographer), Frank Card (Writer & Former RAF MRS), Gail Todd (Rossendale & Pendle MRT), Ged Feeney (MRC Statistics Officer), Georgina Duff (wife of Donald Duff), Gerry Akroyd (Skye MRT), Hamish MacInnes MBE (Glencoe Productions), Harold Burrows MBE (SARDA Wales & North East Wales SRT), Helen Goodwin (Rossendale & Pendle MRT), Ian Bunting (Edale MRT), Ian Dawson (Lomond MRT), Ian Henderson (Llanberis MRT), Jamie Kean (Kintail MRT), James Hotchkis (Scottish Mountaineering Trust), Jan Millar (Lomond MRT & SARDA Scotland), Jane Clark, Jane Suchet, Jez Hunter (Cornwall Rescue Group), Jim Gallienne

(Cornwall Rescue Group), Jim Gilchrist (Journalist with The Scotsman), John Carrie (Ogwen Valley MRO), John Ellerton (MRC Medical Officer), John Gladston (Llanberis MRT), John Griffiths (Maritime & Coastguard Agency), John Grisedale (Llanberis MRT), John Paul Photography, John Rogers, John Usher, Jonathan Barnett (Cornwall Rescue Group), Kenny Lindsay (SARDA Scotland), Lancs Police Air Support Unit, Les Gallacher (Freelance Photographer), Malcolm Creasey (Ogwen Valley MRO), Manus Graham (witness to accident), Mark Leyland (Arrochar MRT), Martin McCallum (Lomond MRT), Martin Moran (Mountain Guide), Mick Beard (Greater Manchester Police), Mick James, Mick Guy (Keswick MRT), Mick Neild (Oldham MRT), Mick Tighe (Mountain Guide), Mike Margeson (MRC Equipment Sub Committee), Mike McErlean, Mike Walker (Dundonnell MRT), Neil Hinchliffe (Torridon MRT), Neil Rawlinson (Llanberis MRT), Neil Ross (Kintail MRT), Neil Sutherland (Moffat MRT), Nick Verrall (Langdale Ambleside MRT), Nikki Wallis (Llanberis MRT, SARDA Wales and SNPA Warden Service), Paul Horder (Keswick MRT), Pete Hill MIC (Mountain Instructor), Peter & Lisa Bell (Bell Stretchers), Peter Deacon, Peter Howells OBE (Central Beacons MRT), Phil Benbow (Llanberis MRT & SARDA Wales), Ray 'Sunshine' Sefton (Former RAF Mountain Rescue Service), Remote Access International, Richard Glover (Assynt MRT), Richard Hartland, Robert Davidson (Ochils MRT), Rohan Holt (Photographer), Roger Clegg (Greater Manchester Police), Roger Wild (Mountain Safety Advisor), Sandy Seabrook (Former Team Leader Lomond MRT), Steve Brailey (Cockermouth MRT), Stewart Hulse MBE (LDSAMRA), Stuart Roy (Photographer & Witness to accident), Steve Penny (Tweed Valley MRT), Ted Atkins (RAF Mountain Rescue Service), Ted Burton MBE (Buxton MRT), The Press Association, Terry Clare (Ogwen Valley MRO), Tim Bird (Ogwen Valley MRO), Tim Bunting (Edale MRT), Tim Walker (Glenmore Lodge), Tom Graty (Photographer), Tom Malone (Graphic Artist), Tom Taylor (ARCC), Tracey Binks (Duddon & Furness MRT), Willie Marshall (Assynt MRT), Willie Miller (Ochils MRT).

glossary

A&E	Accident and Emergency	LDSAMRA	Lake District Search and Mountain Rescue Association
ABC	Airway - Breathing - Circulation		
ACC	Assistant Chief Constable	LKP	Last Known Position
ACPO	Association of Chief Police Officers	MCA	Maritime and Coastguard Agency
ACPOS	Association of Chief Police Officers (Scotland)	MPSRO	Mid Pennine Search & Rescue Organisation
ALSAR	Association of Lowland Search and Rescue	MOD	Ministry of Defence
		MR	Mountain Rescue
ARCC	Aeronautical Rescue Co-ordination Centre	MR (E&W)	Mountain Rescue (England & Wales)
		MRC	Mountain Rescue Council (England & Wales)
ATCC	Air Traffic Control Centre		
BASP	British Association of Ski Patrollers	MRC of S	Mountain Rescue Committee of Scotland
BCRC	British Cave Rescue Council		
BST	British Summer Time	MRT	Mountain Rescue Team
CIC Hut	Charles Ingles Clarke Hut	MU	Military Unit
CPR	Cardio-Pulmonary Resuscitation	NASAR	National Association of Search & Rescue
CRG	Cave Rescue Group		
CRO	Cave Rescue Organisation	NSARDA	National Search & Rescue Dogs Association
CT scan	Computer Tomography scan		
ECG	Electro Cardiogram	NESRA	North East Search & Rescue Association
EMT	Emergency Medical Technician		
ERFR	Emergency Restriction to Flying Regulations	NWMRA	North Wales Mountain Rescue Association
		NVG	Night Vision Goggles
FLIR	Forward Looking Infra Red	OVMRO	Ogwen Valley Mountain Rescue Organisation
GPS	Global Positioning System		
HEMS	Helicopter Emergency Medical Service	OS	Ordnance Survey
		PDMRO	Peak District Mountain Rescue Organisation
HMCG	Her Majesty's Coastguard		
HQ	Headquarters		
IEC	Immediate and Emergency Care	PLS	Point Last Seen
IPP	Initial Planning Point	RAF	Royal Air Force
LAMRT	Langdale Ambleside Mountain Rescue Team	RAF MRS	Royal Air Force Mountain Rescue Service

RCC	Rescue Co-ordination Centre	Cwm	enclosed valley usually of glacial origin – also called coombe, coire
RN	Royal Navy		
RNLI	Royal National Life Boat Institution	Glen	valley
SARA	Severn Area Rescue Association	Gully	narrow valley or split in rock face
SARDA	Search and Rescue Dog Association	Icefall	Steep section of glacier with convoluted crevasses and seracs
SMC	Scottish Mountaineering Club		
SOP	Standard Operation Procedure	Loch	lake
SOS	Save our Souls	Lochan	small loch or lake
SWSRA	South Wales Search & Rescue Association	Prusik knot	used by rescuers and climbers to attach a thinner rope to a wider rope for the purpose of taking a load – when tightened, the knot 'bites' to enable loading but, when the load is released, it can be moved easily
SWERA	South West England Rescue Association		
SRT	Search and Rescue Team		
TRA	Temporary Restricted Air		
UKSAR	United Kingdom Search & Rescue Region (usually used when referring to the Strategic Committee, Operators Group etc.)	Misper	missing person
		Moraine	debris and rocks left by glacier
		Mugger	soft iron nail embedded into sole of climbing boot (middle of sole) to assist purchase when scrambling and general mountaineering – went out of fashion in 1960s
UKSRR	United Kingdom Search & Rescue Region		
USAF	United States Air Force		
WRVS	Women's Royal Voluntary Service	Névé	old snow turned to ice
YDRP	Yorkshire Dales Rescue Panel	Ridge	high crest between two valleys
		Rime	ice build-up on rocks, stakes and other objects
Ampoule	small sealed glass container	Scree	loose rocks/boulders
Arête	sharply defined ridge	Sea King	helicopter used by the RN and RAF
Bealach	low point between two hills or mountains – also called col, saddle or bwlch	Serac	wall, tower or pinnacle of glacier ice
		Tricouni	hard steel nail embedded into the sole of a climbing boot (around perimeter) to assist purchase on rock and ice – went out of fashion in 1960s
Clinker	soft iron nail embedded into sole of climbing boot (around perimeter) to assist purchase when scrambling and general mountaineering – went out of fashion in 1960s		
Coire/corrie	glaciated valley bowl		
Crevasse	split or crack in glacier ice		